WALKING WITH THE WOUNDED

Mark McCrum

WINDSOR
PARAGON

First published 2011
by Sphere
This Large Print edition published 2012
by AudioGO Ltd
by arrangement with
Little, Brown Book Group

Hardcover   ISBN: 978 1 445 89266 5
Softcover   ISBN: 978 1 445 89267 2

British Library Cataloguing in Publication Data available

Printed and bound in Great Britain by
MPG Books Group Limited

To our brave wounded, past and present.
May they thrive in the future.

CONTENTS

Earlier this year I was lucky enough to be part of the most incredible expedition.

It was not just that I found myself in one of the last true wildernesses on earth – though being one hundred and sixty miles from the North Pole, dragging my 'home' on a sledge behind me, being sworn at in turn (and sometimes all at the same time) in Scouse, Welsh, South African and 'officer' English, was extraordinary enough. No, what was truly remarkable and wholly unforgettable were these four tormentors of mine: Steve, Martin, Jaco and Guy. They are British soldiers; fit men, used to hardship, who relished the challenge confronting us. That they went on to achieve the fastest time to the Pole this year should not, therefore, be so surprising.

But what was surprising – mind-blowing, in fact – was that two of them were missing limbs, one had a paralysed arm and the fourth had a broken back which, last year, doctors said would prevent him ever walking again. And yet here they were, powering ahead of me, filling me with a disbelief tinged with panic that they might actually make good on their threat and leave me to the polar bears. I learnt from these men that one should not fear anything in life.

Though clearly very special, Steve, Martin, Jaco and Guy are no more special than the thousands of British soldiers, sailors, airmen and Royal Marines who, like them, have suffered life-changing injuries in the service of our Country since the Second World War. Despite their heroic endeavours on the ice, their lives are changed, their goals in life are inevitably and drastically altered.

Walking With The Wounded – this great expedition, the brain-child of Ed Parker and Simon Daglish, and so ably led by our Norwegian guide, Inge Solheim – has succeeded in capturing public imagination, focusing it on the momentous challenges facing our wounded Servicemen and women as they look to the future. In the same way that Walking With The Wounded has enabled these four fantastic individuals to take life once more by the scruff of the neck, it is incumbent on all of us to make sure that others like them are helped to do the same.

Walking With The Wounded will be back!

Harry.

1

AFGHAN

'The power of the shot threw me on to the ground. It was almost like a back flip. I knew instantly that it was serious. From the way the blood was spurting out, spreading in a dark crimson patch across my assault vest, I reckoned the bullet had cut through an artery. Then it dawned on me that I could no longer feel my right arm. Or move it at all. It wasn't responding. For one sickening moment I thought I'd lost it. Then, as I reached out to grip it with my left hand, I realised it was the feeling that had gone. Glistening with blood as it was, my arm was still firmly attached to my body—it just wasn't responding to the signals my brain was sending it.'

Martin Hewitt was in Helmand Province, Afghanistan, when he was shot. A 26-year-old captain in the Parachute Regiment, he was leading his platoon in an assault on a Taliban position in the Green Zone, the narrow strip of fertile land between the Helmand River and the huge surrounding desert, which the British Army was struggling, then as now, to control. That day the enemy were ensconced in a group of one-storey mud-brick buildings surrounded by a thick screen of bushes and trees. Martin and his men were approaching across open ground, recently ploughed poppy fields, with only a few shallow irrigation ditches as cover. During a lull in the firefight, they had been crouching in one of these ditches, but Martin knew that he had to keep the attack moving.

It was as he'd got up to encourage his men on that he'd been hit in the shoulder, just above his body armour.

MARTIN: The pain was intense, burning, but the funny thing is that within seconds the adrenalin kicks in, takes your mind straight back to the job in hand. It's like having a split personality; half of you is looking at this thing that's just happened to you and the other half knows you've got things you have to do, so you crack on with it.

Fortunately my lance-corporal—Tully was his name—was right beside me. He dragged me back into a ditch so we were below the line of fire, then knelt over me in the mud and pulled dressings from the first aid pouch in my assault vest. He was trying to apply them—but they wouldn't stick. My wound was in such an awkward position, it was hard to put pressure on it. We were going through dressing after dressing, mine then his, but we still couldn't stop the blood. So he ripped off his shirt and tied it tight round my shoulder, but that didn't work either. In the end I got my other hand inside the wound and tried to clamp the artery that way, but it was all too slippery, I couldn't get a grip on it, the artery just retracted into my torso.

But I also knew I couldn't spend too much time worrying about myself. The firefight was continuing and I was captain of a platoon I could no longer effectively command. I needed to get another officer forward to take charge as soon as possible. Simultaneously I had to make sure my men kept the pressure up on the enemy, keeping them pinned down so the rest of the unit could start dealing with me as a casualty. I knew the drill if someone else

2

had been hit. I never thought I'd have to command my own extraction.

Even as we tried to stop the bleeding, I was on my radio telling my commanding officer what had happened and what needed to be done. The enemy fire was accurate and effective, high-velocity ammunition from assault rifles backed up by a PKN heavy machine gun. So air support was called in—F16s and A10 Thunderbolts plus a Chinook helicopter to take me out. On the ground, mortars were launched and fire support was diverted from other areas. We threw everything we had at the main enemy position and then began a fighting withdrawal. Bringing the medical team forward wasn't an option. Even though we'd now destroyed the main target, the fire from surrounding positions was still too heavy.

My focus now was pretty much on staying alive. I could feel myself getting weaker and more lightheaded as the blood drained from my body. My limbs suddenly felt too heavy to move. I was having difficulty breathing; the bullet had collapsed my lung.

Tully dragged me out. We stumbled across the mud. We fell continually, struggling over the three hundred metres that separated us from the first area of cover, a mud-brick walled compound where our supporting forces were based.

Then I got too weak even to stand. I'd lost too much blood. Tully picked me up on his shoulders and did a battlefield version of a fireman's lift. But both of us had been on the go since before dawn. It was now early afternoon and the heat was sweltering, in the early forties. We'd been fighting for five days on the trot. Fifty yards from the compound Tully collapsed with exhaustion.

My officer commanding and the mortar fire controller now ran forward from the compound. They picked me up and carried me back. Three others grabbed Tully. A waiting medic rapidly dressed my wound. He was fantastic. Within sixty seconds: bang bang, job done.

'What were you doing out there?' He grinned. 'You amateurs.'

At that point I was really fighting for my life. People say you see a white light and a tunnel. It's not quite like that, but everything does blur into one; it must be the blood loss from the brain. You're trying to focus on something, and all around is a haze. One of the blokes kept hitting me in the face to keep me awake. In the Paras when things get tough we call on the Regiment. 'Reg it out,' we say. So I kept repeating to myself, 'Reg it out, reg it out, you'll be OK.'

The guys were shouting that at me too. 'Reg it out, mate! Reg it out!'

You think of your family and friends back home. You think, *There is no way I am going to die in some godforsaken piece of desert in the middle of nowhere.*

Then the Chinook arrived, a great grey beast hammering down from the blue sky in a whirl of dust. I couldn't believe how the pilot managed to land in this tiny compound. There was so little distance between the tips of his rotor blades and the walls of the building—a few feet max. And the bullets were still coming.

The first person off was a very pretty blonde nurse. We'd been on tour for so long that none of us had seen any woman for four or five months. And here was this vision. The lads who were

4

supposed to be carrying me on to the chopper were so gobsmacked they dropped the stretcher on the ground. One of my drips fell out. *Cheers, fellas*, I thought.

Once I was on board, I realised I'd done what I needed to do. This nurse was asking me if I'd had any morphine. I said no. I hadn't taken it earlier, because I knew the effects, and I didn't want to slow my thought processes down, or my heart rate. But now I was ready for it.

She brought out the morphine pen.

'Can you feel that?' she asked.

'No,' I replied. The pain was still excruciating.

'D'you want another one?'

'Damn right I do.'

She gave me a second shot. 'Can you feel that?'

'No.'

The third hit finally got to me. It was surreal. Lying down on the floor of the helicopter and suddenly being completely out of it. You can hear the conversations going on around you and you've got other conversations going on in your head. I was still fighting the battle. 'Keep going,' I was telling myself. 'You've got to deal with their depth positions. They're not destroyed yet.'

Then another voice was saying, 'You've come too far, you've over-exploited, you need to regroup.'

Then another: 'Shut up, you idiot. It's over. You're alive. That's all you've got to focus on now.'

*   *   *

Martin was airlifted to Camp Bastion, the headquarters of British Army operations in Afghanistan, where he was operated on twice. Then

5

he was put in a medically induced coma and flown home to Selly Oak Hospital in Birmingham, where casualties of the war are routinely treated. Many come round from sedation thinking they are still on the battlefield; some even ask the nurses where their rifle is or warn them of the continuing danger.

When Martin woke he was surrounded by familiar faces: his mum and dad, his twin brothers, his younger sister, his girlfriend and two officer mates from his regiment. Initially he had no idea what was going on. Slowly it dawned on him that he was back home in the UK, in intensive care.

*   *   *

Two years later, in June 2009, the British Army mounted a major offensive in Helmand Province. It was codenamed Operation Panchai Palang— Panther's Claw—and it aimed to secure various key canal and river crossings and establish an International Security Assistance Force presence ahead of the Afghan presidential elections in August. In what the Ministry of Defence described as 'one of the largest air operations of modern times', 350 infantry were airlifted into the enemy stronghold of Babaji Fasal in the heart of the Green Zone. Guy Disney, twenty-seven, formerly an amateur jockey from Gloucestershire, now a lieutenant in the Light Dragoons, was commanding a troop of Spartan and Scimitar armoured vehicles, providing much-needed support for the men on the ground.

GUY: We had been fighting most of the day to small arms fire and had pretty successfully suppressed everything we'd come across. Around 5.30 p.m. we got to the stage where the infantry company attached to us came under quite heavy attack, so I took my troop of five vehicles to try and outflank the enemy position. I thought we'd managed to cut them off, but then a rocket-propelled grenade came from nowhere, right at my vehicle.

An RPG looks like an American football, only a bit more oblique. It's basically a warhead that, when detonated, creates a molten flush of hot metal which can burn straight through armour. I've still got a piece from the vehicle we were in. The guys brought it back from Afghan with them.

We didn't know what had hit us—at first we thought it was an IED, an improvised explosive device. There was a lot of nasty grey smoke and a putrid stink that I now know was burning flesh. As the officer in charge I was standing up in the turret, which gives you a 360-degree outside view, but you can't see what's going on in the rest of the vehicle.

I looked down. My foot was attached to my leg by a sinew. All the bone was gone. It looked like the remains of a boot hanging by its laces. There was bugger-all left really. I knew fairly quickly that it was coming off. But shock is a great thing for instant pain relief. I didn't think, *Shit that hurts!* I thought, *I'm about to not have a foot. Bugger.*

But in the moment I couldn't worry too much about that. I was straight on to the Net—that's the Army's secure communications network—with the other guys, trying to get a grip on what had happened.

'Is everyone all right?' I asked.

The answers crackled back through my headphones. My driver had been burned on the back of his neck, several of the other guys had been hit by shrapnel, and one of my immediate tank group of seven was seriously injured. I didn't know who at that point.

Everything was pretty chaotic. My driver was reversing out of the ambush and my lead corporal, in the next vehicle, a Scimitar, had opened fire on the enemy's position with his thirty-mil cannon, effectively suppressing them. Then I was back on the Net, this time to base. 'Contact,' I told them. 'There are casualties. One of them is me. I think I've lost my leg. We'll probably need a helicopter.' At the same time my corporal popped smoke— white phosphorus—to blanket us as we moved back. Two of the other guys had got into the bottom of the turret to put a tourniquet on what was left of my leg to stop catastrophic bleeding. Even so I lost eight pints that day. They also gave me a morphine shot for the pain.

We retreated to a place where I and the other casualties could be extracted by helicopter. I didn't find out exactly what had happened till I was on the stretcher myself. I was being carried out by my commanding officer—a colonel—and a sergeant. I was in a pretty shit state by that stage, though the morphine had blanketed some of the pain.

'What's the state of the other guys?' I asked.

'Not so good,' said my colonel. 'I'm afraid we've lost somebody.'

The man killed in action was a private called Robbie Laws. He had been doing a great job looking for mines in the country we were going through. If there was ever an area I was concerned about he'd hop out and do a quick sweep with a metal detector before we drove over it. Knowing he'd died in the contact eclipsed anything I was feeling about myself.

When you're on operations and someone is working with you, they're yours; you've got responsibility for them. I wrote to his parents when I was in hospital, telling them what a great guy he was. But I still think about what happened daily. His death will be with me till the day I die.

As for me, I was chucked on a helicopter and flown back to Bastion. I had been injected with all sorts of things, but I was still conscious. As I was being rolled down the corridor towards surgery, one of the surgeons came past me in his white coat.

'Any chance of saving it?' I asked.

He looked down at what was left of my foot. 'No,' he said. 'Probably not.'

'OK, fair enough,' I replied. It was a bit of a mess.

*   *   *

After two months in Selly Oak, Martin Hewitt was moved to the Defence Medical Rehabilitation Centre (DMRC) at Headley Court in Surrey. Once a country house, set in eighty-five acres of landscaped gardens on the edge of Epsom Downs, Headley was given to the RAF after the Second World War by the Institute of Chartered Auctioneers and Estate Agents in grateful commemoration of the Battle of Britain. It began life as a rehabilitation centre for injured pilots and aircrew, but is now the UK's premier facility for injured personnel from all the services, much in demand in current circumstances.

The DMRC has an intriguing coat of arms, somewhat different to the bold crests and mottos of the regiments its inmates come from. It shows a serpent winding around a sword that is confined by a pair of shackles. The sword is breaking through the shackles of injury with the help of the serpent, which represents the medical profession. The centre's motto, 'Per Mutos', describes the mutual effort of patient and professional needed to overcome injury.

Though Martin's arm was saved, the nerve damage was extensive, and even after thirteen further operations and a great deal of physiotherapy he can only really use it as a basic lever. He can trap and carry a load of laundry across to a washing machine, but there's no dextrous movement or control of any kind. He's had to retrain himself to write with his left hand, sitting down every day and working his way through the Key Stage 1 to 4 handwriting course his parents bought for him, starting off by tracing a single letter, then small words, and finally sentences. Though his new handwriting is actually neater than his old, it still takes him twice as long to write a sentence as it used to do.

His career as a combat soldier in the Parachute Regiment is over. 'Dealing with the ongoing pain wasn't a problem,' he says, 'I just channelled my thoughts into other things and kept myself active. As for the functional loss of my arm, I've learned to adapt. But the psychological impact of not being able to do the job that I trained for and wanted to do for so many years has been by far the hardest thing to deal with.'

Not that Martin has let his injury hold him back in other ways. Through the tri-Service rehabilitation organisation Battle Back he got involved with the

Combined Services Disabled Ski Team and in 2009, as their captain, began to race with them on the international circuit. In 2010 he was invited on to the British National Disabled squad; at the Swiss National Championships in April that year he came fourth in slalom and fifth in grand slalom. He has been racing professionally with the team ever since, winning a gold medal in slalom and a bronze in giant slalom at the Paralympics Winter World Cup in Sweden in February 2011.

*   *   *

After his operation at Camp Bastion, where his leg was amputated below the knee, Guy too was flown back to Selly Oak. From there, like Martin and many other wounded British servicemen, he was transferred to Headley Court. At the end of his first week at Headley he was fitted with an artificial leg. 'The process of getting used to wearing it takes a long time,' he says, 'because the injury has to heal. At first, they were still pulling bits of shrapnel out. The trauma makes your stump swell up too; mine was forty-three centimetres in diameter, rather than the thirty it should be. After my second week I was managing to put the leg on, but you can't do much with it. You have a wound that is bleeding a lot of the time. It's bloody sore.'

Nonetheless, by the end of his first, month-long admission at Headley Court, Guy was walking. Then came a new problem, one which only an expert could have foreseen: heterotrophic ossification. 'It happens a lot to blast victims,' he explains, 'rather than guys who choose to have a leg amputated, so they're expecting it mentally.

It's when the bone starts to regrow. I think it's the body's way of saying: "This has just happened, now I need a new leg."' In Guy's case a bone about half the width of his little finger sprouted from his fibula. 'It's bloody uncomfortable within a prosthesis. It's like a nail almost, touching your flesh inside. It's very sharp and always changing shape.'

Once he was properly up and about, Guy found that one of the hardest things was walking downhill. 'I have no ankle in that leg,' he says, 'and it's something you soon realise you need. An ankle is an incredible thing for going up and down stairs.'

Despite such difficulties, within a year he was back to (almost) fighting fitness. He was playing squash three or four times a week and running as much as he could. He was in the process of trying to get his amateur racing licence back.

Unlike Martin's, Guy's military career isn't over. He is retraining as a forward air controller, the officer on the ground who talks jets in to their targets. His greatest ambition is to be with his regiment when they return to Afghanistan in 2012. 'And if I didn't go in a fighting role, I wouldn't want to go. You may get kicked down, but it's your choice to get up and get on with life.'

2

'THIS YELLOW, BROKEN BODY'

Edward Parker is now in his mid-forties, a wine merchant based in Norfolk. As a boy, he says, he always knew he would go into the Army. His father was in the Navy, his uncle was in the Rifle Brigade, both of his grandfathers had been soldiers. His older brother had joined the Army and loved it. 'I don't remember not having made the decision,' he says. 'I was always going to be in the Green Jackets.'

But at the time he served, back in the 1980s, the Army was, he says, 'very, very different from what it is now, a peacetime army basically.' Ed was posted to Northern Ireland and Germany, and spent time on various excursions in Brunei, Hong Kong, Canada and Kenya. There were 'a couple of busy days' in Ireland, but he hasn't seen action in the way soldiers in more recent wars in Afghanistan and Iraq have done. 'I would never use the word jealous,' he says, 'because there are many mothers and fathers out there who have lost sons and daughters, but yes, there is a little bit of envy. I would have loved to have had a go. Seen how I would have coped.'

Simon ('Dags') Daglish lives in London and works on the commercial side of new media. 'Selling advertising space, effectively,' he says, though this is a modest description of his current role as Director of MultiPlatforms and Partnerships at ITV. He met Edward at Sandhurst and they have remained firm friends since. From an Army family going back several generations, Simon was sent to a military school at the age of thirteen, but after Sandhurst decided not to pursue a military career. 'Much to my father's regret,' he says now. 'I think my mistake was not taking a year off between school and Sandhurst. If I'd done that, I probably would have had a longer career in the Army. And I do honestly wish I'd seen action in some sense or another. It would have been a very interesting test of myself as an individual. But no, I've never fired a shot in anger, never been in battle, never seen anyone wounded.'

Instead he went to work for a while in a chocolate shop in Bond Street. 'I came to London where I suddenly discovered women, nightclubs, easier money and all the rest of it. I hadn't a clue what I was going to do.' Simon toyed with the idea of being an estate agent, but ended up following his father into the media. He started as a runner on the *Daily Express*, went to Australia for a stint working on Murdoch newspapers, before returning to the *Telegraph* and the *Independent* in the UK, always on the commercial side; as the internet burgeoned, he moved with the technology.

When his youngest son, Felix, was born prematurely and suffered a brain haemorrhage that left him with cerebral palsy, Simon rowed unsupported from Cork to north Cornwall in order to raise £25,000 for Tommy's, the charity that funds medical research into miscarriages, still and premature births. 'And when I came back,' he says with a chuckle, 'I found I had a little bit of a sniffy taste for it.' So he took on a bigger challenge, an expedition to the South Pole, retracing Scott's steps using exactly the same kit. Remarkably, his team of four raised over £1 million.

On their return, Simon and his expedition colleagues gave a lecture at the Royal Geographical Society. In the audience was his old friend Ed Parker. 'I'd been wanting to do something like this for a while,' says Ed. 'There was a little worm inside me saying, "Come on, have a bit of adventure, go and do something that's really going to excite you."

But this talk just lit every light on me. I knew three of the four guys very well. After the presentation I went up to Simon and said, "Look, if you ever go North I'd like to come with you." Working on the theory that if you've been to the South Pole, you might as well go to the North Pole too.'

'At that time,' says Simon, 'I thought I'd hung up my explorer's boots. When Ed said, "Shall we do something else?" I was a bit iffy and butty about it. To be honest, I wasn't that keen.'

'I kept floating the idea over him,' says Ed. 'Then, about two years ago, I phoned him up and said, "Look, I really do want to go to the North Pole." We met for a bottle of wine or two and agreed we'd do it, neither of us having the nerve to tell our wives at that point. Then we started very, very gently planning it. We had to do it for something, so we thought we'd do it for wounded ex-servicemen in some way. So we got in touch with Help for Heroes, which hadn't been going that long at that time.'

The initial plan was to involve two of Simon's team from the South Pole expedition; but after consulting their families and thinking about the year-long training they would need to repeat, both men decided against it. 'So we ended up with just the two of us,' says Ed. 'It was at that point that my nephew Harry, who was serving in Afghanistan as a captain in the Green Jackets, got wounded. Badly. In an IED explosion. He lost his left leg in the blast, and his right a fortnight later after an infection had taken hold. The Taliban put shit in the bombs. Literally. Which the IRA used to do as well. It means there's a secondary impact to the blast.

'When my wife Harriet and I first went to see

him, at Selly Oak Hospital in Birmingham, he was hugely ill with this bloody infection. There was this yellow, broken body. It's a very odd sight when you see someone you know and love and they've got a sheet over them and you're expecting to see legs and toes and it just stops at around the knees. He was sweating hugely. He opened his eyes, couldn't smile, but thank God, the sparkle was still there. There was an instant when I looked into his eyes and thought, *OK, fine, he's going to pull through*. But you wouldn't want that to happen to anyone you care about.

'I spoke to Simon at this time and he was very quick off the mark in saying, "Right, OK, we should do this expedition, and we should take some wounded soldiers with us."'

'I didn't know Harry at this stage at all,' says Simon. 'But I was on the phone with Ed talking about what had happened to his nephew and I suddenly thought, *Now here's a reason*. It was my idea to take the wounded with us. We both immediately went, "Yeah, that's a great idea. It's got an angle, it's got a feel to it, we can do something with that."'

'Ed was very upset,' says Harriet. 'He said, "Whatever I'm going to do, I'm going to do it for Harry." At that stage you are only thinking of that one child. Then you realise it could help lots of other wounded soldiers.'

'That was the point,' says Ed, 'at which everything changed. The momentum, the support of our wives, the support of everyone else.'

*　　　*　　　*

16

Things started to move fast. Through a woman he met at a wedding, Simon was put in touch with expedition leader Henry Cookson, a member of the three-man team that had won the Scott Dunn Polar Challenge in 2005, a race on skis to the North Magnetic Pole. Subsequently Henry had got himself into the *Guinness Book of Records* with the same trio by being the first to make it to Antarctica's Pole of Inaccessibility (the exact heart of the continent) without mechanical help. They skied with kites for the full 1100 miles.

'Simon sat next to a girl I'd taken up Kilimanjaro,' Henry recalls. 'When he and I met up and he told me about their idea I explained that I wasn't the guy to actually lead a trip like this. My experience has been the Antarctic and the North Magnetic Pole, but with the North Geographical Pole, you're walking on sea ice which is constantly moving over strong currents. I suggested Inge Solheim, a Norwegian I'd met in the Antarctic. He's done lots of trips to the North Pole, and has huge experience of the polar ice. He's also taken disabled people up mountains in Sweden and a blind man to the South Pole. He seemed like the obvious guy to bring in.'

A meeting was arranged in the very same pub where Simon's South Pole expedition had been hatched, the Cross Keys in Chelsea. The four participants put a map on the table and considered the options.

There are actually five North Poles: the North Magnetic Pole, to which compasses point, which moves from year to year and is currently located over the Canadian Arctic; the North Geomagnetic Pole, which centres the earth's magnetic field, at

17

the moment floating somewhere over north-west Greenland; the Northern Pole of Inaccessibility, the point farthest in all directions from land; the North Celestial Pole, the extension of a line drawn through the earth's axis and out into space; and the North Geographical Pole, the fixed and absolute top of the world, ninety degrees north, where all lines of longitude converge, the place from which everywhere else on the planet is south. This last was their target.

The journey to the North Geographical Pole can only sensibly be made in March or April. 'Otherwise,' says Henry Cookson bluntly, 'it is winter and miserably cold and dark—or it has melted.' Even during this special two months of opportunity, the Pole is a seriously hostile landscape. There are pressure ridges, created when the huge ice sheets crash together, forming walls of broken ice up to fifteen feet high. There are open leads, where the surface cracks without warning to reveal the freezing water beneath. There are rubble fields, where loose ice debris is strewn for miles. There are polar bears, which, belying their cuddly image, are dangerous and predatory animals. And the humidity is higher than in Antarctica, so it feels colder. It's not for nothing that Inge Solheim likes to follow earlier Norwegian explorers in calling it 'the Devil's dance floor'.

Expeditions to the North Pole have always been perilous. Early attempts to reach this fabled destination generally finished in disaster. In 1845 the British explorer Sir John Franklin took two ships into the North-West Passage and was never seen again. An American bid in 1871 ended with the death of its commander and a shipwreck on

18

Greenland. Ten years later the USS *Jeanette* was crushed by ice in the Lena Delta and lost half her crew. In 1897 three Swedish explorers perished when their hydrogen balloon became stranded north-east of Spitsbergen. There were numerous other failed attempts, their participants limping back home in smashed ships with frostbite or scurvy or worse. The first undisputed surface conquest of the Pole wasn't made, incredibly, until 1968, when an American foursome reached it by snowmobile. The first team to reach the Pole on foot was the British Trans-Arctic Expedition in 1969, the year some other men landed on the Moon.

Was it possible for Ed and Simon, in the expert company of Inge and Henry, to take a group of wounded soldiers across this terrifying terrain to reach their goal? Inge thought it was, in principle. Discussions moved on to possible routes. There were two main options: Canadian and Siberian. Canada is closer to the Pole than Siberia, and the journey from Canada marginally less cold. But it was not really an option to do a full trip from land. 'The problem with going from the coast,' Henry points out, 'is that you've got ice floes coming on to the land mass which concertina up, you've got miles and miles of ice rubble, and to cover the distance'— on the shortest route 374 nautical miles—'you'd have to start very early in the season when there is the greatest danger from polar bears.'

The best option, Inge thought, would be to make the journey from the Barneo Floating Ice Camp, a Russian-run station that operates during March and April on the Siberian side. From Barneo the group could be inserted by helicopter on to the ice at a location of 85° to 86° north, which was a more realistic 300 nautical miles from the Pole. At a pace of twelve nautical miles a day, they would take approximately twenty-five days to reach their destination. This route also had the advantage of much better evacuation options should anything go wrong, an important factor considering what Ed and Simon were attempting. In reasonable visibility a helicopter could reach the Pole from Barneo in just under four hours.

There remained the question of whether to go supported or unsupported. The former option meant having helicopters come out to replenish food and other supplies, so that the weight carried by individual team members would be much less; the latter entailed going it alone, dragging everything they needed with them on pulks (as Norwegian sledges are known). Quite apart from the fact that the second option was cheaper, both Ed and Simon felt that if they were going to do this thing, they wanted to do it properly. By the end of the evening they had agreed that their idea was feasible—and they were going unsupported. 'From then on,' says Simon, 'we didn't look back. It was go, go, go, go.'

Ed Parker now contacted the wounded servicemen's charities: the Royal British Legion and the British Limbless Ex Service Men's Association (BLESMA), as well as the new kid on the block, Help for Heroes. The charities were supportive from the outset, but Ed admits to being disappointed with the Army's response. 'The initial reaction when we went to them and said we wanted to take some wounded blokes with us to the North Pole was "no". I was completely gobsmacked by the barriers they put up. We came across one bloke we nicknamed Colonel Porridge. Because the joke was that dealing with him was like wading through porridge.'

At the start of January 2010 a letter and questionnaire was sent out direct to wounded ex-servicemen. 'It was an interesting initial response,' wrote Ed, in the diary he had now started keeping. 'Not as many replied as we hoped, but those that did seem perfect for what we want to do. The answers these blokes have written to our questions are sometimes extraordinary. They describe their injuries like most of us would talk about a common cold. The overriding message was their determination to achieve something remarkable.'

'All the wounded are on an email system from Help for Heroes,' says Guy Disney. 'One pinged in one day which basically said, "We're looking for some chaps to make the first attempt by wounded servicemen to get to the North Pole." I saw it and decided in about five seconds that I wanted to do it. It sounded like an incredible opportunity.'

After a careful look through the forms, Ed and Simon drew up a list of possibles. Two selection days followed, at the Rifles Club in London. Here the candidates were interviewed by Simon, Ed, Henry and Inge, as well as being looked over by a physical fitness trainer, a doctor, and prosthetics expert Jamie Gillespie of PACE Rehabilitation, himself a wounded ex-soldier with an artificial leg. One of the biggest challenges of the expedition would be managing the technical side of taking disabled men to the Arctic: how would prosthetic limbs perform in temperatures as low as −50°C? Might the polymers change, the carbon become

21

brittle, the glue come undone, or the metal core conduct unbearable cold into the centre of the leg?

Guy Disney was one of about 120 who were invited to attend. 'There were all kinds of guys there,' he recalls. 'One who had no legs at all. They were great spirits. To me, they epitomised the typical soldier in the British Army.'

'It was a very humbling experience meeting all these men,' Ed wrote. 'They came with a huge air of optimism. They all wanted to be the one who came with us to assault the North Pole. One Para, who had been hit by an RPG, losing his left arm and suffering huge muscle loss to his left leg, grinned from ear to ear as he told us of his recovery and his undoubted belief that he would be able to make it. I could imagine him dragging himself across the ice, refusing to give up.'

'There was one South African guy, a Para, Jaco was his name,' said Simon, after the selection day was over. 'An RPG had exploded into his arm. He had lost that. Then when we looked at his leg it was like someone had got a spoon and literally spooned out all the muscle, all the way along. He had a colostomy bag as well. He was so badly wounded. But he had such a sunny attitude and he really wanted to do it. Unfortunately there was no way he could have made it. Because he wouldn't have had enough feeling in his arms and legs to determine if he was getting frostbitten or not.'

Tough decisions had to be made, however disappointing for the candidates. Jamie Gillespie was adamant that the expedition would not be suitable for double amputees, as the movement needed to swing a ski would be too great. And there were other issues, which perhaps only veterans of a polar expedition could have known about.

'We had one double amputee,' said Simon, 'and we said to him, "Pick up this pen off the floor." So he bent down. And the only way he could get back up again was to pull himself up with his arms against a table, because he had no leverage on his knees. I turned to Ed after he'd gone and I said, "I tell you what, he couldn't have a crap at the Pole. Because someone would have to help him up every time." It was really simple. He couldn't squat, and you know, hanging over someone while they're having a dump in a forty mile an hour wind is not my idea of great fun. So that was a very good reason to rule him out regardless of all the technical bits.'

'I was scared and impressed by the stories and the scars and the wounds that we saw that day,' says Inge Solheim. 'Some of the injuries were crazy. We were listening to how these men had got shot or stepped on a land mine or been hit by an RPG. At that point I started to realise how important this charity was, and this cause. We deploy people to war zones and we expect them to be ready to make the ultimate sacrifice, or even worse in some cases, to come back paralysed. We owe them recognition for what they have done for us.'

Ed didn't find it easy calling those the team had decided to reject. 'The first person I rang,' he wrote, 'was a lance-corporal from the Grenadier Guards, a thoroughly nice chap who had come off guard to see us. While his wounds were well healed, he had an above the knee amputation, and we had pretty much decided we couldn't risk taking someone with such an injury. The effort required to walk is 300 per cent more than if the injured individual has a knee. While he had good mobility, it was too much of a risk. Telling him was awful. This lad, who has been through so much, was determined to be coming with us, and went so far as to say, "I'll prove you wrong, sir".'

After much sifting and consideration, three wounded men were picked for a testing and selection process in the remote Svalbard Archipelago, several hundred miles north of Norway, over a week in May 2010: Martin Hewitt, Guy Disney and Rob Copsey, an ex-serviceman from the Royal Engineers, who had lost the lower half of his right leg stepping on an anti-personnel mine while on Operation Gabriel, a humanitarian mission to Rwanda in 1994. At thirty-nine Rob was considerably older than the others, but with a maturity that Ed and Simon welcomed. That he hadn't been in Afghanistan was a positive bonus, they felt, giving a breadth of experience to the expedition, and illustrating that the phenomenon of the wounded soldier was not just a recent one. 'I think he's a wonderful balance to all of them,' said Simon, when the shortlist had been drawn up. 'He's very mature. He's got a wife and child. He wasn't injured in one of the recent wars, but some time ago in Rwanda. I think he'll be a very good balancing act for the other parties that are going out there.'

'Rob's story is extraordinary,' said Ed. 'At the time he was wounded, the Army pretty much said, "Here you are chum, thanks very much, goodbye."'

24

3

A SPORTSMAN'S BET?

ROB: We arrived in Rwanda in the middle of summer '94, when the main genocide was over. But there were still a lot of angry people milling around. There were some strange sights. I remember seeing one young kid, who couldn't have been older than twelve or fourteen. He was in army fatigues with an American grenade launcher, and it was armed. He was swanning around Kigali with a gang of his mates, giving us all the evil looks. It was bizarre, he could have just fired this thing at anybody.

You don't take it on board when you see it on the telly. That's just a box in the corner of your room with pictures. When you're out there you smell it and taste it, you see it in a completely different way. The smoke from wood fires, the dust, the stink of rotting flesh—it's horrendous.

We started out at the airport and eventually transferred to the National Football Stadium in the middle of Kigali. The place had been piled high with bodies and before we moved in they all had to be cleared. There was no control, no police or anything. Everyone was just doing their own thing, people coming to try and find lost members of their families. The word was that the stadium had been a torture place and the changing rooms had been used for all sorts of atrocities. There were marks on the walls, bullet holes, machete marks, that sort of thing. So we cleaned all that up and then we moved in. It became a secure base for us.

We got involved with all the other aid agencies that had already gone out there, mopping up and assisting. We were there as engineers, and it wasn't combat engineering. So that was good. We felt we were helping. Water purification was the main thing. Going out to massive refugee camps and delivering water. Some of the guys went to clear a reservoir that was contaminated because it had bodies in it. Then we were doing a lot of repairs. I repaired the roof of the hospital I ended up going into to have my leg off. How ironic was that?

We also provided security for the medics while they did triage with casualties. It was a problem all the agencies had at the time. Once people saw there was aid or a medical person they came running and the facility would be swamped. So we had to control the crowds. It was a matter of moving people into queues. They didn't know how to queue; they saw help and wanted to get it. Once they understood what we were doing they went the other way; they were very friendly—and grateful. You could tell they were often in agony, but they weren't moaning about it. Or bitching to get to the front. If it had been me, I'd have been rolling around on the floor, but they just stood there patiently in line. The whole experience was humbling. These people had nothing. Absolutely nothing.

My accident happened in October, about two-thirds of the way through our tour. A task came up: it was a damaged Bailey bridge in Kigali that needed repairing so it could be opened to traffic again. It was highly urgent and one particular sergeant major, Richard Brown, was well known within the Corps of Engineers as being a very good bridge man. The night before we went in, we were all briefed and told that a bomb disposal recce of the bridgehead had been done. Which meant no bombs, no mines, no threat.

The next day we went to the site and started gouging out parts of the demolished bridge. A Bailey bridge is heavy, so this was hard going. As we worked we noticed some soldiers of the Rwandan Patriotic Army (RPA) on the far bank of the river, shouting at us and holding up their weapons, AK-47s and rifles. We ignored them and carried on. It was highly unlikely, we thought, that they were going to try shooting at us.

Around midday we broke to have some food. After lunch I happened to be at the head of the guys, walking back down the embankment to get a sledge hammer that was propped up against a transom beam. I was about to start knocking out this big pin to take part of the bridge down. As I stood on a girder, there was a very loud bang, right underneath me.

Everything goes slowly then. I'm now astraddle this girder. My left leg is behind the girder and my right is on the other side. I'm thinking, *What the bloody hell was that?* Then: *Get down you idiot. You're being fired at by those guys over the river.* But then I have a sudden sensation of intense heat. It's like dipping your toe into a really hot bath and immediately pulling it out. Except that you can't pull it out. This burning heat is now creeping up my leg. I look down at my foot. My boot is black and smouldering; my army fatigues too. There's a crater around my foot. *Oh shit*, I thought, *I've stepped on a mine or something.*

It was only then that I fell over. To the right, landing so hard on my elbow that I sliced it open.

27

As it turned out, that was a good thing to have done. Because if I'd fallen to the left, I would have landed on another three mines. They were all in such close proximity, they probably would have finished me off. It's amazing that none of us had stepped on them during the morning.

Sergeant Major Brown was there, shouting at everyone to freeze.

'Retrace your exact steps back up to the road,' he yelled, and everyone started tiptoeing back up to the vehicles. Then he ran down and got me.

'Oh shit, my foot, my foot,' I was shouting.

'Shut up!' he shouted back at me. And I did. I suppose it was his way of taking control. Then he put his arm round me and walked me out of there. It was a brave thing to do, because where there's one mine there's usually three; and that day, in that place, as they discovered later, there were more.

Once I was flat in the back of the Land Rover they cut my boot off and got a dressing on my foot. There wasn't lots of blood spurting out like you see on TV. The front of my foot had just vaporised—from the toes to the bridge. All the bones were shattered. At that point the pain really kicked in. I was breathing really heavily, like a woman giving birth. Sergeant Major Brown was beside me holding my foot and a guy called Paddy was holding my hand, going, 'Come on, Rob, come on, you'll be all right, mate.'

All of a sudden the Land Rover skidded to a halt. I could hear a load of shouting from outside. There was a chain across the road and an RPA roadblock. These guys had AK-47s and they were saying we'd have to turn round. Sergeant Major Brown wasn't having that. He scrambled out the back and there was more shouting. The next thing I knew he'd got one of them by the scruff of the neck and round to the doors. He was pointing at my foot and yelling. I was aware of a black face and the whites of his eyes as he gawped at me.

'OK,' he said. They dropped the chain and we were on our way.

We drove on down a dirt road. I could feel every bump and every rock. I was focussing on one rivet hole in the roof of the Land Rover. To one side the daylight was streaming in. It looked more and more like a single beam.

'Come on, Rob!' Paddy was shouting, 'Stay with us, Rob!'

All of a sudden it was as if I was above the Land Rover, looking down at it bumping along the dirt road. I could see myself looking up at the roof, Paddy shouting at me and the sergeant major holding my foot. There was dust flying up behind the vehicle and I could see that too. I could see the bushes and thorn trees on either side of the road.

Then Paddy slapped me on the face a couple of times and I was back on the floor of the Land Rover. To this day I can't explain what happened. Perhaps I was unconscious. But it felt as if I was really there, high above the road, watching myself.

Now I was on a stretcher, being run into the casualty room where they cut my fatigues off and gave me pain relief. They were Australians and they kept calling me 'Sir'.

'Don't call me "sir",' I said. 'I'm not a bloody officer, I'm a sapper.'

I had the amputation that day. When I came round I was in the ward that I'd helped repair.

I stayed in that place for a couple of weeks, being

29

looked after by Australian nurses. Even though I realised I'd lost my leg, I was still in awe of some of the locals who'd been injured. There was a boy there who'd got shrapnel to the head from a mortar round. He'd lost an eye, but he was the happiest kid around. There were many others in the ward who were in a much worse state than me. It made me think, *OK, you've got to deal with this now, mush. Crack on with it.*

Peter Inge, the Chief of the Defence Staff, was there at the time and he himself came to see me. He told me he was very sorry about what had happened. If there was anything he could do, he said, I should let him know. He wrote to my mum, as well. It was very good of him to do that, but much later I heard a rumour about the whole incident. That there had been a sportsman's bet between Inge and Brown. Inge had apparently said that if Brown could build the bridge within twenty-four hours, he would send a magnum of champagne to his mess. I always wondered if this was true, and if the mine that injured me had been overlooked as a result.

There were no complications with my amputation, no secondary infections or anything, so after a fortnight I had a second operation to close the stump, then I was flown home. I went with a guy called Captain Button, who was going back because his wife had died. He was supposed to be looking after me, I think, but he was equally shell-shocked, because his world had crumbled too. We flew to Mombasa in an Italian air force military plane, then we did the rest of the journey on British Airways.

We were like this odd couple, wandering around Mombasa International Airport. I was wearing a

KSB walking boot on my good foot, a pair of jeans and a 9 Para Squadron sweatshirt. That and a pair of crutches I'd been given. Captain Button was in similar garb. We'd just come out of an operational theatre and we were minging. I was about seven stone and Button was miserable as sin. The looks we were getting were comical. People avoided us.

We then found ourselves in club class. Two stinking, scruffy soldiers in a cabin full of business people in suits, all immaculate. I couldn't bend my knee, so I had to ask the guy in front not to recline his seat. 'Where the hell have you two come from?' he asked. So we told him. He and his colleague were gobsmacked. They didn't even know the Brits were in Rwanda.

Back in the UK, I spent a month in Woolwich Military Hospital, then I went to Headley Court. It was very different then from how it is now. The last major war had been Gulf War One, which was very light on casualties. Most of the guys there had got injured through sport or accidents at work. But I met other amputees, including Jamie Gillespie. He'd been in 9 Para as well and had had a motorcycling accident.

It was a sad time, because we were fighting to try and stay in the Army, but it was also a fun and fascinating time. There were five of us amputees and we all helped each other. There was a natural bond, because we'd all lost limbs. There was a lot of black humour too. Calling each other a one-legged git or nicking each other's prosthetic limb and hiding it. We did all sorts of silly stuff. Broke into the gym one night and put a load of stink bombs under the mats where the chief Physical Training Instructor would stand. The next day an awful ammonia smell rapidly filled the place. In the end they had to stop the lesson, evacuate us and open all the doors. It was childish, really, but I think at the time it was a way of coping with what we were going through and what we knew was going to happen, which was being medically discharged from the Army. We knew it was coming, but none of us wanted it.

It's harsh. The Army fights wars and is good at it, but it's not so good at the back stuff. What you soon realise is that it's your relatives and friends who have to pick up the pieces. And if not them the charities. The Royal British Legion, BLESMA, Combat Stress, St Dunstan's, who help the blind ex-servicemen and women. Help for Heroes didn't exist at that time.

That was basically my motivation for wanting to raise money for Walking With The Wounded. Because I'm acutely aware how difficult it is for men and women from the services to rebuild their lives after such a life-changing event. In the fifteen years since I lost my leg, I have met hundreds of amputees, and I'm humbled by a lot of them. I know one guy, for example, who's a double amputee who also lost an eye. He was injured in '89 in Northern Ireland, and he was completely forgotten about. He fell through the system. He was militarily discharged and that was that, he was on his own. But he's managed to rebuild his life. He has married and had several kids. I never once heard him moan. Not once. That is the attitude of a lot of the guys.

Mine was like that to start with too. I was back riding a motorbike the January after I'd lost my leg. Headley Court went mad. They tried to nick

32

my keys and hide my crash helmet. I set myself challenges. Two years later, in 1996, I ran the London Marathon. I wanted to prove to myself, and also my friends and family, that I was OK, that I'd got over the loss of my leg—and of my Army career. But the truth was, deep down inside, I hadn't.

The day after I was discharged I applied for a job at Sea France, loading the ferries. You're basically a car park attendant, taking tickets, directing cars to the top deck or bottom, on your feet all day. I was absolutely crapping myself when I went for the interview. I thought that if they found out about my leg they wouldn't employ me. So I did the best walk I could, didn't say anything, and I got the job. About three months later I told them and they were gobsmacked. But they didn't sack me. I had proved I could do the job.

About five years after my injury I had a really black period. I was angry, I was depressed, I was drinking too much. One Sunday my parents, my mum and stepdad, invited me round for dinner.

'We're worried about you,' they said. 'You're not yourself.'

'I'm fine,' I said. 'Leave it. I'm all right.'

I was half way through my dinner and I started crying. I couldn't stop and I didn't know why. The three of us decided I needed some help, so I took myself off to a hospital that specialises in mental health problems, Ticehurst House in Sussex. I only did a two-week programme—post-traumatic counselling—but it was the best thing I could have done. Slowly I turned myself round.

A few years later, I was at a do in Aldershot, and I saw Sergeant Major Brown again. He got the Queen's Gallantry Medal for what he did that day; he was later commissioned and is now a major. (Peter Inge is Field Marshal Lord Inge these days.)

It was about midnight and we'd had a few beers. I saw Brown and I thought, *I need to do this.* So I went up to him and I said, 'Richard.'

He turned round and looked at me blankly.

'It's Rob Copsey,' I said.

Then he realised who I was.

'Yeah,' he said. 'How are you?'

'I'm fine, Richard,' I said. 'I just want you to know that I am fine and I don't hold any grudge against you.'

I put my hand out and he shook it. Then he nodded and turned and walked away. I think he was a bit choked, to be honest. I didn't see him again that night. He disappeared. But I felt relief for saying that. I needed to do it for me. Because feeling so angry and carrying it around for ages doesn't do you any good.

4

A PRINCE AT THE POLE

In tandem with selecting the wounded men who were going to come to the North Pole with them, Ed and Simon were working hard on finding sponsors. Even going unsupported as they planned, they were looking at £200,000 to get themselves and two soldiers to the Pole and back. They were both aware that it was a lot of money to raise and equally keen that donations should go 100 per cent towards the wounded rather than on paying the costs of the expedition.

At the end of January Ed and his nephew Harry Parker flew to Scotland to address an 'awayday' organised by Lloyds Development Capital, a private equity company whose CEO had already expressed broad support for the idea of the charity. In his diary Ed wrote: 'Harry hasn't flown since he was on a plane back from Camp Bastion under sedation, so the trip up north was a big deal for both of us. But I found the support and goodwill he received from so many complete strangers very encouraging. When the captain of the plane asked Harry what had happened to him and then congratulated him on still smiling, I felt a definite lump. People really do care about what these boys have done in our name.

'We were warmly welcomed by LDC and Harry spoke about what it's like to be a soldier on the front line, something which I suspect was pretty alien to most of the 100 or so people in the room. He talked briefly about what had happened to him and the challenges that face the wounded as they try and prepare for a new future—all in a matter-of-fact way that had an enormous impact on those we were addressing. I spoke too, briefly, about the walk and the charity. I think they probably looked on me with pity and surprise. A 44-year-old planning to pull a sledge to the North Pole with no polar experience. Sure! But when we talked about the charity, it definitely seemed to resonate.'

'I often wonder,' said Harry, 'just how much of it is me being an effective communicator and how much they're just gawping at me.' Barely six months after being blown up he had only recently started walking without sticks. He had taken to wearing shorts, so that his two iron legs were clearly on view. This wasn't because he was an exhibitionist, but because it made it easier to take off the prosthesis when it became uncomfortable. It also allowed passers-by to know what they were dealing with: 'I think it looks weirder if I've got trousers on. In London especially, people passing, going up the tube escalator or whatever, are otherwise going, "Come *on*! Get out of the way."'

Harry was only slowly coming to terms with his new role as a wounded soldier: 'This injury really wasn't part of my big plan. But it's part of who I am now, so I've got to get on with it. I'm quite mindful that you can get pigeonholed. I really don't want to become this professional wounded person. I was happy to help Ed with his charity, but only because it was Ed and I believe in what it's all about.'

While other approaches to possible sponsors were made, the organisers were not turning away any ideas for money raising. A friend of Ed's wife Harriet had suggested a series of 'Support the Walk' lunches. 'We started off writing to two hundred and fifty people,' says Harriet, 'asking them to host a lunch, with the idea that those people then went home and had another lunch, so you get a pyramid of awareness building up, and hopefully also money. It was astonishing how it snowballed. Some people did coffee mornings, some did dinners, it didn't matter, it ended up raising a lot.'

'One thing which continues to amaze me,' Ed wrote, 'is the enthusiasm and support people are giving us over this.'

Another intriguing development was the possible

involvement of Prince Harry, either to offer support for the expedition's press launch in March, or even, just possibly, to accompany the team for part of the walk itself. Dags had a friend in common with the Prince and had talked to him about the expedition at a social event: 'It was Lawrence Dallaglio's Eight Rocks party in Battersea. Harry was there with a mate. I went over to him and said, "Thank you very much for your support." He said, "I wish I could come with you." I said, "You're more than welcome." We laughed about it and that was about it. But it was something that stayed in our minds. Wouldn't it be great to have Harry along? So Ed then went through the official channels.'

'If we were able to have him join us from Barneo for the last degree,' Ed wrote in his diary, 'it would be fabulous for our publicity. I'm sure it would help gain more corporate sponsorship too. It seems there's a little horse-trading going on. He either walks with us or does the launch! My view is that he will hopefully do both, but we obviously mustn't push our luck too much. We are enormously lucky to have his support at all.'

*   *   *

A second selection session at the Rifles Club at the end of February brought more possible candidates for the shortlist. A Welsh ex-PTI was, Ed noted, 'thoroughly engaging, with the grit and determination of ten men', but he had an above-the-knee amputation, something the selectors were cautious about, as the lack of mobility and the energy required to walk without a knee was significantly greater. The clincher was that he had sustained his injuries in a motorcycling accident in Germany. Ultimately, Ed and Simon felt that the expedition had to be about soldiers wounded on operations. 'It will be agony telling him he's not coming,' wrote Ed, 'as he was so up for it.'

A place, however, was to be offered to Matt Kingston, a Royal Marine who had lost a leg below the knee after he was shot through the ankle during a firefight near Afghanistan's Kajaki Dam. In the two and a half years since he'd been wounded, Matt had, on a prosthetic limb, run the London Marathon, cycled to Paris and climbed Mount Everest to Base Camp One.

'Following this last session,' Ed wrote, 'we now have our shortlist of four, and it's a really good mix. Three below-knee amputations and one lame arm as a result of a gunshot wound to the shoulder. More encouragingly, we have two officers and two other ranks, a Para and a bootneck, a cavalry officer and a customs officer. While three were wounded in Afghanistan, one was wounded a few years back in Rwanda, so not all the emphasis is on today. Who will or won't come? Already I know the decision which two to take will be a horrible one. For the moment, I remain a little concerned that Martin Hewitt, who was shot in the shoulder, might have difficulty with his arm. He has limited nerves and blood flow in it and I fear there is a real danger that he could sustain cold damage without knowing. We do have a duty of care to these guys and we mustn't take undue risks.'

Fortunately the expedition had been offered expert help in making these tricky but essential assessments. Ed had successfully approached the Institute of Naval Medicine at Alverstoke in

Hampshire, which in addition to its work for the Fleet is an internationally recognised centre for maritime and occupational health advice, training and research, with such intriguing-sounding departments as the Submarine and Radiation Medicine Division and the Diving and Hyperbaric Medicine Division, as well as the world's only Cold Clinic, where tests on individuals' suitability for extremely cold environments are routinely run.

In early March, Ed, Simon, Inge Solheim, Henry Cookson, Rob Copsey and Matt Kingston presented themselves at the Institute. Martin Hewitt was away in Canada skiing at the Paralympics and Guy Disney was on an Army course, but the nucleus of the Walking With The Wounded squad was there. 'It was the first time we had seen Rob and Matt since the initial interviews,' wrote Ed, 'and it felt great having a day together, starting to form into a team. We were amazed after we arrived to be shown into a small room where we were greeted by no less than seven staff. We were all rather nervous as we thought that we were going to be dunked into the cold pool, but luckily that wasn't in store for us.'

Instead the group had their body mass, blood pressure and lung capacity measured, before being rigged up to an electro-cardiograph (ECG) machine, to test heart fitness. Next up was the VO_2 Max test (which involves pedalling on an exercise bicycle with a tube in your mouth, while your body's capacity to transport and use oxygen is analysed). 'This meant absolutely nothing to me,' Ed wrote, 'but it was explained that we would each in turn have a session on the bike. Every minute the resistance is increased. The plan is to

39

keep pedalling at a constant rate until you can't pedal any more. Inge, our Norwegian guide, went first. None of us knew what was a good or a bad performance, although we all assumed Inge was in pretty good shape. I was second. Bear in mind that I went for my first run just over two years ago, when I decided it was time to get fit again, and during that run I had to walk after only half a mile. Since then I've run a fair amount and been training hard in the gym, but this was the first time I'd been physically tested since leaving the Army in 1992. I started off OK, but as the minutes progressed it got harder and harder. But our team and all the medics were watching, urging me on. I went through Inge's time, much to my surprise, and felt there was still something in the locker, so I kept going and managed a couple more minutes before I hit the wall. One should never brag, but by Jiminy, I ended up with the longest time and the highest score. On a day when the competitive nature of us all was reawakened, it felt fantastic! During the drive back to London with Dags, I was delighted to do a little nose rubbing.'

More important than Ed's personal triumph, perhaps, was the assessment of the capability of the two wounded members for the cold weather training and selection in Svalbard in May. Matt Kingston was deemed to have sound overall fitness and good balance and strength in both his legs. When Rob Copsey took his turn on the VO_2, however, it became apparent that he had developed a habit of favouring his left leg over his damaged right. Questioning by the medical team revealed that he had never been offered or received any physiotherapy since his injury. Despite his many

40

physical achievements since then, including the running of marathons, Rob had effectively been using one leg. But both men were passed fit to go.

A discussion between the organisers and the head doctor, Dr Dan Roiz de Sa, about one of the two absent candidates, however, was less positive. As Ed had thought, Martin Hewitt's injuries meant that the blood circulation in his right arm would be poor, while as a result of nerve deterioration there was a strong possibility that he wouldn't be able to feel any cold damage as it occurred. This was a real danger, a risk that the organisers might not ultimately be able to take.

*   *   *

Back at their various home bases the team put into practice the advice they had been given by both the Institute and Inge. In addition to regular runs and gym sessions they were all also encouraged to drag tyres, this being the best agreed method of building up the core strength necessary to pull sledges for hours at a time across the snow-covered ice pack of the North Pole.

The alarming reality of what they had let themselves in for was indeed growing on Ed. One evening he went with his wife Harriet to a talk given by Tom Avery, an explorer and author who had been to both Poles, breaking the record for the fastest ever trip to the South Pole by using kites. He had also replicated the North Pole expedition made by Peary and Henson back in 1909, using similar dog teams and wooden sledges. (Peary's claim to have reached the Pole has long been disputed, but Avery's experience made him believe that it might, after all, have been genuine.)

'While Tom was telling us about the South Pole,' Ed wrote, 'there was something a little mundane about it. But when he started talking about the North Pole, he instantly became animated. It was the more challenging of the two, he said, more nerve-racking, more unrelenting. He spoke of its beauty, its remoteness, of it almost being alive. Then of standing, briefly, on top of the world, something that I have an ever increasing desire to do. As I watched and listened to him I felt a thrill welling up, a hint of adrenalin, and definitely some anticipation and apprehension. But what I saw was a place I now really wanted to go. In contrast, next to me, poor Harriet was watching with complete horror. As Tom spoke of the dangers from polar bears, the open water leads, the moving ice and the cold, I think she became more and more frightened about what is to come. She has to think, not just of herself, but of the children back here too. She has to imagine the worst case scenario, and listening to Tom she heard many different instances which weren't good.'

'To start with,' says Harriet, 'Tom talked about the South Pole. Then he said, "Anybody thinking about going to the North Pole faces death every day." I almost gagged. I made this extraordinary noise. He then showed us some quite graphic photographs of pressure ridges and leads and dogs falling into them and having to be hauled out. There was one picture of a tent with a lead underneath it that had opened up overnight, so they had woken up to find themselves either side of it. It was a very interesting lecture, but it made me realise that this was actually an incredibly hostile place to go, and a dangerous thing to do, and was my husband mad?'

'On our way home,' Ed wrote, 'Harriet asked a very wise question: "How would you feel if it was me going?" Which was incredibly difficult to answer. I think my first feeling would be to protect the children from it all, then an element of anger about her selfishness in embarking on such a trip. Does the fact that we are doing this for the wounded impact on the decision? Of course. But there is still a very personal side to all this. Dags told me recently that the hardest bit of his South Pole trip was saying goodbye to his family. I know it will be the same for me.'

But by now Ed knew there was no going back; the beast he and Simon had created already had its own life. The official press launch at the Rifles Club in Mayfair on 19 March only took things a step further. Especially as Prince Harry had now agreed to come down and lend his support.

By this stage Ed and Simon had a PR agency on board. Captive Minds had come recommended by Inge Solheim, as they had worked on an expedition he had been involved with a couple of years before; its directors, Marcus Chidgey and Alex Rayner, initially agreed to work *pro bono*. Now Marcus swung into action. 'Creating the right scene,' says Alex. 'Having the right backdrops, the right messaging.' The agency took Rob Copsey down to his home town of Dover and filmed him dragging three big black tyres across the pebbly beach, his prosthetic leg exposed underneath a pair of black shorts, balancing himself with ski poles. It was a powerful piece of footage that was shown across several TV networks. 'There was a very quick turnaround,' says Marcus, 'from the day we met Ed and Dags, to them being given a date by Clarence House. It was set up so rapidly in fact that we were making the warm-up video overnight.'

For Ed, the launch day began at 5.40 a.m., with a taxi to BBC Television Centre for an appearance on the BBC *Breakfast* programme. He and Rob Copsey were joined on the crimson couch in the studio by a bearded Inge Solheim, who provided the voice of experience to balance the enthusiastic novices. Breakfast television led to the World Service, then to Channel Five and on; by the time Ed arrived at the Rifles Club at lunchtime the outside broadcast units were double parked down Davies Street.

Dags was as surprised as his fellow organiser by the turnout: 'We thought that there might be a couple of photographers and maybe a freelance cameraman who could flog something to the BBC. But then the phone started ringing and the BBC wanted to be there and ITV and Sky wanted to do live broadcasts and there were all these bloody great satellite trucks on the street outside, and we were kind of going, "Whoah."'

'We were given the nod by Clarence House,' says Alex Rayner, 'literally the day before, that Harry might be quite keen to go along on the expedition. That meant that the media interest did get very excitable the night before.'

The Prince got to his feet, at the centre of a line-up which included Ed, Simon, Inge, Rob and Matt, and told the gathered press, as expected, that he was absolutely thrilled to become patron of this wonderful expedition. But at the end of his short speech came the bombshell. 'You'll be glad to know, maybe,' he said, in characteristically self-deprecating style, 'that if my military commitments allow me I would love to join the team. I hope to join for maybe five days before the end if I'm allowed—and invited.' He grinned at the organisers, Ed and Simon, on his left. 'Hopefully,' he went on, turning to Matt and Rob on his other side, 'I'll be able to keep up with you guys otherwise it'll be fairly embarrassing. Let's get an army flag on the North Pole before my brother lands a helicopter there.'

The laughter that followed was drowned out by the sound of journalists reaching in handbags and jacket pockets for their Blackberries. If all went well this would in due course make for the kind of headline that tabloid sub-editors dream about: A PRINCE AT THE POLE. And sure enough, the next morning, the *Daily Mail* led with HEAVE HO HARRY! PRINCE PREPARES TO JOIN THE WALKING WOUNDED IN TREK TO NORTH POLE.

'After everyone went home,' says Simon, 'I was down in the garage in the basement with Ed and there was a moment of silence. And then we looked at each other and said, "Jesus Christ, what was all that about?"'

'The single most inspiring moment of the day,' Ed wrote in his diary, 'was when my mobile rang again, for the umpteenth time, as Harriet and I were driving back to Norfolk. A man who had lost his leg to diabetes phoned me to say how proud he felt about what we were doing. He acknowledged he wasn't a military amputee, but he thought that we will act as an inspiration to all amputees. To be able to get the attention of people like this, and for it to mean something to them, means a whole lot

45

more than I would have expected. Walking With The Wounded is now real, very real. No pulling out now, just pulling to the Pole. Hoofin' as Matt would say!'

The success of the launch had an immediate impact. TV production companies were falling over themselves in their keenness to make a film about the expedition. Meanwhile, the BBC's security correspondent, Frank Gardner, expressed a desire to cover the continuing news side of the story (he had been a Territorial Army officer for six years and was himself confined to a wheelchair after an attack by Al-Qaeda sympathisers while on assignment in Riyadh, Saudi Arabia).

'We were literally deluged with TV companies saying they would love to do the documentary,' says Marcus Chidgey. 'We felt that the TV deal could be a big fund raiser for the charity, so Dags and I went round a load of different companies to see what sort of people they all were, and how they might handle it.'

'Dags was wary,' says Alex Rayner, 'that the TV side might overshadow the enjoyment of undertaking the expedition.'

'Sometimes,' adds Marcus, 'you can get the wrong TV crew. They might dramatise something that doesn't actually happen. They want to create a story that isn't there. That was definitely a concern.'

The interest from sponsors also picked up dramatically. Several new names had seen the TV coverage and were now keen to get involved. None of this could come too soon. As Ed put it with his usual honesty: 'There is a certain funding issue in the short term. We are starting to spend money and neither Dags nor I have very deep pockets.

46

We do need to start getting sponsors on board.' At the same time numerous equipment suppliers had come forward offering free kit for the team, which would make yet more money available for the charity.

At the start of April, the organisers received their first firm pledge of sponsorship: £25,000 from Elmfield Training, a UK-wide vocational training provider which had a special interest in the possibilities of working with wounded soldiers. The timing couldn't have been better. The money would be more than enough to finance the final selection process in Svalbard in May. Shortly after that, Lloyds Development Capital, the firm Ed and Harry Parker had spoken to in January, committed to a generous contribution. Then Ed and Simon were invited to lunch by London-based fund manager Artemis; before the pair could even roll out their presentation, they were offered a minimum of £50,000. Later that week, Carillion, the property company, committed to £40,000.

Then came a call from international financial brokers BGC Partners, who had once been part of Cantor Fitzgerald, the company which had lost so many of its employees during the horrific events of September 11, 2001 (all 658 who were in its offices on the 101st to 105th floors of the World Trade Center perished on that day). Since then, both firms had donated all profits from a single day's trading in September to the bereaved families and to other nominated charities both in the UK and in the US—at over £10 million, a figure not to be sniffed at. 'Dags said they were interested in getting involved in a big way,' wrote Ed, 'but apparently wouldn't go over half a million pounds! What!!

47

I think we might be about to find ourselves a headline sponsor.'

Meanwhile, the guys from Captive Minds had worked with Henry Cookson to create a Facebook page, something no respectable charity—or expedition—could now afford to be without. 'It was interesting,' says Alex Rayner, 'that we put our social media site up about three days after the Rifles Club event almost as an aside. Within seventy-two hours of it going live we had six and a half thousand members. That is a very quick build. We've done stuff for Premiership rugby clubs that has taken a year to do that.'

Martin Hewitt had now returned from the Canadian Paralympics and Guy Disney had finished his training course, so there was a chance for the four candidates to finally meet round a table with the organisers. 'On Monday,' Ed wrote, 'I received a call from Matt asking me how important it was for him to attend the meeting. "Very," I said. It transpired that he had run the London Marathon the day before and after ten miles something in his foot had gone ping. Being Matt, being a bootneck, that didn't mean the end of the run for him. He ran and walked for the next sixteen miles in excruciating pain in order to finish. A bit of me was very unimpressed. Matt informed me that the longest run he had done prior to the Marathon was only three miles—which is simply ridiculous. Who runs the Marathon having only run three miles? Well, Matt. And bearing in mind he is one down in the leg department, it's simply extraordinary. Why had Matt potentially compromised our expedition? But if you think about it in a little more detail, here is a man who has lost his leg who is showing everyone he can still do it. From our perspective, maybe we should be encouraged that this extraordinary guts and determination exists in one of our team. But we must also ensure that Matt doesn't come North having only pulled his tyres a mile or two!'

The meeting, over plates of sandwiches and glasses of Coke and beer in one of the boardrooms of the Rifles Club, was a success. 'The dynamics between the four of them seemed good,' Ed wrote. 'Martin and Matt will compete, being a Para and a Marine (though Martin might need to be told to shut up from time to time). Guy is considered, and clearly sizing the others up, and Rob remains the mature, solid, ambitious core to the four. I felt that they are all very much up for the task, although we do need to ensure that for the next twelve months this is the single most important part of their lives. We need 100 per cent commitment.'

Next stop: Svalbard, cold and remote enough to give the team a taste of the conditions they would be experiencing in just under a year's time. All four wounded soldiers were going, plus organisers Ed and Simon, polar guides Inge Solheim and Henry Cookson, and prosthetics expert Jamie Gillespie, with a specific brief to see how the three artificial legs would handle the low temperatures. Trailing them at a distance would be Alexis Girardet and Rob Leveritt, cameraman and soundman from TwoFour Broadcast, the TV company that Dags, Ed and Captive Minds had finally selected from many rivals to make the documentary film of the expedition; as well as winning Best Independent Producer at the 2010 Broadcast Awards they had sound experience of filming in sub-zero conditions, having made the film—*On Thin Ice*—about Ben Fogle and James Cracknell's attempt to win the Amundsen South Pole Race in January 2009. More important, they seemed to have the right attitude. 'They get it,' said Ed.

To foster a spirit of competition, and for TV purposes, Ed and Simon had told the group that, as originally planned, just two of the four soldiers would end up being selected for the final trip. But privately both organisers were hoping that all four would prove up to the challenge. With substantial sponsorship in place, and more in prospect, they could now afford to take a larger team than they had originally anticipated.

'I think Simon and Ed are being quite clever,' said Rob Copsey, a few days before they left for Norway. 'They may already know what they're going to do, but we don't know that. So it's making us train and focus. It's going to be blimming hard, I think. Especially the endurance ski march. But it will be a really good taster. To see if this is actually for us and if we really want to do it. And prosthetics-wise it's going to be a big challenge. If the prosthetic isn't right or doesn't fit, or you can't work with it in a cold environment, it isn't going to work. That's it, end of exercise. I'm going to be forty if I get to go. A lot of these lads that are getting wounded now are eighteen. If they see a forty-year-old amputee can walk to the Pole, maybe they will say to themselves, "Yeah, I'm going to be all right. If that old fart can do it, with one leg, maybe I could do it next year."'

'WOULD EVERYONE PLEASE STOP GETTING SHOT!'

MATT: I grew up on the beach in Clacton, which wasn't the nicest of places in the world. My dad was a fisherman, so I used to do a lot of fishing with him when I was younger. Then we moved to Norfolk and lived in an old abandoned watermill that we renovated as a family. When I was seventeen Dad took over a ferry business; it takes foot passengers from King's Lynn to West Lynn and back again.

After college I went travelling. When I came back I joined the Royal Marines. I'd always liked the idea of the military, and because of my background with my family I put two and two together and the Marines were the result, soldiering with the maritime aspect. The 32-week course that all Royal Marines do is basically a commando course, which is one of the hardest courses, bar Special Forces, that you can do. In our troop we started with sixty-five blokes and only between twelve and fourteen finished. It's gruelling and tough, but enjoyable at the same time. It definitely makes you proud to wear the green beret. It's great to be part of something that is so much of a brotherhood. There are only six thousand of us within the whole military.

In training I was given a King's Badge, which is an award for best Marine in the troop. Because of that I got promoted quite quickly. Within six months I was a lance-corporal, which saw me as second-in-command of an eight-man team in Afghanistan a year later.

We flew out in September 2007. I was twenty-two at the time. Obviously you have some nervous anxiety; we'd heard rumours that one in six guys was getting injured. But there's always the excitement of going out to do your job properly, because that's what you've been trained to do. There's a lot of difference between running around with a blank firing attachment on your weapon and running around with real bullets winging over your head.

There's a joke within the Corps that if you've got your green beret on your head you're bullet proof. Obviously that isn't the case. But you do feel confident in your skills because you've been trained to such a high standard; and you know that the lads around you have too.

The day that I was shot we were fighting to protect the Kajaki Dam, on the edge of the desert at the northern tip of the Green Zone. It was my first tour and we were only seven and a half weeks in. We hadn't really seen that much action. We'd put the odd round down here and there, but we hadn't gone properly toe to toe with the enemy. Every time we got near them we just dropped bombs on them. It wasn't sticking bayonets in people's heads.

The mission that day was to reach the FLET, that's the forward line enemy troops. Reach them, engage them, keep them at the distance they're at. Our main objective was to maintain a roughly three-mile Taliban-free zone around the dam.

There were three of us up on the roof of this deserted mud-brick building: me, Ben, my machine gunner, and my grenade launcher Smithy. We were protecting another troop who were ahead of us on the ground.

At first there wasn't much fire coming in, just a few rounds, quite high, and not really anywhere near us, so we weren't too fussed. Then some started sneaking a bit closer. They were AK rounds, so we couldn't really see where they were coming from. It's hard enough finding anything in the desert, let alone where people are shooting from. The Taliban do a shoot-and-scoot technique, where they just fire through a hole in any wall they can find and then run on to the next one. You can't even see the muzzle flash.

Then a few rounds came in really close. Ben grabbed me and threw me back off the roof, into cover behind the building. As the dust settled, I felt this weird sensation in my foot, a warm fuzzy feeling, like someone had poured hot water on it.

Ben said, 'I think I've broken my ankle.' I got up to help him and as I stood on my foot I felt a burning, horrible pain. I looked down and I had two little red dots on either side of my desert boot.

'Fuck it,' I said, 'I've been shot.'

'Shit,' Ben said, looking down at his boot. 'So have I.'

We yelled up to Smithy, who was still on the roof. Complete silence. For a moment we just stared at each other. At that point we both reckoned he was dead.

I shouted back for a medic and the rest of the team came up. There was a bit of banter and a bit of laughter, because it was like that scene in *Lock, Stock and Two Smoking Barrels* when the guy says, 'I've been shot,' and the other guy says, 'Would

53

everyone please just stop getting shot!'

One of our boys got up on the roof to see what had happened to Smithy. He was alive, but he'd been hit in both legs; through his Achilles in one and the back of his calf in the other. The Taliban had caught us by coming round the side, where we had no cover. They'd flocked up and shot all three of us in a line on the roof in one burst of fire. All on the lower limbs, luckily. I don't suppose that's what they were aiming for.

Somehow we had to get out of there. It takes four guys for each injured man, because all your kit and equipment has to go as well: extra link for your machine gun, extra ammo, extra grenades, mortar rounds, water—you're carrying eighty, ninety, a hundred pounds with you. For the three of us being extracted that's twelve others to carry us, which means fifteen blokes from a thirty-man troop are out of the battle.

The Taliban weren't going to miss an opportunity like that. They surrounded us in a three-hundred-degree arc and hit us with everything they'd got. There were over twenty-seven firing points confirmed by the helicopters on that day. We were basically pinned down until the Apaches turned up, and Camp Bastion was forty minutes away. In the meantime we were crawling, hopping, getting dragged, doing whatever we could to try and get out of that situation. We were all of us a magnet for bullets. At one point I remember lying behind a three-foot-high wall and the rounds were zinging over the top. I was trying to get a cigarette out of my shirt pocket and I thought, *We're all fucked. There is no way we can get out of this.* Then another guy, a Marine engineer who was with us, got shot in

54

the front of the leg. So that was four of us down.

The Chinook which was going to be taking us out couldn't get any closer than a kilometre or so. CH47s are susceptible to fire from the ground. Plonk one down in the middle of a firefight to put casualties in, you lose a helicopter. So they have to come down somewhere else, wherever it's free from fire. Which meant putting us on ladders, stretchers—whatever the guys could get—then running the distance with us.

They were just phenomenal that day. They carried us to the point where they were being physically sick with the exertion. Rounds were still coming in at us, but they just cracked on. Finally they managed to get us on a quad bike and take us down the *wadi* to the chopper on a trailer.

Once all four of us were up on the Chinook the medics gave us gas for the pain. Believe it or not, as we sat there sipping from a nozzle Ben and I were laughing.

'How the fuck did we get out of that?' we said. It was a pretty heavy contact. We couldn't understand how we were still alive.

*   *   *

Like Martin Hewitt and Guy Disney, Matt was flown back to Camp Bastion and then home in the flying casualty ward to Selly Oak. From there he followed the others down to Headley Court. 'My injury was just a scratch compared to some of them,' he says. 'There were double amputees, triple amputees, amputees who were blind, people who'd lost their genitals. But they were all still smiling and joking and fooling around. Blokes in wheelchairs nicking other people's wheelchairs, just for the banter. I think it's the black humour that keeps the guys going really. It's funny. There's a really good atmosphere, though obviously some days are better than others. The only thing wrong with the place is it's not big enough.'

Matt didn't actually lose his foot for another eleven months. But the round had gone straight through his talus, the essential ankle-bone that supports the tibia, the larger of the two bones in the lower leg. He was told that if he kept his foot he would never walk properly again. He was offered a choice of ankle fusion, which locks the foot at ninety degrees with a pin, or amputation: 'With a fusion you're always going to get fractures and other problems. With amputation you've got the admin of socket fitting and you don't have a foot, but if your prosthetic foot breaks, which is very rare, you just get a new one. I weighed up the pros and cons and told them to chop it off. There's no drama. I can run on it. I can climb mountains on it.'

Exactly as he had done. Thrilled to have been chosen for the Svalbard selection, Matt recognised that the North Pole expedition was a challenge of a different order. 'This isn't just a bimble up a mountain or a jog round town,' he said as the prospective Walking With The Wounded team left for Norway. 'It's a massive feat of endurance, team work and hardship. I'm a little bit anxious, but excited. Hopefully, if I get to go, this is going to be the turning point to something new.'

56

6

ONE DOWN . . .

Spitsbergen is the central island in the Svalbard Archipelago, a remote group several hundred miles north of the main land mass of Norway, right on the edge of the permanent polar ice pack and just 880 miles south of the North Geographical Pole. At over 15,000 square miles it's the largest island in Norway, and the thirty-sixth largest in the world. The entire archipelago has a population of 2753, alongside an estimated 3500 polar bears. Most of these hardy folk live in Longyearbyen, the capital of Spitsbergen, which looks more like a barracks than a town, with rows of prefab type buildings painted orange-red and green set in a steep valley on the edge of the dark waters of Adventfjord. Eerily beautiful, the place feels as remote as it is. It has long been one of the key bases for exploration of the Pole.

On Thursday 12 May, the six prospective members of the Walking With The Wounded team flew in to Longyearbyen airport, the sight of snow-covered mountains and the fragmented ice pack below them causing a flurry of excitement as they came in to land. With them on the plane were Henry Cookson, Jamie Gillespie, and not one but two TV crews: Alexis and Rob from TwoFour and the BBC's Frank Gardner with attendant producer and cameraman. They were met by Inge Solheim and two of his expert guides, Rune Malterud and Stian Aker (the very pair who had beaten Cracknell and Fogle into second place in the South Pole race).

The tyro expeditioners were surprised to find the place warmer than they had expected, with temperatures hovering around 0°C. May is high summer in the Arctic, with 24-hour daylight, and a sun that floats along the top of the surrounding mountain range rather than setting. At last it was all starting to seem real.

Inge drove them to the Basecamp Hotel, an atmospheric hostelry with rough-hewn wooden interiors, bunk beds, driftwood furniture, slate tables and animal skins on the floor. Ed found it wonderfully eccentric, imagining himself bedding down in the sort of cabin that Scott or Amundsen might have slept in a hundred years before. After a pre-dinner briefing in the bar from Inge, they headed out on foot to a nearby restaurant. Everyone sat round the same big round table, soldiers, organisers, polar experts and TV people.

For the next three days the soldiers would be eating dehydrated rations, so tonight they tucked in. Ed enjoyed a hefty steak and watched with some amazement as Martin Hewitt made himself a spaghetti carbonara sandwich. It was still daylight when they made their way back to the hotel at midnight. The rooms had blackout blinds on the windows, but the sun shone bright round the edges. Ed found it a very odd phenomenon; despite a whisky nightcap or two he didn't sleep well.

The next morning the soldiers were taken to a warehouse to test their equipment and be introduced to their pulks, state-of-the-art Norwegian sledges with sleek carbon fibre bodies and waterproof-material tops that open and close with a hardy zip. Inge and his team showed them how to pack the pulks, with heavier items of kit at the bottom for stability, and lighter, more accessible items near the front and top. So fuel canister and cooking utensils went in the compartment at the back; in the middle, tents, guy ropes, tent pegs, snow shovels, sleeping bags, blow-up mattresses, emergency medical equipment, rations. At the front came a day bag, containing all the kit you needed to have handy during the day: snacks, Thermos flasks with water and soup, extra items of clothing to add if temperatures dropped. The final weight was 30–40 kg, less than half of the 100 kg that each of them would ultimately be carrying to the Pole.

'While we packed up,' Ed noted, 'the banter between the team began to evolve. Matt, Martin and Guy are all strong characters, confident in themselves, and even though they have only just met, they are forging a strong bond, all mercilessly ribbing each other. Rob is a little more restrained, less sure of himself in self-confidence, and although he clearly enjoyed the banter amongst the others, he found it hard to contribute and join in. As for Simon and I, we were able to give as good as we got! Our wounded team members think that because Dags and I are so old (according to them mid-forties is "so old") the expedition would be better if done for Age Concern. From then on the tent Dags and I shared was referred to as "The Care Home".' Guy and Martin, meanwhile, were sharing 'The Officers' Mess'.

By 5 p.m. on Friday, two hours behind schedule, they had finally loaded their sledges and were dressed in their snow kit: a thin woollen vest next to the skin, doubled with long johns; a thin fleece and a black waterproof jacket and trousers on top of that. They were then driven up to the road head, where the narrow strip of tarmac petered out into the snow. Here, for the first time, they clipped on their Nordic cross-country skis, which are narrower than normal skis, with boots that attach only at the toe and have no ankle support, making balance precarious for novices. 'I did a short hundred yards on my own,' Ed wrote, 'and quietly pottered back with no one looking, as I found it rather tricky. I hoped that with a sledge attached to my back it might be a little easier, as it would stabilise me.'

Rob Copsey was surprised that there wasn't more instruction on how to use the skis: 'Basically, we had to work it out for ourselves. Look at Henry and Inge and see how they coped.'

'Inge's style,' says Martin, 'is very much to teach you as you go along. He let us learn for ourselves at the start. Then he intervened when he felt it was appropriate with a few hints and tips. I went right in behind him and watched what he did; everything from his body movement to his route selection.'

'It was noticeable,' says Guy, 'that Martin wasn't too bad with the skis, and the guys with both legs and arms were fine. But my pulk was dragging me backwards and I couldn't get a grip with my leg. I was falling over continually and going back downhill again. It became quite miserable to be honest.'

Slowly the guys moved off up the long snowy valley ahead of them. Ed was thrilled to be finally on the go. 'It was an extraordinary sensation,' he wrote. 'After eight months of chat and planning, here we were as a fledgling team, on the snow, in the Arctic, skiing off. Three amputees and Martin with his right arm which is nigh-on useless. For the first time I felt that things were moving ahead, that talk was becoming action.'

Though Guy was quietly struggling, and Matt too was having trouble with an ill-fitting leg, it was Rob Copsey who was finding things hardest. His prosthetic limb had been supplied by the NHS, and was nowhere near as hi-tech as those the Headley Court physios had provided for Matt and Guy. Rob had tried to make a hospital appointment to get it changed before he came out, but had had no joy: 'It was a centimetre short and it didn't fit. So it was rubbing on my knee and on the bony bit of my stump as well. I soon knew I was going to have problems.'

After three hours the team reached the top of the valley and skied through a narrow pass. Now, as they moved on to the downhill slope, there were new difficulties. Suddenly the pulks, weighed down with 40 kg of equipment, seemed to have minds of their own. Most of the group were struggling as pulks sped off willy-nilly down the slippery slopes, or cannoned painfully into the backs of legs. 'We all fell over,' said Jamie Gillespie, 'even the guys without prosthesis. It's difficult to control cross-country skis going downhill, and often the sled would slide past you and pull you down the hill. It was very funny here, but it wouldn't have been funny at the Pole.'

By the time they finally reached their designated camping spot, a flat area of snow in the middle of nowhere, the laughter had died down and tempers were starting to fray. Not a bad test of things to come, Ed thought.

Setting up camp provided new challenges for

the wounded servicemen. 'Putting up a tent,' said Martin, 'takes me five or six times longer than somebody with the use of two arms. As does firing up the Primus stove. With a prosthetic leg you can get a lot of your mobility back. Unfortunately there's not a piece of equipment that you can use to regain the dexterity you have with your hands.' With help from tent mate Guy, however, the Officers' Mess eventually joined the others, a fourth crimson dome against the snow.

'It was my first night in a tent since I had left the Army,' Ed wrote, 'and that was a very long time ago. Having to do all the cooking, melting snow for water, cleaning up, getting everything ready for bed, came back in no time. It wasn't difficult and Dags and I soon had it running like a well-oiled machine. Supper was a sachet of soup followed by freeze-dried bolognese, eaten out of the bag. Followed by a mug of hot blackcurrant. The key in this environment is remaining hydrated and it is very misleading how much liquid one needs.'

The group settled in for another Arctic summer's night, the sun still bright on the empty white landscape outside their tents. Before bedding down Inge erected an electric trip-wire around the camp, in case of a small-hours visit from a polar bear. With 3500 of the animals in the archipelago such an intrusion was a real possibility and the group were carrying a pump-action twelve-bore shotgun, just in case. Inge kept an ear out throughout the night, as he always did on expeditions (though at the Pole it would be for the tell-tale cracking of ice). Apart from Ed, kept awake again by the light shining through the skin of his tent, the others slept soundly. Far from being cold, they were stewing in thermal sleeping bags designed for temperatures of −35°C.

At 8 a.m. sharp they were woken by Inge, shouting at them to get up. The morning routine began, a taste of what life would be like every day on the expedition proper. Cookers were fired up to melt snow to make water for porridge; more snow was melted to make tea; then more for washing, before sleeping bags and mats were packed up, tents emptied and taken down, and pulks packed and made ready to go. Toilet facilities were a hole in the snow, in a 'dirty area' twenty yards from camp. 'All ablutions took place in front of the assembled audience,' Ed wrote, 'which met with much mirth and commentary. Makes things a little more tricky. Loo paper has to be burned afterwards. The Norwegians are very environment conscious.'

Eventually the soldiers were on their way again, into some of the starkest, most remote terrain any of them had ever seen. The virgin snow was like heaped icing sugar. The sun shone from a pale blue sky. Fluffy white clouds sailed past them, low and fast, here and there blurring the sharp outline of the mountains. It was undeniably beautiful.

On this much-anticipated twelve-hour endurance ski, it soon started to become apparent how the core team of the wounded might work. 'Guy had few problems,' Ed wrote, 'and embraced the challenge, urging us to do more. Martin was very strong in the harness. As a disabled skier he is very capable on skis. Matt had some difficulty with his leg, but was grimly determined to keep going. Our worry was Rob. His situation is different to the others. He was wounded sixteen years ago, and

63

now works as a customs officer, in a world which I suspect is dominated by the modern attitude to health and safety and union rules. While I don't think this is the core to Rob, the military world he left many years ago is not part of his mentality any more. He seemed to lack the mental strength the rest of the team had. His belief in himself was not evident. He was clearly in discomfort all day and was struggling against his amputated leg. Put this in context—how many amputees would attempt to do what he was doing? Very few, and his efforts mustn't be belittled. But we are preparing for an expedition to one of the harshest places on earth, and even the slightest self-doubt is dangerous, not only for him but for the team as a whole. Rob inevitably turned up last whenever we stopped, arriving with a cheery cry of "The weakest link has arrived!" or "The hand-brake is here!" He was smiling, but it was not an attitude which resonated with the rest of us. We need positive, not negative, thought. During the day I lobbied Inge and Henry about all of the team, and it was on Rob their concerns were centred. I could also detect that the other three wounded weren't as confident in his abilities, and a loss of confidence would be a concern.'

'The thing with the other guys,' said Rob, 'is they're like what I was like fifteen years ago. They're still in that military mindset. When you ask them, "Is your leg sore or hurting?" it's, "No, no, I'm all right, mate." But I'm now a bit more mellow, a bit more honest, and when they were asking me if I was sore, I was like, "Yeah, I am." I was in agony. I had two huge blisters coming up on the hotpoints of my stump, so I was having to compensate by

64

putting most of my weight on my good leg, and there was a blister coming up there too.'

'As a guide,' said Henry, 'you can often pick out the person who's not going to make it, early on. "Oh," they say, "my foot is hurting a little bit." Unnecessary comments, but they let it be known. They're softening the blow for later on and giving themselves a fallback.'

*   *   *

The team skied for twelve hours, at one point leaving firm ground to cross a snow-covered frozen lake. 'You can hear the ice creaking below you as you go,' said Ed, 'and it's a horrible sound. I haven't shared this with anyone other than Dags, but that's my real fear about next April, falling through the ice into the freezing water. Forget about rescue helicopters. If you can't climb out of that in double quick time you won't last long. And leads open up the whole time at the Pole.'

There was another reality check for the group when Matt stumbled on the tracks of a polar bear. Gathering round, they realised just how big an animal it was. Each individual paw print looked like something an elephant might have left and the soldiers could clearly see the individual pock marks of each nail, clawing into the snow. This wasn't the cuddly creature depicted in children's books and they were glad that they had their shotgun on board.

By the end of the day they had covered seventeen miles. Ed was pleased, but neither of the guides were much impressed. 'Inge is stern,' says Matt, 'but he tells it how it is. He came straight up to me and said, "You're a very strong contender for the trip, you're just fat and unfit." But you have to respect what he says, because at the end of the day, he's got his life and other people's lives to look out for.'

Rob was less happy with the group leader: 'Inge's very direct. I found a couple of his viewpoints I disagreed with—and I told him so. I don't think he liked that particularly. Don't get me wrong. I thought what he was saying was right. But he was looking at me as if I should have known these things already. Why should I? I wasn't going to let him talk to me like I was some kid.'

'I look at what people do,' says Inge, 'and listen to what they say, and from that I try to decide: Does this person have the right mental attitude? Does he mix well with the group? Will he be willing to do what it takes to get there? I am always allergic to excuses and explanations, totally allergic.'

Jamie Gillespie had meanwhile been keeping a beady professional eye on all the amputees, himself included. He was aware that of the three candidates with artificial legs his old Headley Court mate Rob was faring the worst, even though he was quite obviously trying as hard as everyone else. 'I was angry that he wasn't as comfortable as he should have been. His socket wasn't a good fit. He was ripping his leg to bits.'

There was another issue too with the prosthetic limbs. As Jamie had anticipated, sweat building up between stump and socket was proving a problem: 'The guys were having to take their legs off after about an hour and a half of walking. The temperature was only zero, which meant they were able to sit down, take their legs off, dry their

66

stumps, take their time and put their prosthesis back on. But up at the Pole, in minus thirty to fifty they won't be able to do that. The sweat will freeze and could easily lead to hypothermia or frostbite.'

The tents were up in ten minutes the second evening, even Guy and Martin's. 'Still too slow, if temperatures were significantly lower,' wrote Ed. 'One thing which has become apparent is that Martin finds it very difficult to help with the admin once we stop to pitch camp. He was sharing with Guy and they were comfortably the slowest. It became clear that we will need to help him in order to avoid his partner having to do everything. In our discussions it became apparent that three-man tents might make sense so that Martin would have two people to assist him.'

Cookers were soon alight, however; snow was melted and dinner eaten. Even though they had been pulling their pulks for twelve hours, Ed found himself wide awake for ages. 'The sun was still high in the sky and it just seemed so wrong to be trying to sleep.'

*   *   *

Sunday proved altogether easier. Camp was broken more slickly and as the group moved off down the long valley they had climbed the first evening, they were either more comfortable on their narrow Nordic skis or had the confidence to abandon them altogether. 'The last day was fantastic,' said Matt. 'We were right at the top of this valley and we just thought, *Fuck it*. We took our skis off, got on top of our pulks and slid down three miles head first.'

Ed had been physically fine. 'But as soon as we

67

got to the vehicles, my bones started feeling tired and weary. My body seemed to know we could stop. It was a great feeling to have completed the last couple of days and Simon and I both felt we had really achieved something, learning a lot about the wounded, and also having the opportunity to operate as a team for the first time.' It had only been the mildest taste of the hardship they would face the following year. But useful nonetheless.

'The magnitude of what we've taken on has hit home thanks to this trip,' said Martin. 'We had very comfortable conditions out there. The pulks were light in comparison to what we're going to be taking. I realised that I'm going to have to adapt a lot of my personal equipment, so I can get access to things quickly with only one hand. My jacket, for example, will need industrial-sized zips, instead of the small zips that are so hard to do up in the cold. Or perhaps I'll use Velcro instead. The key to survival in this environment is speed—we can't afford to stop too frequently in the temperatures we'll be facing.'

Despite all his difficulties, Rob too had found the long weekend a good test. 'I learned a hell of a lot from it. I think I've got to be stronger in the head. It's good that I can acknowledge that. I certainly identified a few issues that I need to sort out. But I'm still positive, I still want to go.'

*   *   *

Safely back in the UK, Ed and Simon had a problem. After further discussion with Inge and Henry, they had reluctantly made the decision not to take Rob on the expedition. Ed didn't relish the prospect of

68

making that phone call, especially after all the hard work Rob had already put in, both in training and in helping promote Walking With The Wounded. 'Both of us,' Ed wrote, 'were acutely aware that this expedition means an enormous amount to him and we were dreading being the bearers of bad news. But if you take on the responsibility for organising something, you need to accept that these sorts of conversations are sometimes necessary. For Simon and me, the safety of the whole expedition is the key, and we can't have the slightest bit of doubt about any team member. We both know we've made the right decision. The phone conversation was fortunately a fairly easy one, made so by Rob's dignity and good grace. He spoke at length of his frustration of not having prosthetics that were good enough for the task, and that he felt let down by the NHS. Clearly his leg had been very painful during the training, as had his foot which had been affected by the new boots. We left Rob with the thought that we would be delighted for him to help the project in a different way.'

Unsurprisingly, once he had recovered from the initial shock of rejection, Rob was seriously disappointed. 'I felt they didn't really give me any real reason,' he said a few days later. 'They just said they had a duty of care, and maybe I'd struggle— and it's true I did struggle in Norway. But I don't think they took into consideration the facts: which were that the leg I was using at the time didn't fit, and they knew that. When I got back I had to go into casualty to have my blisters cut out. On both legs.

'Maybe there were some other issues too,' he continued. 'I don't think the three other lads particularly warmed to me. I don't think they can relate to me, to be honest. I was very much the civvy and they were the squaddies, still running along at a hundred miles an hour with their hair on fire. They're what I call head bangers. They're not going to say that something hurts. They're just going to get on with it. Which is maybe the way to do it. I think Simon and Ed picked up on that and thought, *We don't want a wedge between the guys.*'

'I felt really sorry for Rob,' says Simon, 'because he got such a bum deal. The trip to Svalbard was about us seeing if people were up to doing the journey or not. Rob turned up with a prosthetic limb that was crap and didn't fit him properly. As a result he struggled. I think that played a lot on him mentally and by the end of the three days he doubted whether he could really do it. With that doubt, in our minds came doubt. Once that gets in there, there's no way of getting it out. We weren't going to get another chance to test the ability of that leg in extreme circumstances until October. If Rob's leg wasn't good enough by then, we had no chance of replacing him. So we had to make the decision there and then.'

Meanwhile, the three younger candidates were confirmed as team members, and Jamie Gillespie had his work cut out to make sure that Matt's and Guy's prosthetic challenges were overcome. After this trial weekend, Jamie was more aware than ever that frozen sweat was a problem. He was now thinking that perhaps the expedition should take an extra pop-up tent to block the sub-zero wind while the amputees removed their legs and dried their stumps during breaks.

Another issue was going to be weight loss. Over

the course of the three- to four-week trek, each team member would lose up to a stone and a half. This would cause further problems with the artificial limbs, which are designed to fit a specific body size. To deal with the issue of shrinking stumps, Jamie was planning to design a leg that the guys could adjust themselves as they progressed.

The toughest challenge of all was going to be preventing the dreaded 'rub', when skin at the base of the stump peels away to reveal raw flesh. Even over the course of a three-day stint, that could cause severe discomfort, as both Rob and Matt had discovered. On a longer outing, the problem would be worse. 'The thing that is going to make or break this trip,' Jamie said, 'is infection. If the skin breaks down, which it's likely to do, and infection sets in, there's nothing you can do about it. The leg will swell up and be unbearably painful. At that point they're going to have to be evacuated.'

7

PROFESSIONAL ADVENTURERS

INGE: I grew up in the mountains in Norway, in a little village called Otta. It's in the Rondane, which means the round mountains: they are round on one side and very steep alpine mountains on the other— it's a beautiful place. As a child in that area you get used to the cold. In the winter we'd walk to school in minus thirty-five. We just put some extra clothing on and walked faster. I never had frostbite, though I had a few nips. Every Norwegian kid gets frost nips.

I learnt to love being outdoors, challenging myself out in the wild. Not that we call it that in Norway. We just call it Nature. From the age of seven I was out there, walking alone. I wasn't interested in football, and anyway I was crap at it, so I tended to go out exploring on my own instead. It was the best thing, being out there, looking at animals, philosophising, sleeping under trees and waking up in the morning with a moose passing through my little camp. Nature is kind in Norway. Nothing is out to kill you. It's very safe.

Not that I didn't like people too. I did, and of course I did what was expected of me, taking normal jobs and so on. I started a pizza restaurant in Otta when I was fifteen. Then I worked for a bit as a teacher. After that I moved to Oslo and went into the finance industry. I worked for a fund management company, then I was a stockbroker for a few years.

Every young Norwegian does military service. After the compulsory year there's a selection for the reserves, and if you volunteer for that, you train every year. I did winter training with soldiers, which I still do for a couple of weeks a year. My military service taught me how to focus on getting the job done with no ceremony or fuss: just do what it takes. I like that simple approach.

At the end of my twenties I'd had enough of the office life. I followed up on my dream and my passion, which was being outdoors and doing expeditions full time. Not that I'd ever stopped all that. Even as a stockbroker, I had a month's extra leave so I could go away on expeditions, guiding people in Spitsbergen and in the Arctic. That was always part of the package. I couldn't do my job without it.

I set up my own company, Storm Adventures. We do expeditions for private individuals and organisations. We also work with film and TV companies, on productions like *On Thin Ice, Seventy One Degrees North, Beyond Boundaries.* A film shoot is a kind of expedition. We are experts in taking people to remote areas.

This lot will get a shock when they get up to the Pole for the first time. It will be more uncomfortable than they think. Harder actually than you can possibly imagine. But it will also be more rewarding. You can have better times up there than anywhere in the world. You get into a strange kind of meditative state. There are so few visual impulses and references that your focus turns inwards. You get a lot of time for yourself and your thoughts. Little things, like the colour of the ice and the patterns in the snow, become more important. If we had snow here now, and there were patterns in it, because of all the other visual impulses, you wouldn't notice them. But out there you do. People say, 'Look at that cloud!' Clouds they wouldn't notice normally.

It's a world of ice up there, and it's constantly shifting. There is no clear route. You have to find your way on a micro level, the fastest, safest, easiest way through the ice rubble and over the pressure ridges. You don't want to get stuck. You can potentially fall and break your leg. You also want to avoid thin ice, moving ice, open leads; those are terrifying if you fall into them.

The leads go east–west. Sometimes it's more efficient to cross them than try and walk around them, as they can stretch for miles. We will have two immersion suits with us, which will be used by me and one other team member, probably Ed or Simon. I will go over first with a rope and operate a ferry system, pulling the rest over on a raft. One person stays behind to make sure everyone gets over safely. He then swims over after us and then we get back to walking again.

Sometimes you have to do that with thin ice too, where it's not yet formed properly. Break it and swim through. There are different ways of reading the ice to see how thick it is. One is visual. I look at the colour. Then I look at the surface. The ice gives off moisture when it's thin, which forms into frost roses. From those I can tell how old it is, how thick it is, and so on. Then I probe it with my ski pole. If that goes through within two or three jabs of the same hole, it's not safe. I'll also check air temperature. There are many things to think about before you walk out on thin ice. If there's a lot of spindrift it can cover a thin crack with snow and you can't see it. When you're skiing you can't just look forwards. You have to constantly be looking to the side to see if there are cracks that may be opening up. If you step into a big open lead it could drown you. Before you know it you are soaking wet and potentially even under the ice. That's not good at all.

HENRY: The word 'explorer' always makes me feel a bit uncomfortable. I never knew I'd end up doing this, it all happened totally by chance. My parents ran an upmarket travel company and we lived in Wiltshire. I went to Harrow, then to Newcastle University. I was mucking around a bit up there, didn't go to enough lectures and got flung off the course. I had to go back a year, but I ended up getting my 2:1. I had an Army bursary and I was due to go to Sandhurst after uni, but I decided four years in the Army would just be another jolly, delaying the inevitable proper job. So I did the obvious, which was go into the City, even though I knew I'd hate it. I did that for three years, but it was soulless, so after procrastinating for quite a while, I left. There was still a spark there somewhere, I just didn't quite know where to put it. I had a plan to go to Africa, but my parents had a bit of a hooley with a divorce so I ended up faffing around in London doing all kinds of odd jobs.

Then I had a conversation over far too many whiskies with a friend. He'd heard about the Polar Challenge, which was a 360-mile ski race to the North Magnetic Pole. I am naturally quite a lazy person. If anyone had ever said Henry Cookson is running a marathon, people would have laughed, and I'd have laughed as well. But before I knew it I was verbally committed to this thing. My thought was, *What the hell! I'm going to do something totally stupid.*

The idea was one big trip to tell the grandchildren and that would be it. Then bugger off to Africa or whatever. To cut a long story short, we ended up winning the race. We smashed the record by two days, beating Arctic-trained Marines and people who'd clambered up Everest, the sort of person whose ideal weekend is sitting in a tent in the Lake District while I'm in a dirty nightclub picking up a big bar bill.

It wound the other competitors up to a certain extent. These three guys, Henry, Rory and Rupert, all from a public school background, never really taking the training seriously. There was a film crew there for the event and they were told beforehand, in no uncertain terms, 'Don't bother wasting your footage on these guys. They're a bunch of Muppets who won't get anywhere.' Before they knew it we were charging out in front. That record still stands seven years on.

I suppose our secret was having a sense of humour about it. Polar travel—they call it the polar plod—is mindless, mundane and boring. So you have to find ways to amuse yourselves. We had paid a significant amount of money to enter this race, and the irony was we were putting ourselves through abject misery. We found that quite funny. The worse it was, the more hysterical we got. We were laughing when Rory got frostbite on his face or my arse was bleeding.

We didn't have any knowledge of what to do. We didn't know how to do blister admin. Our feet were mushy. Our food was disgusting because we'd thrown it all into one big bag. It was appalling. But because we found all this stuff humorous, I suppose our mental energy was that much more than the others'.

We did it in eleven and a half days. The organisers were expecting it to be sixteen. So we beat the Marines and we won. Then, on the back of that, talk turned to the Antarctic. Rory wanted to do that trip with the same team and he was happy to pay for it. So I ended up spending a year of my life putting together an expedition. Instead of going to the Geographic South Pole, which has been done and dusted to shit, I found in my research a place called the Pole of Inaccessibility, which is the exact centre of the Antarctic. The only people who'd ever been there were a Soviet expedition in 1958 using tracked vehicles. It took them about two years to get there and when they did they left behind a statue of Lenin.

If you go to the Geographic South Pole, you're never more than 350 miles away from help. Then when you get there you find this huge American base. It's like a shopping mall. They've got a bowling rink and all sorts of things. Seventeen Hercules flying in and out every day.

The Pole of Inaccessibility is fifty per cent further to go. It's higher, which means it's colder. Once you leave the base on the coast, that's it. And when you get there, there's nothing—except the statue of Lenin. All the experts had told us it wouldn't be there after forty years. It would be buried in snow drift. But after fifty-three days of kite skiing we got there and there it was, still sticking out of the ground. It was great, made of cheap plastic. It was fabulous to do a true first, especially as three amateurs out of nowhere.

After that I decided that I could make a life out of this. My idea was to be a guide rather than a professional adventurer, because to do that you need sponsors and then you have to get into that endless competition for column inches. To get a sponsor you have to come up with a new concept, which is probably surrounded by bullshit. Being a guide allows you to work on your own terms. You can pick and choose the trips you want to do.

So I went to Alaska for three months and did everything the wrong way round. Here was this Brit who was in the *Guinness Book of Records*, but he'd never actually camped before on snow and ice. So I did courses in mountaineering, kayaking, hiking and canoeing.

The polar stuff is very seasonal. So I do a lot of Africa trips as well. There's a big difference between doing a trip, however big, and looking after other people. Some explorers aren't suited to it, however brilliant they are at climbing mountains or crossing deserts. There's an assumption that being a guide just involves being able to read a map and get people from A to B. But that's a very small part of it. It's managing people's expectations, it's calming them down if they're getting too ahead of themselves, it's pepping them up if they're feeling low, it's judging a situation.

I keep my expeditions small. It tends to be word of mouth that gets me the business. Mostly people approach me. They may have a place in mind or they may have no idea. For example, I had a girl come up to me the other day who wanted to do something on quad bikes and go somewhere fucked up. I said, 'What's your budget?' Sometimes there's somewhere in particular I want to go that I know is interesting. I put a trip together in 2009 to northern Ethiopia, a place called the Danakil Depression, which is fabulous. Kilimanjaro's an easy one to sell, because everyone wants to do it, but I refuse to go the normal way; having been very lucky in doing unique things that no one else on earth has done I don't want to run into other people. So I have a way up the back where you avoid all the *hoi polloi*. The truth is that to get off the beaten track costs more cash and takes longer. Most people might have the money, but they don't have the time; or they have the time and they don't have the money. The beasts you are after are the ones with both, who are rare.

There are lots of guides out there who have more

experience than me and have been to more places than me. But if you're out in the wild all your life, you may not have the connections. I have a wide circle of contacts. Simon Daglish sat next to a girl at a dinner who'd been on one of my trips. That was how I got involved. Then I brought in Inge. He's done lots of last degree trips to the North Pole: that's the ten-day trip, when you walk from eighty-nine degrees north to ninety degrees north. It's for people who've got the money but not the time. That's where Inge learnt his trade. He has huge experience of sea ice—and you need that. It can be a complete maelstrom up there. You've got thin ice, you've got polar bear worries, and you've often got bad visibility too. It's basically a frozen ocean with ice on top of it, with very strong currents moving around underneath and the wind above it. The ice can be pushed together and it concertinas up and you get pressure ridges. Or they can collapse and you get open water leads. You've got to find your way round them, which means using your gut feeling and your judgement on whether to go east or west. You might walk for many miles one way when it could have only been a few hundred yards the other way before you'd be able to cross. Then there are bits where the ice floes are moving next to each other and to get six people across it's 'Go, go, go!' By the time six have crossed it's too far apart for anyone else.

I did a last degree trip with Inge in April 2009. From those eight days I'm confident I picked up the skills I need. One night we had the ice break up right under one of the tents. We were stuck in a three-day storm and in the middle of night two there was the most almighty crack. The tent sank into it and broke up. During the ensuing panic everyone had to double or triple up in the remaining tents. It was pretty terrifying.

I didn't recommend Inge for nothing. He is fucking good at what he does. But part of the nature of a polar guide is that they have huge self-belief, and for one guy to look after seven other people is a massive task. I just want this thing to work.

8

'A FUNNY OLD TIME'

Having reluctantly let Rob go, the expedition were now looking for a fourth team member. Ed and Simon put the word around and asked Help for Heroes and BLESMA to circulate a new email to their members. 'We have a much clearer idea of the sort of person we want,' Ed wrote, 'so hopefully we will find someone quite quickly.'

But now there was a new—and completely unexpected—problem. The Royal Marines had been in touch to say that they didn't want Matt Kingston taking part in the expedition. 'They say his safety is their primary concern,' Ed wrote, 'and they don't want him being put in harm's way. But this is another huge blow. I believe that a Lt Col on the Corps Adventure Training has made this decision, but it was without any contact with us.'

Ed and Simon decided to go to the top. They made a direct approach to the Commandant-General of the Marines, General A. K. 'Buster'

Howes. But his position, they were soon told by aides, was clear; he had to support the decision of his medical team.

'Now this seems odd,' Ed wrote. 'The Institute of Naval Medicine has given Matt the all-clear, and they are the pre-eminent cold specialists in the world. So I wonder who these "medical experts" are. I believe that General Howes is going to call me to discuss Matt's involvement, but as yet I've heard nothing. I would hate to lose Matt as he is such a good man, hugely determined, and a core part of our team. It does strike me they are being rather hasty in their decision. If we could discuss this properly, show them the medical report from the INM and I could take Inge down to meet them, I feel confident we could persuade them otherwise.'

There was more bad news. BGC had been in touch to say they were not, after all, interested in being involved as a sponsor. Both Ed and Simon were disappointed. It was BGC who had made contact in the first place and they had always seemed so enthusiastic. The organisers had to console themselves with the thought that perhaps, after all, the upbeat fellow they had been dealing with wasn't the one calling the shots.

Just as they were starting to wonder what else could go wrong, there was a call from hedge fund managers Artemis, inviting the pair back into the office for another lunchtime discussion. Ed and Simon went with bated breath, but fortunately, at last, there was potentially positive news: Artemis reiterated their commitment to £50,000 and were now, they said, considering offering more financial support in return for being the headline sponsor. They would be in touch with their decision shortly.

There was another twist in the tale: Prince Harry was about to visit New York with a small group of wounded soldiers, including Guy Disney, with the aim of furthering links between the American and British charities who were seeking to help wounded servicemen. The Prince was scheduled to throw the first ball of a New York Mets baseball game before taking part with the soldiers in a race for the disabled in Central Park. Ed now received a call from the Prince's private secretary at Clarence House, wanting to know if it would be OK for the Prince and the soldiers to wear Walking With The Wounded T-shirts during both events. 'This is obviously fantastic profile for us,' wrote Ed. 'But it might go further. The organisation putting together this run is called Achilles International. It uses sport to assist disabled people in achieving feats they didn't think they would be capable of. Within Achilles is a sub organisation called the Freedom Team, which is a group of disabled servicemen. What if one of our team was an American? It would certainly fulfil Clarence House's objective of forging closer links. It would also take us to America, the impact of which would be huge to our project. Would it be too big? Hardly seems possible. The more noise we make the better.'

In the meantime the organisers had a conference call with their two remaining team members to canvass thoughts about who might replace the two they had lost. Guy suggested a Rifles officer who had been blown up in Afghanistan the previous June, suffering two broken legs, damaging an arm and losing peripheral vision in one eye. He was hoping, he told Ed over the phone, to return to operational duty, but knew he was still not ready.

'Maybe more of a long shot,' Ed confided to his diary, 'but I've always maintained I wanted a Rifleman on the expedition. The officer said he would think about it over the weekend. It would be great to get back to four. Since we put the word out that we were looking for another member, the response has been limited. I wonder if a lot of the boys just think it will be too much?'

Martin had another idea for the fourth (or would it be the third?) new team member. Jaco van Gass had been one of the rejects from the first selection session at the Rifles Club in January, the South African with the sunny attitude and the colostomy bag whom Ed and Dags had been so sorry to have to turn down. Jaco was in the same regiment as Martin, the Paras; indeed the platoon he had joined in Afghanistan was the same one Martin had commanded before he'd been shot. Since January, Martin said, Jaco had made a remarkable recovery. The colostomy bag had gone in March, and by April he had started learning how to ski. He had then been spotted by the sergeant major in charge of adaptive adventurous training and recommended to Martin as a possible recruit for the Combined Services Disabled Skiing Team, of which Martin was captain. Together with his skiing team's coach and performance director, Martin had got Jaco on to an indoor ski slope for a trial and all agreed that he was a potential racer. He was put on a training programme to build up his damaged leg and maximise the power of what muscle he had left.

Jaco had been more than up for this challenge. His work only required his attention for three or four hours a day. The rest of the time he was spending getting fit. Training regularly in the same

83

gym, Martin had been watching his development.

'He's developed muscle mass,' he told Ed and Simon, 'where we didn't think it could happen. His leg is now extremely strong. More than that, this guy has got the right mental attitude. I've now got him on the ski team, which means he'll be cut loose from work and be doing nothing but training to race. His level of fitness can only continue to improve. I think you should have another look at him.'

There was still no news, however, about Matt Kingston from the Commandant-General of the Royal Marines. General Howes's ADC had called to say that he was en route back from Afghanistan and did want to speak to Ed, but as yet there had been nothing more. In a moment of panic Ed called his contacts in the Army to double check that Guy and Martin weren't suddenly going to be pulled from the project too. But all seemed to be well. 'I think they rather like the idea of us getting to the North Pole as a group of soldiers with no Marines present,' Ed wrote.

Nor had Ed heard back from Artemis: 'which is a worry. We do need to get a title sponsor sorted as soon as possible and we need to move things on.'

* * *

In Ed's home county, thankfully, enthusiasm for the project remained unabated. On 6 June he met a group of boys from his son Jack's school, for a walk along the North Norfolk Coast Path. Ed dragged his tyres along the route and talked about the expedition and what it was trying to achieve. 'Halfway along the cliffs we stopped and for a brief

84

moment I was able to explain about the wounded and their future and what we owe to them. It is important to me that schools are made aware of the extraordinary sacrifices these young men and women have made and how we must be prepared to look after them in the future. I know the impact of my words would be altogether more hard hitting if I had one of the team with me. But still, it was great to be out with them all and a number had a go at pulling the tyres along, and did brilliantly. Maybe one or two explorers exist in their midst.'

The following Thursday brought mixed news from the Marines. On the down side, confirmation that Matt Kingston would not be allowed to join them on the expedition. He had, his superiors pointed out, been allowed time off the previous year for the Khumbu Challenge, the armed forces expedition to climb peaks around Mount Everest in Nepal, and that, they felt, was enough. However, on the up side, the senior command hadn't entirely ruled out the idea of *a* Marine being involved, if a suitable candidate could be found. 'I was able to explain,' Ed wrote, 'precisely what we are aiming to achieve and how. I suspect that they previously thought we were a bunch of amateurs out on a jolly. Following my conversation with them, they are going to reconsider.' The lieutenant-colonel Ed had spoken to had said he would go back to the Commandant-General and see what he had to say. 'I do hope the answer is yes. With Dad having been in the Navy for his career, I feel I have a slight link with the Marines and it would be lovely to have them represented when we finally stand on top of the world.'

Back in Norfolk, Ed was buoyed up by

another sponsored walk, this one organised by his daughter's pre-prep school. And this time, fortunately, he had one of his soldiers with him. 'The children, aged three to eight, were walking up to three miles and Guy and I joined them with a couple of tyres each. Their enthusiasm was wonderful, and they were very inquisitive about Guy's leg (he was wearing shorts, so all was on show). None of them had ever seen a prosthetic leg before and they were absolutely fascinated. They weren't as embarrassed as adults might be and they were hugely direct with their questions. Guy was brilliant with his answers and I think the children were pretty in awe of him.'

Later, one mother confirmed the excitement her daughter had felt at meeting the man with the iron limb. 'Mummy,' she told her, when she was picked up after school, 'Guy Disney is so cool. On the fourth of July last year a great big firework went into his truck, which is called a tank, and blew off his leg and he didn't even cry. He now has a metal one, and doesn't even have a foot, and is going on a big walk to the North Pole and we all think that when he is there he should ask Father Christmas for a new leg.' Over fish fingers at teatime she added: 'Mummy, today I learnt how people die and you don't even have to be in Afghanistan. People dig holes in the road and bury bombs and if you step on them you are blown up. When I grow up I don't want to marry someone in the Army!'

Also in the class was another little boy called Alex, who had cerebral palsy after a difficult birth. 'He can walk,' said Harriet Parker, 'but he's got a different gait. And he's quite shy. He's always last in every running race, but he's at this mainstream school and he certainly has his physical difficulties. So Guy was talking to the children about his leg and suddenly Alex stood up, in the middle of the class, and said, "I've got one of those." Everyone turned round to look. "I've got two of those," he went on. And he rolled up his trousers where he had his callipers on.

'The teacher indicated for the whole class to be quiet, because Alex doesn't normally come out of himself that quickly. At that point Guy didn't realise what was wrong with him.

'"Have you broken your leg?" he asked.

'"No," said Alex, "I've had these since I was born." His eyes were huge. You could see him thinking, *There's a hero, there's a real proper soldier, I want to be a soldier and he's got what I've got and I can do what he does.* He was standing, talking just to Guy, completely oblivious of the rest of the class, who were all sitting there cross-legged, eyes on stalks.

'"Can you jump?" he asked.

'"Well, I can't jump very well," Guy said, "but yes, I can jump."

'"I can jump," Alex said; and he started jumping, and Guy copied him and did a rather floppy jump.

'Then Alex said, "Can you run?"

'Guy said, "I'm not very good at running, but I'm getting better."

'"I can run," Alex said. "I run everywhere now *and* I can play hockey."

'You saw that little boy change before your eyes. You really did see him grow pride. He went home that day and he told his parents about what had happened and they came in to the school a couple of days later with two hundred pounds

87

for the charity. Little Alex had gone round all his family and friends and said, "There's this soldier like me at school and I want to be like him." Alex is disabled. He'll always be disabled, but you could suddenly see him thinking, *I can do this.*'

* * *

Perhaps good karma from the children had turned the organisers' luck, because the end of the week brought excellent news. A call had come through from Artemis, confirming their interest in becoming title sponsor; in return, they were pledging £150,000. 'To think that someone is willing to commit this sort of money to our "little" project is so exciting,' Ed wrote, 'and a little humbling. It means people believe in what we're doing, which gives us a huge boost in confidence.'

Finally too the Commandant-General of the Royal Marines had been in touch directly. 'We had a perfectly civil exchange,' Ed wrote, 'and Gen Howes made it very clear why Matt would not be able to join us, though he did say the scope of the expedition was not as extreme as they had initially thought. Somewhere in the system is an ex-bootneck who has been saying some fairly strong things about us without seemingly being fully furnished with all the facts, and luckily we have now had an opportunity to explain ourselves. Gen. Howes said he was happy for the Marines to look for another potential candidate to join us, and I followed it up with Lt Col Joyce, but I don't honestly think they'll find anyone. They are making conciliatory noises, but I don't feel they are behind the project and have an institutional suspicion of people outside the military who want to help. There is a misguided arrogance within their ranks which assumes a greater understanding of many matters, particularly that of operating in the Arctic. At least the Army is on side.'

Another insight into the sorry affair of Matt's departure came from the ever-frank Henry Cookson: 'The fact is he was used as a pawn. There was an ex-Marine out there, who shall be nameless, who was highly critical of the expedition. He was briefing elements in the Marines who then told Matt, "You can't go on this trip." Matt was still desperately keen, so he said, "OK then, I'll leave the Corps." At which point they said that if he did, it would jeopardise his pension. So he had to stay in the Marines and not go on the expedition. Basically, the Marines think the Arctic is their area, so why should a bunch of civvies be sorting it out.'

*   *   *

The depleted team were now set for their next planned group training session, a weekend of tyre-dragging along the huge sandy beaches of north Norfolk, not far from Ed's home at Holt. After their experiences on Spitsbergen, the banter was unremitting and nicknames were the order of the day. The organisers were Dags and Parks; no surprises there. Guy was Disco or, as Dags liked to call him, Tom Thumb. And Martin, for reasons sadly not suitable for publication, was Dog.

It was now mid-June, but the English weather obliged with near-Arctic conditions: a freezing, grey, windy day. As the four men assembled their tyres by the golf club on Brancaster beach, then

89

headed off down the wide empty swathes of sand, the sea far out on a low tide, they were continuing to bond in interesting ways. 'We pulled along the beach for a few hours,' says Martin, 'then Dags noticed some rain clouds coming in. All our tyres were similar in size, but there was one at the back of Dags's set which was significantly bigger than the rest. He very tactically decided that he and I should swap tyres just before the rain came. He didn't give a reason, just looked at me with a look almost of disgust and said, "You can take this and I'll take the easier one." I said, "OK Dags, I'll take the big one. Let the disabled boy take the biggest load. You crack on with the smaller one." I thought, *He's getting old, he's probably not as fit as he once was, I'll help him out.* But as soon as it started raining, the tyres filled with wet sand. Resistance more than doubled. It was phenomenal hard work. I didn't say anything to Dags, but I couldn't keep pace with them. Eventually they stopped and asked if I wanted a hand. I said, "No, no, I'm going to finish it."'

'It was miserably wet, miserably cold,' wrote Ed, 'and the sand was turned into glue by the rain. The tyres became harder and harder to pull, and we slowed to a crawl. Dog had the heaviest set of tyres and he was soon well behind us, but there was no way he was going to give in. When we finally stopped he bent double and was dry retching from the effort. We all laughed, but we did realise the effort he had been putting in.'

'I had a slightly bigger tyre on the way out,' says Dags. 'Dog was teasing me, going, "Look at the old man struggling." So on the turn I said, "Right, Dog, we'll swap tyres." I was absolutely thrilled to know that by the time Dog got to the other end of the beach he'd been sick from exhaustion.'

After a three-hour pull along the coastal path in the afternoon the team repaired to the Jolly Sailors in Brancaster for a well-earned supper. In among the banter, there was serious chat about how the project was shaping up. 'Talking,' says Martin, 'about what we wanted to achieve for the charity and drawing up a programme for the coming months; how we were going to maximise the profile of it, how we were going to get the media involved, and how we could all contribute to that—quite apart from synchronising our group training.'

There was more tyre-dragging the next morning, back on a beach that was mercifully once again dry. Ed and Guy were a hundred yards or so behind Dags and Martin when they were stopped by a couple of curious ladies walking their dogs. 'We explained what we were doing,' wrote Ed, 'about the expedition and who we were (no interest in me . . . it's all Guy!) and after we had chatted for a minute or two, one of the ladies looked at Guy and simply said, "Thank you". It was such a meaningful comment, said with great sincerity and respect for Guy and all those many young men and women and it showed how people really do care about what our armed forces do on our behalf.'

At lunchtime on Sunday they dispersed. Martin was flying to Corfu to spend a few days on holiday with some of his mates from the Paras. Guy was going back to his base down the road at MoD Swanton Morley, Ed and Dags home to their respective wives in Holt and Battersea. They wouldn't meet up again until September, when it was hoped they would have a third and even a fourth member for their next planned training weekend together on Bodmin Moor.

'It was a funny old time,' Dags recalls, 'because we were suddenly down to two people. We were a team that wasn't a team. And there weren't at that point two replacements readily available on the horizon. We were very worried, to be honest. Ed was saying to me, "Maybe we'll just take three."'

9

A GREAT BIRTHDAY PRESENT

JACO: I grew up in South Africa, on a farm, near a little town called Witbank in the Eastern Transvaal. I'd always wanted to join the Army. When my grandfather and my dad were young there was still National Service and hearing the stories they told me was always fascinating. They had been all over Africa, doing unbelievable stuff. But the South African Army is not the same as it was when they were in it. There's not really respect for soldiers any more. If you say you're in the Army in South Africa these days people will laugh at you. So it was always the British Army I wanted to join.

But in my last year at school I fell in love and everything came to a standstill. Genevieve was a year younger than me; she was stunning, an absolutely beautiful girl. She was very cultural too, in the choir and all the plays. We spent a lot of time together, even after I left school. But then things changed. She started going on courses and meeting different people. It began not to feel right any more. We probably got a bit too serious, thinking about the future. Eventually we decided to call it a day.

I was working for my father and still living with my parents. I felt I needed to get out of the house. I badly wanted my own flat, but that would mean getting a mortgage and furniture and being able to feed myself. It wasn't falling into place. So I went to my parents and said, "I've always wanted to join the Army, I'm going to do it now." They asked me if I was sure. I told them I was one hundred per cent sure. Then I started looking up stuff about the British Army on the internet.

Ian, one of my very good friends from school, heard about my plans and wanted to come with me. We used to play rugby, centre pair. I'm not being big-headed but we were probably the best centre pair ever; we knew each other's moves so well. Ian was now without a job, he had no income or anything. By this stage I'd set the ball rolling, sorted out my visa, accommodation and so on. 'Mate,' I said, 'you're more than welcome.' So it ended up me and him, coming over to the UK together.

We landed at Heathrow on Saturday; my sister lives in London so we stayed with her. On Monday morning we were straight into the recruiting office. I said I was there to join the Army. They asked if I knew much about it or what I wanted to be doing. There are hundreds of jobs in the Army, from infantry to engineers to doctors to clerks. I said I wanted to start at the bottom.

The recruiting officer who was there that day was from the Rifles. Obviously they were trying to recruit blokes who had come in off the street for their regiment. So he was pushing the Rifles at us.

As we were talking a Parachute Regiment officer came down the stairs. He heard us talking and came over.

'You guys are from South Africa?' he said.

'Yes, we are.'

He had a good look at us. 'You guys are fit, aren't you?'

We grinned at each other. 'We think so, sir. We hope we are.'

He nodded. 'You're looking for excitement? You want to travel the world?'

'That's exactly what we want.'

'Another thing,' he said. 'A lot of your mates from South Africa, they've joined the Parachute Regiment.'

'What's the Parachute Regiment?' I asked. He got out a couple of DVDs and leaflets and gave them to us. 'Here you are,' he said. 'Take them home and have a look.'

Back at my sister's we watched the DVD. 'This is what I want to join,' I said to Ian. We went on to the computer and looked at the website, started finding out about 2 and 3 Para, the training, everything. The next day we went back in and signed up.

The interview process took about five months. During that time Ian and I got a job with a company called Show Force, who build stages for the entertainment business. We stayed in a house full of South Africans; it was a good time. After a couple of months Ian came up to me one day and said his dad was really supportive about him joining the Army but his mum was worried. He had a shoulder injury he'd picked up playing rugby and he wasn't sure they'd let him in anyway.

'To be honest with you,' he said, 'I don't know if I'll fit into the Army.'

So he pulled out and carried on with the rigging work. It didn't matter to me. I did my interviews and then some tests, and one day I got a letter through the post saying 'Congratulations' and asking me to come in and do my oath to the Queen.

But then I had to wait some more, because South Africa had brought out this new mercenary law. Our government didn't want any South Africans joining Commonwealth or foreign forces. You had to make a choice. You could stay with the force you had joined, but if you did you would be classed as a mercenary; the moment you set foot in South Africa you'd be arrested and thrown in jail. Or else you could leave the Army and return to South Africa. I waited eight months for the green light. Then one day I received a letter saying nothing had happened about the mercenary thing, so the British government had decided to carry on with basic recruiting. I finally enlisted on 11 February 2007.

I headed up to Catterick in Yorkshire to do my basic training. It takes twenty-eight weeks. Out of the eighty-two who start, only twelve will pass out. It's true what they say: 'They break you and then they make you.' It's a culture shock, being told what to do. You need to get used to it. On week six, if you're still there, you get handed a beret. It has a green backing behind the cap badge. They feed you little bits, give you just a taster of what it's like having the Maroon Machine on your head.

We were very lucky. We passed out on Friday and had to report to Brize Norton on the Sunday to start our jumps course and get our wings. You need to do eight jumps to qualify, so we were banging out two or three a day. I was qualified in three weeks.

We were all new to the platoon and everyone was getting to know us. I was half way through a fireman's course when this corporal turned up.

'Who's Jaco van Gass?'

'I am.'

'D'you know you're going to Afghanistan in two weeks' time?'

I couldn't believe it. 'Good joke, man,' I was saying. 'Good joke.'

Someone had pulled out. To this day I don't know why I was chosen. I was brand new. There were other guys available, with three, five, fifteen years' experience. It was a quick learning curve. Kit was being thrown at me. I didn't know what to pack, what to leave, what to touch.

So at the start of 2008 I was in Afghanistan. It took a bit of getting used to: the dust, the heat, the dryness in the air. But I loved every second of it. I was given a lot of responsibility. Our emblem is *Utrinque Paratus*, which means 'Ready for Anything'. Whatever is thrown your way, you just have to deal with it. I was brand new, still a private, but I was acting as a lance-corporal. Being involved with the Afghan National Army you need to show your leadership otherwise they just go 'He's low rank' and won't listen to you.

After four months we had a bit of leave, then we were back into rotation with the rest of them. It was our company's turn again in the summer of 2009. This time I managed to do five months. Me and this other single guy Stefan, we volunteered to give up our time off. Other guys have got wives and kids, girlfriends, we just had ourselves and our friends. So there were no roots, nothing calling us back. But

96

in the end, because of health and safety, you have to take your R & R. The Army has to make sure that if something goes wrong with you, you go a bit cuckoo or something, you can't point the finger at them.

So it was actually two weeks before we had to come back. I was fit as I'd ever been, tanned brown as a nut, with a little bristly black moustache. You're not allowed to grow beards out there, so me and the guys had a competition to grow 'taches. I was rather proud of mine. It gave me a military look.

It was 19 August 2009, the day before the Afghan elections—and also my birthday. We got a call in for an operation. The whole thing was explained to us, how we were going to go in, where we were going to land. We were going after an IED factory. These guys were suicide bombers who were going to target various voting stations, so it was essential we capture them. We took off in the helicopter around eleven at night. It was fairly dark, not much of a moon.

I was attached to a sniper, carrying telescopic ladders for him; we used them to get into compounds and up on to walls and roofs. I'd also be on the radio feeding him information while he was observing. He might say, 'I can see a guy walking out of this building. He's moving from the north-east . . .?' I'd be putting all that information through on the Net, reporting exactly what we're doing, then getting instructions back. As well as the enemy stuff, you might get friendly fire coming in as well, so everyone needs to know exactly where everyone else is on the ground.

That night the operation went well. We got the

blokes we were after. We had all the evidence too: bomb-making equipment, suicide vests and so on. We were taking them off target, moving away from the village we'd been in towards the desert where we would be picked up by the helicopters again. You need to get well away. If you're near a built-up area there's a risk of RPGs or gunfire coming your way when the helicopter lands. For the Taliban it would be like Christmas if they could shoot one down.

We were headed cross country on a little path. We'd walked a couple of miles when it came over the radio that two guys had been spotted moving on some high ground right above us. In the darkness you could just make out the two little buildings where they were. So we pushed off the track with a whole section of the Afghan National Army and moved forward to the area where the guys had been seen.

We had an interpreter with us. He was shouting out various commands, telling these guys to stand still or lie on their tummies, that kind of stuff. They didn't react. He shouted again and then one of the blokes started running away. He ran into one of the buildings and the next thing we knew he'd come out with an AK-47 and was opening fire in our general direction. As soon as he did that we dropped him, but there were others there too and they were quite well dug in. They had trenches and fire points and now we were receiving fire from a number of positions.

We returned fire. The muzzle flashes in the darkness show you where the enemy are shooting from; with your night vision you can see even more clearly. The fight went on for quite a while, dying down then picking back up again, as it usually does. Me and my sniper started doing 'Buddy-buddy', which is when you go fifty-fifty. So while I'm shooting, keeping the enemy suppressed, he's changing mags on his rifle. As soon as he's done he shouts 'Back in!' then he starts firing rounds and I'll do my magazine change. It was one of the better fights I'd been involved in. By this time it was early morning of 20 August and I was thinking, *This is a great birthday present.* I thought that we'd get back to base and be gobbing off like ten men about what we'd been doing.

Then an RPG was fired from our left flank. It was too high to be any danger to us. My partner was doing his mag change and I could hear a massive noise going over our heads, then exploding in the distance. An RPG is basically a rocket that you shoot from the shoulder. It's very inaccurate. It has a little trigger on its nose, so it needs an impact to set it off. It will keep going till it hits something with that trigger. If it doesn't hit something it will eventually die out.

As I fired two more rounds, I could hear the noise again. It was a second RPG and this time it was coming lower, right at us. As I was shooting I caught a glimpse of it out of the corner of my eye, its red trail behind it, bouncing along the ground at us. I thought, *Wow, this is going to be close.*

I was still on my knees, firing, and my partner behind me was about to get up. As I turned away, this RPG clipped the ladder I was carrying on my back then bounced off that on to my arm. The bone must have been just hard enough to initiate the trigger, because the explosion was right next to me. It threw me four or five metres across the open ground.

I was aware of a deafening blast, then after a couple of seconds, it felt like, I realised I was on my back. I was trying to get up, but I couldn't, with the ladders strapped on me. I knew I wasn't where I had been, but all I was thinking was, *I've got to get back into the firefight.*

I still had my rifle in my right hand. So I brought it up to fire. That was the point I realised I'd lost my left arm. As I tried to bring it up to hold the rifle steady, it wasn't there. The rifle just fell through. It took me two or three attempts to take in what had happened. My arm had been blown off. At that stage it didn't really bother me. I couldn't feel any pain. Finally I got up into a sitting position on the ground and started firing with one hand. I was very confused.

Then a bit of pain started coming through in my leg from the shrapnel. I looked down and saw that I was actually glowing. My shirt was on fire and I was burning. I put my rifle down and tried to pat out the flames with my hand.

My partner meanwhile had got some shrapnel in his legs. That was burning too and he was screaming. I was thinking, *You need to sort out that arm, stop the blood, treat yourself.* Your tourniquet and med kit are very easy to reach, in a pocket of your battle vest. So I got my tourniquet out and got it round my arm and tried to apply the pressure to stop the blood. But with one arm I couldn't crank it up enough. To stop the blood in a wound like that you need to squeeze it right up to the bone.

When I'd been doing med lessons during my training, it had sometimes felt a bit daft—to be doing this stuff when you'd otherwise have a bit of time off. But now all that knowledge kicked in. I'd always thought, *If something happens to my mate I'll know what to do.* It was never in my mind that I'd be in that situation myself.

I lay back down and I could see one of the other guys coming over. He was trying to get his night vision to work again because the shock of the blast had knocked it out. I was whispering at him because I didn't want to give our position away.

'Reece! Reece! Get my radio, get my radio.'

My radio had been blown off me in the blast. It was on the edge of the track where I was now lying. Reece picked it up but it was totally broken, it wasn't going to work now. Then he crawled over to me in the middle of the road.

'Shit, Jaco,' he said. 'You've lost your arm, man.'

'No shit, Sherlock,' I said. 'I know I've lost my arm. Get some help over the radio.'

So he called the medics. Then he tried to tighten up the tourniquet. Luckily the medics were nearby and were soon there. They pushed my rifle away and started fixing me up.

'Mate,' this medic was saying to Reece, 'that bleeding needs to stop. You've got to tighten it right up.' He cranked it up so hard I thought that he was going to snap off the only bit of arm I had left. Then they locked it off and gave me morphine. Mine had been blown away by the blast, so I had to use theirs.

By this stage my leg was in agony, the pain in my ankle was unbelievable.

'Have I lost my leg?' I kept asking. I could see it but I couldn't move it. I didn't know about the third of my thigh I had lost, or the shrapnel in my side. All I could feel was this pain in my ankle.

In the meantime the others had called in air cover. That seemed to kick in really quickly. Two planes, hammering down on the enemy positions.

From there on in everything just happened. The guys had called in the helicopters to pick us up. They took about thirty-five minutes to arrive. As the first one touched down, there were four Afghan guys running up with my stretcher. They dropped me and I fell off on to the dirt. There was a lot of shouting while they got a bollocking from the other guys. Four of them then picked me up and lifted me into the chopper. There was a doctor there ready, so I got treated straight away. I was only just conscious now. The guys around me were trying to keep me awake, slapping me and shouting, 'Jaco, Jaco!' But my eyes just kept going. I thought, *If I die now, I die.*

I came round when we got back to Bastion. As they were lifting my stretcher into the ambulance, they dropped me again. So I was semi-conscious in the ambulance. Then I remember going through the hospital doors. I could feel the nurses' hands as they stripped me of my clothes and boots. The next thing I knew I was in Selly Oak.

I lost a massive amount of blood. The shrapnel in my side had punctured some of my internal organs. They opened me up, took them out, washed them, looked at what had gone wrong and fixed me up. Then they put it all back together. My heart stopped on the operating table and they had to bring me back to life. I had a collapsed lung and various other problems. Not that I knew anything about it.

When I came round I was in intensive care, with tubes in my arms. My mum and all my family were

Ed and Simon training in Cornwall, Sept 2010

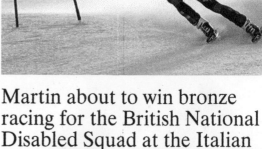

Platoon Commander
Martin Hewitt in full
battle gear at the end
of an operation in
Helmand Province,
Sept 2007

Martin about to win bronze
racing for the British National
Disabled Squad at the Italian
National Championships at
Sestrière, Italy, January 2011

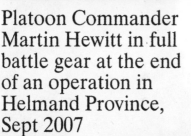

Guy Disney on
operations

Guy's shattered leg
immediately before
his operation

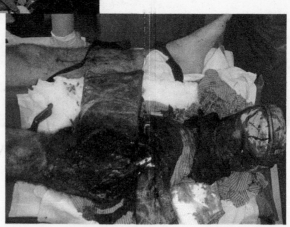

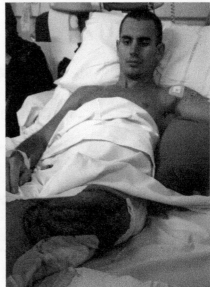

Jaco on operations in
Afghanistan

Jaco in hospital at Selly Oak

Man of war: Steve
returns from a contact
in Afghanistan

Steve in a back brace at a
Welsh Guards homecoming
organised by Cardiff City
Football Club

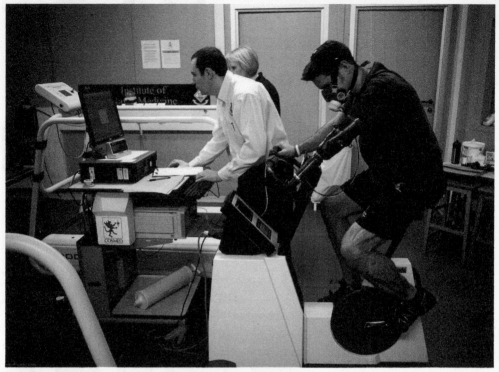

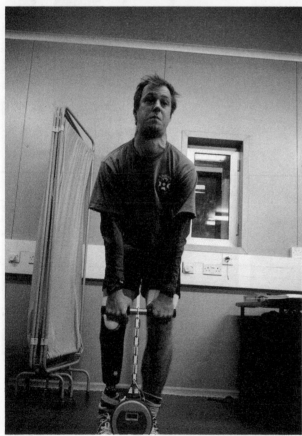

Jaco is tested on the VO$_2$ Max machine at the Institute of Naval Medicine

Guy hits the wall at the INM

Initial bonding: the team on their first training exercise together on the North Cornish Coastal Path

'A funny old time': The depleted team dragging tyres in Norfolk in June 2010

Guy Disney leading the team above the lakes at Beitostølen, January 2011

The team stop to set up camp on a lake: Beitostølen, Day 4

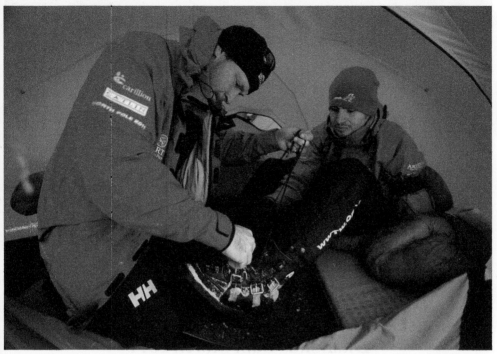

Ed Parker helps Jaco with the tricky task of tying his boot laces

Jaco assisting Steve with his daily physio exercises after a day's man-hauling

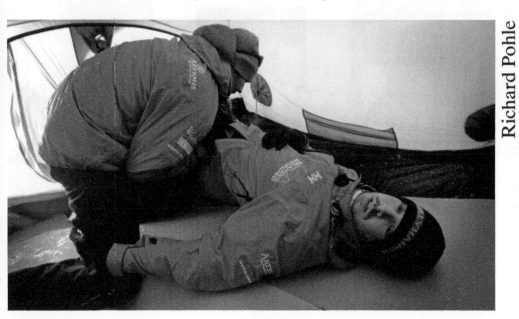

Battersea Power Station illuminated for the Ice and Diamonds Ball: March 2011

Room at the top: the full team outside Number Ten Downing Street

there from South Africa. I was very confused. The last thing I could remember was being in a firefight in Afghanistan. Now there were lights in my eyes and the nurses and my family were saying, 'Jaco, you're OK, you're in a hospital in Birmingham.'

I ran my hand across my upper lip and my little 'tache was gone.

'Where's my moustache?' I asked.

'They had to shave it off, Jaco,' my sister said, 'when they were operating on you.'

I was gutted. That 'tache had been my pride and joy.

My family weren't sure that I knew I'd lost my arm; or that my leg was so badly damaged.

'How are you feeling?' my mother asked.

'I'm feeling like a bloke who's just lost an arm and a leg,' I said.

They laughed. Out of relief as much as anything.

'You've lost your arm,' they said, 'but not your leg.'

When I fell back to sleep I was still dreaming about Afghanistan. I was back in the firefight and I had to keep firing. I could hear helicopters coming in and out.

I was in intensive care for between seven and ten days. I had a neck brace and a colostomy bag. My stomach had been punctured, so I couldn't eat solid food. Eventually I was moved up on to a ward. There were other wounded guys there as well, three of us in a little bay. That was good. We were able to swap stories, talk about what had happened to us, how we'd got injured, where and why. Some of the other families get involved with you as well. They might bring you a bowl of fruit, some yoghurt, something to read, a DVD. That was absolutely great.

I lost about eighteen to twenty kilograms during my time in hospital. Your body goes through shock and is trying to heal itself, which is why you lose so much weight. I had to get stronger to be able to do basic things. Even sitting up and feeding myself was difficult to start with.

After a while I moved to Headley Court. This is when you start learning to become more independent. You start trying to do stuff on your own: going to the toilet, dressing yourself. That was quite a challenge to start with, with just one arm.

I heard about Walking With The Wounded from the guys during the unveiling of a memorial to the regiment's casualties in Afghanistan. When I got back to Headley one of them rang me up. 'Jaco,' he said, 'I heard about this fantastic challenge. I'm going to mail it through to you.'

I read through it and it was everything I wanted to do. So I went up to London for the day for the assessment. I had a lift with another lad. As we rocked up at the Rifles Club, at least five others from Headley Court appeared.

'You never said you were coming,' they said.

We were laughing. We see each other all the time and everyone had kept it quiet.

There was a physio there, a doctor, and the two organisers, Ed and Simon. They each had a quick look at us and asked us to do various tasks. Picking up things from the floor and so on. At this point my wounds were still fresh. I was only a month and a half out of my wheelchair. I wasn't even running by that stage, just barely walking.

All the others got calls within forty-eight hours saying they weren't strong enough. But I hadn't

104

heard anything, so I thought I was in with a chance. After a couple of weeks I still hadn't heard, so I rang Ed. Somehow he had got confused and hadn't got the right number for me. He was very apologetic, but he said they couldn't consider me because of the colostomy bag and also because my wounds were so severe.

So I forgot about it and cracked on. At the start of March I had the reversal of the colostomy. Then in April I went out to Germany with Battle Back to learn how to ski. I'd never been on skis in my life. That was the beginning of everything, because I realised from there I could do other things too. By June I was fit enough to run a half-marathon in Kenya.

I was back with my regiment by then, spending every morning in the gym, training. I knew Martin anyway, because he's in my unit and also on the Combined Services Disabled Skiing Team. I knew he was involved with Walking With The Wounded too. One day he approached me and told me that while they had originally planned to take just two soldiers, they had more funds coming in, so they'd upped it to four and there were two spaces available.

'Are you still interested?' he asked.

'Martin,' I said, 'you know I've been following you guys on the website and on Facebook ever since January. Of course I'm interested.'

10

FRESH BLOOD

On the first weekend of September 2010, the holidaymakers enjoying an evening drink on the bumpy little green at the front of the Maltster's Arms in Chapel Amble, north Cornwall, were joined by an unusual-looking group. Four fit young men with visible disabilities of various kinds, and two older blokes with all their limbs intact. They appeared to be having a good time, bantering away with each other noisily as dusk fell. After a while they headed into the dining room for their evening meal.

This was the six-strong Walking With The Wounded team, getting to know each other for the first time. Besides the original four—Ed, Simon, Martin and Guy—there were two new members, for whom the upcoming weekend of training on Bodmin Moor and the North Cornwall Coast Path would act as probation.

The first recruit was Jaco van Gass. A day after he had told Martin he was up for joining the expedition Ed had called him, and after a brief chat had arranged for him to have a face-to-face meeting with Simon in London. Dags was impressed. The Jaco they had interviewed in January at the Rifles Club and the one who stood before him now were like two completely different men, he told him.

The second candidate for the Pole was Jaco's mate Steve Young, a sergeant in the Welsh Guards, who had also been wounded in Afghanistan, when the Mastiff armoured car he was travelling in had been blown up by an IED. The blast had broken Steve's back and for a while it had looked as if he might never walk again. Though he still had both his arms and legs, his back remained a serious problem for him.

At the end of June Steve, like Jaco, had taken part in the Safaricom half-marathon in Kenya, regarded as one of the toughest in the world, across the savannah plains and through the acacia woodland of the Lewa Wildlife Conservancy, 140 miles north of Nairobi.

'Out in Kenya I got quite pally with Jaco,' says Steve, 'and he was talking then about this Walking With The Wounded trip. I thought it sounded amazing. Then one evening Jaco was saying how he loved Kenya and the African warmth. "If I had the option of Kenya or the Pole," I said, "I would choose the Pole without a shadow of a doubt." He must have kept this in mind, because a couple of months later a place became available on the team. He rang me up and said, "Are you still interested?" I said, "Definitely." So I went down to Bodmin with him to meet the rest of the boys. Understandably, with something like this, you're going to be in very close proximity, so you've all got to get on.'

The following morning Dags led the soldiers on a six-hour walk across Bodmin Moor: up the short, steep, rocky slope to Rough Tor, then on across the low, heathery valley to Brown Willy, a name that provided a good topic for banter. To make the fifteen-mile trek a little more interesting, they were each carrying a Bergen army rucksack containing 60 lb in lead weights.

'I had never been to Bodmin before,' Ed wrote

107

in his diary, 'but it turned out to be remarkably like Brecon—without the rain. A very beautiful spot. Saturday was a good day, giving us all an opportunity to be with one another again, and to see how Jaco and Steve fitted in. Both did brilliantly, although I was a little concerned about Steve's back. Prior to Saturday, the furthest he had walked since being injured was 3.5 miles, and the most weight he had carried was 20 lb. Bearing in mind that his doctors had initially warned him that he would probably be paralysed from the waist down, that in itself was an amazing achievement. He needed to stop every hour or so and stretch his back in order to deal with the pain he was in. Despite this, he managed the full distance, so he clearly has the grit and determination we are looking for. It will be interesting to get him on skis in a few weeks' time and see how the motion affects his back.'

Dags was also checking out the newcomers' potential. 'Dog was at the cottage before I'd met Steve,' he says, 'and had been chatting with him for an hour or two, so I asked him, "What d'you make of Steve?" Dog said, "I don't say whether I like somebody without knowing them better." *Uh-oh*, I thought, *that doesn't bode very well*. But as it turned out, by the end of our first day on the moor, everybody was really chummy.'

'When I first met Steve,' says Martin, 'we talked about his background and what he'd done. He was a recce platoon sergeant in the Welsh Guards at the age of twenty-five, which tells you something immediately. That platoon normally has some of the best soldiers in the battalion. So for him to be a sergeant at that stage, tells me he's doing well.

He's from the Rhondda, not far from Merthyr. I've a lot of work colleagues from that area, so I know what kind of sense of humour those boys have got. I know they're quite robust as well. I immediately thought, *This guy is going to fit well into the team.* He was Welsh, which amused Ed; he likes taking the piss out of the Welsh accent, as do I. But then I thought, *A Scouser and a Welshman. How are we going to articulate ourselves in the media industry with our regional accents?'*

'I was on probation at that point,' says Steve. 'None of the team were chosen, or so we were told. But it was good doing it, because the old Army mentality came back. When I was having my physio back home, it was like being pampered, in kid gloves. Out there I was back with the lads, doing something I loved; going over the hills. It was a hard old slog. But that's when the team gels, when you go through something like that.'

Ed was equally impressed with Jaco. 'I last saw him in January,' he wrote, 'when his injuries were shocking and he still had a colostomy. That has now been reversed and his physical recovery has been nothing short of miraculous. While he does have a significant loss of muscle on his left leg, his ability to tab was as you would expect from a Para! I think his mental strength is extraordinary and he is clearly determined to succeed.

'It was fascinating talking to him over the course of the day. He loved being a soldier and was clearly good at it. But he realises he can no longer do this, and so he needs to leave the Army at some point. But he has no idea what he wants to do, or what is even available for him to do. He is not a sitting in an office man—he needs something more energetic

109

to drive him. The dilemma is the same as for so many wounded soldiers, and it is something I hope we can help with. One thing I've been thinking about is an Employment Forum, where companies who have expressed an interest in employing wounded servicemen set up a stand and the wounded are able to meet people, talk about what they do, learn a little about what is available, what skills and training they need, and start forming an idea of what lies ahead. It would also give these companies direct exposure to those they could potentially employ. Something to work on.'

With the sponsorship now in place to cover the costs of the expedition, and donations still coming in, Ed had been thinking hard about who might be worthy recipients of his new charity's help. Over the summer he had visited the Warrior Programme in Fulham, where work is done with both ex-servicemen and the homeless, particularly those with post-traumatic stress disorder. He had then gone with his nephew Harry to see the work of Enham Alamein, a charity for disabled people in Wiltshire, which was founded in 1919 as a rehabilitation centre for ex-servicemen returning from the First World War. 'Here in the middle of Wiltshire,' Ed wrote, 'was an infrastructure already in place to provide exactly what I believe the Forces need in order to help servicemen successfully resettle when they leave. Early intervention is the key. The more those leaving are offered means the less chance there is of them becoming homeless or ending up in the prisons of the UK. There are many organisations out there which mean well, but they are all operating independently of one another and nowhere in the chain are the MoD or military

110

providing any influence or guidance—why not?'

After six hours on the hills, the team finished around 4.30. In another conversation along the way, Guy and Steve discovered they had both been involved in the same incident in Afghanistan, when a Viking, an armoured personnel carrier in which Steve had been travelling, had rolled into a canal and Steve had technically drowned before being pulled out and resuscitated. Guy was one of the first on the scene, and had watched while the medics brought three of the soldiers back to life. He had then driven these casualties in another Viking to a rendezvous with a rescue helicopter: 'As we were driving along, the two guys who had just drowned were in the back and one of them was regaining consciousness. When he did, he completely flipped out, because the last thing he remembered was being in the back of a similar cab, then rolling into the canal and drowning; he was still half naked. This guy was tapping my leg. "You've got to stop," he said. "You've got to get us out of here."

'I said, "I'm really sorry but we can't stop because any second a fight could start." The Taliban are very good at watching and waiting. It would have been a prime opportunity, to have a scrap with us while we were disorganised, with a vehicle half in a canal and people not really knowing what was going on. Eventually this guy saw the point. "OK mate," he said, "Crack on." So we got them into the helicopter and off they went, never to be seen again. But it was amazing. The chap who was half naked was Steve.'

There were more war stories over supper that evening in a pub on Trebarwith Strand. In Afghanistan, Guy and Martin had served as

111

officers, while Jaco and Steve were other ranks. Jaco admits to being a little bit wary with his two new team-mates to start with: 'I wasn't obviously going to say "sir" to them, but I was probably being fairly polite. I soon got to the point where I felt more comfortable. Maybe after taking a bit of banter off them.' At some point over the weekend the subject of rank came up. 'Relatively early on one of us said, "Listen, we all know each other's background, but there's no ranking system once we're together now."'

'We refer to each other on first name terms,' said Martin, 'or nicknames, which in the military just would not happen. But this is very much about us working together and supporting one another. To do that efficiently we don't need an autocratic militaryesque regime.'

'It's a really interesting dynamic between the four of them,' said Simon, 'that I've thought about quite a bit when we've been out training or on exercises. It's completely at odds with the normal way of functioning for serving officers and soldiers—and they are all still serving. I think the fact that Ed and I are there makes it into a civvy trip for them. We have nothing to do with the Army any more, so that makes it less formal.'

After a week of unbroken Cornish sunshine, Sunday morning brought rain, sweeping in under dark grey clouds over the sea. The terrain, too, was more challenging, as the team took their heavy Bergens to walk the steep ups and downs of the North Cornwall Coast Path between Tintagel and Port Gaverne. For the two without arms, this presented no unusual difficulties. Steve's back was pretty sore, but he was keeping his discomfort to himself. Guy, however, was visibly struggling. Going downhill with an artificial leg had always been a problem for him. Now, like Rob in Spitsbergen, he realised his prosthesis didn't fit as well as it should. 'It was fine to start with, a few blisters, a few rubs. But the leg itself has a carbon fibre rim around the top, which is pretty sharp. After a while this was slicing into the back of my leg. It got pretty sore. I was cut to shreds.'

Ed was aware of Guy's problems, but overall, he thought, the weekend had been a success. 'The revelation for Simon and me,' he wrote, 'was how well Jaco and Steve fitted in. Both are extremely likeable individuals, with a strong sense of humour and an ability to stand up for themselves.' There was another bonus: 'From the word "go" we have wanted to avoid this expedition being seen as an Officers' Jolly and the involvement of these two will make a huge difference to the perception of the team.'

Ten days later the two new recruits were taken to the Institute of Naval Medicine to be put through their paces. Ed accompanied them, keen to have another go at the VO_2 Max test after Martin had boasted of achieving a higher score than him. 'Vanity aside,' Ed wrote, 'it did transpire that Dog had been very slightly misled and actually my VO_2 Max score remains the highest.' More important, Jaco and Steve were passed fit for purpose, albeit with some changes to their fitness routines: 'Endurance is the key, so Steve was advised about how to alter his training regime in order to start building up his body in the right way for what we need to do. I do like the way Steve is so open, and so clearly listens to what he's being told.'

Even as Ed and Simon began to think they might finally have found their team, there came a new setback, as reservations about Walking With The Wounded resurfaced within the senior ranks of the Army. Ed had heard on the grapevine that Colonel Porridge was creating problems again, telling people that the expedition should not be allowed to go ahead. 'It worries me,' he wrote, 'that he persists with this hugely negative approach. I am convinced it is because he doesn't fully understand what or how we are preparing, or thinks that we haven't paid enough attention to the welfare of our injured soldiers. I need to put out as much information in the higher echelons of the Army as I can, so there's a clear understanding of what we're trying to do. It does make life more complicated, and to have another episode similar to the one we had with the Marines would be disastrous.'

Then an alarming letter arrived from Martin and Jaco's commanding officer: 'I wrote to him some months ago to keep him in touch with the expedition and everything we were doing, stressing how keen I was to have two of them involved. The noises I had back from Martin were that the regiment was very positive. But on Thursday their CO wrote to say that he was deferring the decision about their involvement to their new COs as both are being moved to new Personal Recovery Units. After a quick chat with Martin, who told me he'd already spoken to his new PRU boss, and he was very keen Martin was involved, I was a little more relaxed. Martin then called Jaco's PRU CO in London and apparently he too is keen. But I do find it frustrating that a definite decision has yet to be made by the Army. I understand that nobody wants these boys to come to any further harm, but someone needs to take ownership of this expedition within the military, someone who can make a decision and give us the unequivocal green light. I do understand that the Army's attentions are focussed on fighting and winning the war in Afghanistan, but people must stop regarding Dags and me as some sort of threat.'

*   *   *

However unsettling all this was, it was essential for the team to stick to their training schedule. Individually and collectively, they had to continue building the extreme level of fitness required for the challenge the following year. Next on the agenda was the group's participation in the annual 30/30 Endurance Race on Exmoor, when small teams carry Bergens containing 30 lb of weight over a thirty-mile course between ten checkpoints across the rough terrain of the moor. The event would serve, too, as a final test for Jaco and Steve.

The new recruits drove down together, arriving first at the rendezvous in a pub in Exford. Martin appeared next, followed by Ed, Dags, Guy and Inge Solheim, who had flown in from Norway. The 30/30 is a traditional military-style navigation exercise, where competing teams are given grid references at each checkpoint for their next target, so the afternoon was spent poring over the map, getting familiar with the terrain they would be walking over the following day.

Then the guys lined up on the village green for a photo shoot, its results destined for the Walking With The Wounded website, which the PR agency had recently put together. Alex Rayner was on hand with the branded expedition kit provided by sponsors Helly Hansen, and the team were photographed wearing the bright red jackets and trousers with the Artemis logo over the pocket. Later Alex and TwoFour's documentary crew, Alexis Girardet and Rob Leveritt, joined the boys for supper in the pub. 'A massive scoff,' says Jaco, 'which was needed. Thirty miles and thirty pounds is going to take it out of you. So we had starters, steaks and a couple of beers too to help with the calories.'

Then an early night, in bunks in the local youth hostel. They were up at five, grabbing toast and tea before heading up to the village hall for the 5.30 a.m. start. 'It was clear from the lack of conversation,' wrote Ed, 'that there were nerves across the whole team. This was a big deal for all of us. The wounded boys hadn't embarked on anything like this since they were injured, and Dags and I are just plain old! I suspect the person least fazed by it was Inge.'

Nor were Team Wounded yet that media savvy. They had arrived for the day's challenge wearing camouflage trousers and T-shirts. 'It was a bloody nightmare,' says Alex. 'I gave them all this beautiful smart kit and said, "See you tomorrow morning at four thirty." Then they turned up in some ragged T-shirt.

' "So where's the kit?" I asked.

' "I've left it behind. This is my lucky T-shirt."

' "We're going to have to have a chat about branding. You see that logo on the jacket. That is called a sponsor. That is why I'm wearing it." '

Team Wounded headed off into the darkness

116

and promptly got lost. There was fog on the hills and visibility was down to ten metres. Coming down from a crag on to a narrow road, they went west instead of east and lost a good half-hour. 'We went down the wrong valley,' says Dags. 'I don't know who was responsible, Ed or Martin, but it was quite funny watching the blame game going on.'

Back on track, they pushed on to the first checkpoint, where their heavy Bergens were put down for five minutes while they rested their backs and had some water and food: flapjacks, sweets, jelly, easy calories to keep the energy quotients high. After a short consultation with the two marshals about the grid reference of the next checkpoint, they were back on their way. Jaco noticed that of all the team, at this point, Ed was working hardest: 'I wouldn't say he was struggling, but due to the nature of his build, he was slower.' Without saying anything, the others discreetly dropped their pace.

At Checkpoint 5, Guy was let off. His leg still did not fit as it should, so he'd already said that he was only going to do twelve miles before calling it a day. As it happened he had managed sixteen, carrying the full 30 lb, but the carbon fibre rim at the top of his prosthesis continued to chafe badly: 'It was frustrating having to stop because I have that "never quit" mentality. But I was pretty sore, the end of my stump had gone raw basically.'

Alex Rayner had been following the team in his vehicle, meeting them at each checkpoint. 'It was thick fog, you couldn't see a thing. I was parked up with the TV crew, listening to these voices coming up through the mist. You hear them for about half an hour before you see them. When Guy got in the car I said, "D'you want to drive or do you want to map read?" He said, "I'll drive. Last time I did map reading I got shot."'

After Checkpoint 5, the terrain became rougher, the ground covered with big grassy tussocks, evocatively known as 'babies' heads', which would, Ed thought, have been very hard going for Guy. The soldiers had been overtaken—at a run—by the local team, but as they passed through Checkpoint 6 they realised they were doing well, getting ahead of several other competitors.

Then, as they reached Checkpoint 7, one of the marshals approached with the news that they were being taken off the race. 'It was only 3 p.m.,' wrote Ed, 'and though it was clear we weren't going to be able to finish the course, it was far too early for us to stop. I was furious. We had not come all this way to be pulled off the 30/30. I threw my teddy a little out of the cot.'

'We had a punch-up,' says Dags. 'Not a physical one, but it wasn't far off! We'd been going like billy-o and by that stage were third in the race. We knew we could do a whole lot more, but for safety reasons they weren't going to allow us to go on. There was a marshal there who was saying "Rules is rules." But we hadn't yet pushed ourselves to the point where we were really shattered, which was what we wanted to do to test ourselves. Ed sounded off massively. Then one of them radioed back to base camp, but they came back with, "No, no, you've got to pull them off." We said, "We're not going to pull off, thank you very much. We're going to carry on. Stuff you!"'

Fortunately, at that moment, Ed spotted an old acquaintance who had just arrived at the

118

checkpoint. He was a legendary Army figure and one of the race's committee members. 'A silence fell over things,' says Alex, 'and Ed turned to this character and said, "Sir, are you going to allow this to happen?" He was saying, "I've got nothing to do with it, really, nothing to do with me." But then he skirted round and had a quiet chat with the marshals. They were Hereford men who referred to him as "the boss".'

'There was a big old kerfuffle,' says Dags, 'but in the end they said, "OK then, off you go."'

'I think that was a real low point for Dags,' says Martin, mischievously, 'realising we'd won our argument and he now had a load more miles to go. His feet were sore and he hobbled off like an old man with a hunched back.'

'From a personal perspective,' Simon admits, 'I was fucked. When they'd said, "You're off," my mental head had said, "Right, we're off. That's it, that's life." Now I had to get back into it, which I found really difficult.'

Ed's determination paid off, as the team pushed on through rugged terrain to Checkpoint 8. 'By now,' Ed wrote, 'things were beginning to hurt. Dags was feeling his feet a bit and Steve had a couple of corking blisters on his heels. But we were doing fine and I was delighted to see that with a bit of hardship we were sticking together well. Jaco and Martin's shoulders were both hurting as a result of carrying heavy packs, which aggravated their injuries, and for the first time since we've started training as a team, Martin shut up! He must have been tired.'

'Ed came through in the end,' says Jaco. 'When we were fatigued, his resources kicked in.'

On they slogged, reaching Checkpoint 9 almost in the dark. 'The marshal told us it was over,' wrote Ed, 'and this time there were no complaints. We were delighted to stop.'

As it turned out, only two teams had finished the course. Walking With The Wounded had come in third place, far better than anyone had expected. The winners were local men, keen fell runners who had been training for the race for the last year and had used a GPS to find their route. According to this instrument, they had actually walked forty-two miles over the day, while Walking With The Wounded had covered thirty-six miles to reach Checkpoint 9.

That evening, at the prizegiving in a local village hall, the team were the first to receive a trophy— and from the very gentleman who had helped them out at Checkpoint 7. 'There was a standing ovation,' says Alex. 'I don't think there was any doubt then, in the minds of the people there, that this team were going to get to the Pole. It was a hell of a trek.'

'We were thrilled,' wrote Ed, 'by how we had all done as individuals, but more importantly as a team, beating eight others with able-bodied people in them. As a personal confidence boost, it was huge. But what I was most pleased by was that as a unit we had worked together, looked after each other, and been doing it for each other.'

'It was a good thing to spend a day working hard together,' says Inge Solheim, 'because that is more or less the hard work we are going to see every day in the North Pole. The best thing was just to walk and talk to them in the fog. Conversations were light, the banter was there, and they were all enthusiastic. No moaning or complaining.'

It looked as if, with Jaco and Steve, Ed and Simon had found their dream team. Subject to final Army approval of course. 'We've now got two officers and two soldiers,' said Ed. 'You've got Guy, who is public school educated, and Martin, who is not, then a South African and a Welshman. It's a really lovely quartet of characters and backgrounds. At one point I was really worried it was going to be a bunch of yahs.'

11

'I CAN'T DIE LIKE THIS'

STEVE: I grew up in Tonypandy, in the Rhondda Valley. All through school I pretty much knew I wanted to be a soldier. I was that typical kid running around with toy guns, always up in the mountains building dams and tree houses. My father used to take me to lots of rugby games and I would meet these old guys, D-Day veterans and the like. I loved listening to their stories. Then I watched all the war films I could. I remember there was a careers open day when I was at school. There was a military stand there and I made a beeline for it.

When I left school I went straight into the Army. My mum was a bit reluctant about signing me up, because I joined as I turned seventeen. I was a boy soldier. But my father said, 'If you don't sign him up now, he'll join anyway when he's eighteen and he might regret not being in at a younger age.'

After training I joined the battalion. Obviously

121

it was the Welsh Guards. To start with we were in London in a ceremonial role. Then we moved to Aldershot, where we prepared for the first operational tour I was going on. I was deployed to Bosnia in 2001, aged nineteen. I quickly got into the reconnaissance platoon and did my first tour as a recce soldier. You're involved with intelligence gathering. The reconnaissance platoon generally has the best soldiers in the battalion: the keenest, the fittest, the most motivated. I love being around people like that.

When I came back I decided to stay in the recce platoon. The next deployment was to Northern Ireland. We did six months in Londonderry, then eighteen months descaling, pulling the troops back. A lot of the stuff we did was hush-hush, surveillance work. It was very enjoyable.

After that, Iraq. We deployed in October 2004. It was counter-insurgency at that stage. We went with the Black Watch group up to Camp Dogwood as a surveillance asset. It was nicknamed Camp Incoming because of the amount of indirect fire we were getting; we were being hit twelve times a day with mortars and Chinese rockets. That was my first experience of actually being engaged with the enemy. I got blown up by an IED, what they call a daisy chain, where you have a whole string of explosives. I was in a Snatch Land Rover, escaping from an incident where we had managed to get surrounded by a couple of hundred people in a marketplace, throwing stones at us, climbing up on our roof. That was a bit hairy. Thankfully nobody was killed.

My battalion deployed to Afghanistan in March 2009. We were in Camp Bastion for about six days. I was just biting the bit to get out on the ground. Then they asked for volunteers to go up to the forward operations base, the FOB, so I put my hand up. All eight of the lads in my section volunteered to go with me, up to this base at a place called Salab. We were only there a week when the captain of another platoon was shot and killed at Haji Alem, which was an old drug dealer's fort; it was like something you might see in a film about the Foreign Legion, with four corners, thick walls and turrets on each corner. The captain replacing him took me with him as his platoon sergeant.

Haji Alem was an awesome place. It was very easy to defend, because you were elevated above the surrounding terrain, which gave you good open arcs for shooting all around. But the Taliban were more than happy to attack us. And we were more than happy to take them on. Every day we had contact. We were getting some good firm kills.

Some of the firefights we were involved in lasted the best part of a day; they were eight, ten, twelve hours long. During one of these the Taliban managed to block our resupply lorries and we ran out of water. It was hot and dry and there was nothing to drink at all. You could see the lads running around with their lips stuck to their gums. There was no way a chopper could come in either, because the Taliban were so close to the fort they might have brought one down with a lucky RPG.

Then Operation Panther's Claw kicked off. My battle group pushed north to a place called Shawqat. This was a Taliban stronghold, so the fighting was intense. They were better soldiers up there, more disciplined. They would stand and fight, they wouldn't run away. This was what I had imagined Afghanistan would be like. Full-blown fighting. It was a good time to be a soldier. I'd watched all those films and wanted to experience it for real. I'd wanted to know how I'd react in a situation like that. I loved it.

We were pushing up a road that ran to one side of the Shamalan canal, trying to take control ahead of the Afghan elections. The idea was to secure the area so people could vote. Both east and west of the canal was enemy occupied. We were trying to seize a number of bridges that crossed the canal, then either destroy them or put obstacles on them so the Taliban couldn't use them. At Crossing Point 7 we got stuck for three days. We were running low on water and food. We had got to the point where we were picking up old potatoes the locals had left on the ground and using gun oil to fry them for chips.

In the early hours of the fourth day we got the nod that we were going to push north again. Two Vikings rocked up outside the compound we were in and we got the lads in the back with all their kit as well. We couldn't believe how tightly we were crammed in, eight of us in a space that was about seven foot by five foot and five foot high. I had a Bergen under my legs and another on my lap. I thought, *If we have a contact now, or an IED, we're not going to be able to get out.* I actually said, as we set off, 'Boys, if we roll, we're fucked.'

Our worst nightmare came true. After only a few miles, we were driving along by the canal, when the Viking suddenly went off the road. The vehicle rolled into the canal and sank under the water. There was one lad in a hatch on the roof who managed to jump free, but there was no escape for the rest of us.

124

To start with we were all yelling, because we were rolling like we were in a washing machine. Then we came to rest with a thud and the water flooded in through the doors and the cracks of the vehicle. It was pitch dark. My face was pressed against the corner; I could feel metal on either side of it, then water rushing down my cheeks. There was no way I could move. One of the boys was pushed against my back, screaming right in my ear. I could feel the handle of the hatch with my right hand, but there was no way I could get it open, because I was pinned down with kit, and anyway there was thick sediment on the other side.

I was panicking and hyperventilating, but we were under water now. So I was gulping it in, I could feel it coming into my chest. Then retching, because it was filthy and I could taste diesel oil and brake fluid as well. There was vomit and shit and piss from the other lads in there too; it's a natural reaction to urinate and defecate when you're dying. They were kicking me and thrashing around, going mental because they were trapped.

I was still desperately trying to shift myself, but I couldn't, I was jammed in. A lad crammed right next to me had grabbed my hand now, was squeezing it hard. I could hear the other lads yelling, but it was like being in a swimming pool, muffled. I could still recognise their voices.

This is not fucking happening, I was thinking. *I can't die like this.* Then my lungs were full of water and I'd stopped choking and panicking. *Shit*, I thought. *This really is happening. So this is how I die.* I sort of accepted it then. Apparently it's the lack of oxygen in your brain, you become euphoric; you relax and drift away. So I just lay there, stuck where I was, as images flicked through my head. People say your life flashes before you, but I didn't see myself at all, I saw my family. My father. My mother crying. My last thought was of my beautiful fiancée Emma. Then I passed out. Afterwards, this lad Barber, who was next to me holding my hand, said that my hand went limp. He kept squeezing it but there was no reaction. He thought I was dead.

When I came to there was noise everywhere. More screaming. My head was out of the water, I managed to get a gasp of air, then I went back under again. Somebody was trying to climb over me to get out of the vehicle. Somebody else shouted, 'Leave him! Leave him! He's gone, leave him!'

Then someone was pulling me, hard. I could see light then. There were hands all over me, pulling me out. My kit was caught on something, so a lad tried to dive under the water to get my kit off. This all happened quite fast.

There were lots of lads there now. I recognised a couple of faces. My platoon commander was crying. Then he was grabbing me and screaming my name. 'Steve! Steve!' Slapping me hard in the face to bring me round. I got dragged up on to the bank and I was coughing and vomiting. They left me then, because obviously I was OK. There were lads still in there who could be dead and gone. The medics were trying to save them.

I was in shock. I wanted to go back down the bank to get my lads out. The other boys were pushing me back, telling me to leave it, there was no point. They'd got everyone out of there now, they said. I squatted down and I was looking at two of my lads, boys that I'd trained and that I was meant to look after, and there they were, lying dead on the bank. The medics were working on them, but they didn't seem to be getting anywhere.

A lot of vehicles had moved up now, to help and offer protection. Luckily for us the Taliban must have thought it was a big British offensive, because they didn't attack. If they had seen us there, boys with no armour or weapons, tops off, diving into the water to get everyone out, they could have caused havoc.

Finally we were taken in another Viking to a rendezvous with a Black Hawk, to be flown back to Camp Bastion. The officer in charge of the vehicle was Guy Disney, but I wasn't to know that then— or how and when we'd be linked up again. With me were the two lads I'd seen earlier. Amazingly, the medics had managed to resuscitate them. They both burnt their lungs on the diesel, but everybody got out with their lives.

I flew home and had two weeks with Emma. At that stage Panther's Claw was all over the news. The Welsh Guards had taken a lot of casualties and the reconnaissance platoon had lost over two-thirds of its people. I was obsessed with it: newspapers, television, I kept wanting to know what was going on. In the end Emma said, 'Come on, let's get away from it all.' So we went to west Wales to chill out and leave it behind.

When I got back to Bastion, I was having problems with my shoulder. The medic sent me to see a physiotherapist, who said I wouldn't be able to go back on the ground because I'd torn ligaments when I was pulled out of the Viking. I couldn't hold a weapon. But the operation was in full swing. Every day you'd see the helicopters bringing casualties in. My platoon had gone from twenty-nine men to eleven at that point. I felt guilty. I wanted to get back out there with the boys. Somehow I managed to get myself sneaked on to a combat logistics patrol, which was going out on the ground.

That was quite an experience, because the last time I'd been in an Army transport I'd nearly drowned. This was a Mastiff, a huge, six-wheeled, heavily armoured vehicle that is designed to resist explosions. I had to really work myself up to get in the back and then once we were off and the Mastiff was rolling from side to side I had a sort of panic attack. I must have smoked twenty or thirty cigarettes in the space of an hour trying to calm myself down.

We'd been in there about two and a half hours and I'd just started to get used to it again. I had smoked all the cigs I had. Then a lad sitting opposite me got his cigarettes out.

'Lend us one, would you?' I asked.

'*Another* one, mate!' He laughed.

I leant across to get it off him and that was the last thing I remember, because at that moment we hit an IED and there was a big bastard of an explosion. I didn't so much hear it as feel it—as if it was in every part of my body, right deep down inside me. I got thrown up to the ceiling, then upwards and forwards.

It all went dark again, because the hatch had been blown shut. I came to on the floor. I could hear the lads screaming around me and there was dust everywhere. I was crouched in the foetal position. I tried to stand and I managed to get half way up when I felt pain like I'd never felt before in my life. It was centred in my back, but it was so intense it took over my whole being. I couldn't speak. I sank down and just curled up like a child.

The sergeant who had been in the front of the vehicle was going through the drills we're all taught. He was crawling back, checking people to see if they were OK.

'Something's wrong,' I was moaning. 'Something's wrong.'

So he and a couple of the lads pulled me to the side and started checking me for damages. I could see there was blood in my crotch and my combats were shredded there.

'Check my bits,' I said to one of these lads. 'Are my bits still there?' At least I'd got my priorities right.

He ripped my combats open and gave me the thumbs up. Thank God for that, I thought. Then I started vomiting, because the pain was so intense. This lad gave me a shot of morphine, but it did nothing for me.

I was shaking all over, going into shock. 'Give me another,' I said.

'Sorry, mate. Got to wait.' I knew from my training that it was fifteen minutes before you can have a second dose, but I couldn't bear the pain. I just wanted it to stop.

'Steve, mate, you're OK, you're OK.' He was trying to comfort me, there was nothing else he could do.

After fifteen minutes he gave me the second shot, but that didn't work either. I was still in agony. But I knew, somehow, I had to get myself out. The vehicle had been immobilised by the explosion. The lads were now outside on the ground. The longer they were there, the more we would become a

129

target for the Taliban.

After about an hour the lad who'd been with me climbed up on the roof to give us a bit more protection with his rifle. So there was just me and the driver left inside. He was on his radio, so I could hear what was happening outside.

I could see the escape hatch right up above me. I kept thinking, *I've got to get myself out of here.* Eventually I managed to reach up and grab hold of it. The driver heard me and turned round.

'Stop! Stop!' he shouted. 'What the hell are you doing?' He jumped in the back and laid me down again.

'I've got to get out,' I was saying. 'It's all taking too long. We're becoming a target, I know we are.'

'Stay there!' he said. 'You've got a spine injury. You can't move.'

'OK,' I said. 'But get us some water, mate.'

He crawled forward towards the cab and as he did so I sat up and grabbed at the hatch again. I managed to pull myself up with my arms, but as my legs swung, the pain was unbelievable. Everything just went white in my head. My ears were ringing and I vomited again.

But somehow I managed to get on to the roof. I slumped to the side then and passed out from the pain. The lad who was already there was trying to keep me conscious, giving me water, holding my head in his lap, talking to me. He pointed out bits of the vehicle to me. There was one big lump of armour which weighs in excess of a ton. That had been blown three hundred metres away into a field.

By now there were helicopters circling above us. They landed and everything started happening fast. There was an American medic on the roof with me.

'Don't move him,' he said, 'we need to get a spinal brace for him.' But I had it in my head that I had to get off, so I started crawling along the roof. The lads were screaming at me to stop, but I somehow got to the front, started sliding down the windscreen. As I came down this big lad Cook grabbed me and pulled me off. He was holding me like I was a baby in a cradle. Then he lowered me down on to a stretcher.

I got stripped of all my ammunition. They wanted to take my weapon too, but I was adamant I was holding on to that. So they carried me across to a helicopter, with my rifle on the stretcher beside me. It was a Black Hawk with American medics on board.

One of them started checking me over.

'I'm in a lot of pain,' I told him. 'My back hurts like fuck.'

'On a scale of one to ten,' he said, in his American drawl, 'how much pain?'

'I think you need to make that scale a bit bigger,' I said. 'I'm about twenty or thirty. They've given me morphine but it's made no difference.'

He gave me a shot of ketamine. 'Give it two minutes, man,' he said, 'and you'll be away in cloud cuckoo land.'

The ketamine did the job. The pain vanished. I couldn't feel a thing. All I was aware of was rotor blades whirring above me.

They flew me back to Bastion and gave me an MRI scan. Then an elderly Danish lady came in and held my hand. She was soon joined by a doctor. He was Danish too.

'Sergeant Young,' he said. 'You've got problems with your spine. You've broken your back and

131

you've damaged your spinal cord. You may never walk again.'

I was lying there, with this Danish woman gazing at me with a look of deep sympathy. I was thinking, *Fuck, shit, this is really happening. I'm never going to walk again.*

'Are you OK with that news?' the doctor said. 'Would you like someone to stay with you?'

'Just leave me alone,' I said. 'I just want to be left alone.'

So they pulled the blue curtains around me and left me there for it to sink in.

I was flown back to Selly Oak. After two or three days there they told me I would walk again. There had been so much swelling around my spinal cord that the medics thought it had been damaged or cut. But it had been compressed.

'You will get back up on your feet,' they said, 'but it'll be with a frame.'

But by that stage I'd started to think, *The news is getting better each time. I'm going to walk again, whatever it takes. I'm going to do it, I'm going to do it.*

It was quite a strange injury to have. There were lads coming in around me who had been torn to pieces. One lad just along from me had no legs, one of his arms was missing, and his lips and his nose had been torn off, so he practically had no face left. And there was I with not a visible scratch on me.

The worst part of it was going from the peak of physical fitness, leading men into combat, to not being able to do anything at all. To start with, I even had an eighteen-year-old lad to wipe my backside for me. He wasn't doing it properly, so I could feel I was getting sores on my bum cheeks and on my back. Eventually I thought, *OK, enough*

132

of this, I'll do it myself. It got quite funny then. They made me sign a waiver to say I was willing to take the risk of wiping my own behind. Then they pulled the curtains round me and left me with a cardboard pot to do my business in, with another plastic pot around it to take my weight. I managed to roll myself over on to my side and put this double pot behind me. Then I somehow got up on to it.

I was still having real problems with my digestive tract, because of all the diesel oil and brake fluid and shit that I'd ingested when I was in the Viking in the canal. So my excrement was like black treacle at that stage. Soon I could feel that I'd filled the pot, but as I was trying to pull myself off it, the cardboard gave way and it exploded everywhere. Right up the wall and everything. I think that was my lowest point. I had to swallow my pride and press the buzzer.

The nurses came in laughing. 'We told you you couldn't do it,' they said.

Panther's Claw was in full swing at that time, so there were a lot of casualties coming in and they needed the bed space. They offered me surgery, but there was only a thirty-three per cent chance of that improving anything, so I declined. In the end my regiment bought a special spinal bed for me and they released me home. Emma looked after me, along with my mother. It was a long road. Four months in a spinal bed. My weight plummeted. I went from fifteen stone down to about ten.

One remark stuck in my head from Selly Oak. One of the nurses was sat by my bed and she said, 'What people don't realise is there are two wars being fought. There's the war in Afghanistan, with the soldiers, and then there's the war back home,

133

with the families.'

From home I eventually went on to rehab at my base in Wales. To start with I was walking with a full body brace and crutches. Gradually I built myself back up. I met Jaco there. When we were both on the mend, we decided to go for the half-marathon in Kenya.

It's not a very visual injury, but it is debilitating. It's changed my life. I'll have good days when it's hardly an issue. On other days I feel like an eighty-year-old man. I basically have a back like a question mark.

12

TRIALS ON THE SNOW

At the start of November, Ed and Simon finally had a chance to put to rest any dissident voices within the Army. They were invited to give a presentation about the Walking With The Wounded North Pole expedition to a panel of experts, drawn largely from within the military. Aware that final decisions on Martin and Jaco had not yet been made, Ed took the request extremely seriously. 'We knew,' he says, 'that there had been a fog spreading through one level of the Army, doubting us and saying essentially that the expedition shouldn't happen. At the same time, at a slightly higher level, there was an understanding that if we did it well, the expedition would be beneficial for the Army; they could see things from the PR point of view as well. So I put my heart and soul into preparing this presentation.'

In addition to fellow organiser Simon Daglish, Ed took with him Inge Solheim (flown over from Norway), Guy Disney (convincing and courageous wounded officer), and Jamie Gillespie (ex-military prosthetics expert, a leader in his field).

'Just to give you an idea of how well briefed and educated these experts were,' says Dags with a chuckle, 'one question was, "You are using helicopters during your expedition. Tell me about their night flying capabilities." Well, mate, I'm sorry to say there is no night at the Pole in April. It's twenty-four-hour daylight up there. That's what happens when you go in summertime to either end of the world. Brilliant question.

'We were constantly asked stuff based on "Ha ha, I'm going to catch you out here," rather than them being interested in understanding what we were planning to do. Thankfully, one of the people in their team was a well-known explorer and adventurer and he backed us the whole way. He actually said, "This is the best organised thing I've come across in years."'

'At the end,' says Ed, 'the senior officer present, a general, stood up and said, "Very rarely do we get a presentation of this quality from the Army itself." I think he was trying to make the point to one or two of his colleagues that not all civilians are idiots. That some of us can run things effectively—profitable businesses and the like. At that point the Army changed from being somewhat cautious around us to saying, "How can we help?" To which the answer at that stage was, "Actually, we're fine, thank you very much." But having this official thumbs-up made all the difference. It was a huge weight off my shoulders.'

With the Army's approval, the team was set. Now it was time to try out its members on the snow together and, equally important, sort out their kit. On Thursday 11 November Ed, Simon and the soldiers, along with Marcus Chidgey of Captive Minds, flew to Oslo to meet up with Inge and Henry.

In consultation with Inge, Ed and Simon had decided that Henry would not now be part of the team going to the Pole. Inge would bring in his own guides from Storm Adventures to work with the expedition on the ice, while Henry would remain in Longyearbyen. Here he would be able to concentrate on managing the logistical side of things, as well as providing useful liaison with the press and the royal party.

On Friday morning they all tried on various items of kit, beginning with specialised polar footwear. 'The boot one needs to survive in minus 40°C,' wrote Ed in his diary, 'is no ordinary boot. You must imagine what else you have on your foot in order to get an idea of the boot itself. First one wears a thick sock (imagine any thick skiing sock). Over that one puts a wool liner. This is a fairly stiff woollen bootie which eventually merges to one's foot's shape. On top of that comes a fleece outer sock. Only then can one get into the boot! This is leather with a long toe with three holes in it, which fits into three studs on the ski and is tightened by laces and buckles. For some of the team (Martin and Jaco) these will be extremely difficult to fasten, so we plan to take the boots to a local cobbler in Norfolk to see if he can adapt them with Velcro.'

Laces and buckles would not be the only difficulties for the team in the extreme temperatures they were preparing to face. Anything that required the dexterity of two hands was going to prove a serious challenge for Martin and Jaco, from zips on clothes to ties on tents. Guy Disney's main requirement was obviously a decent prosthetic leg, but he would also need easy access to this, so that he could adjust it without having to pull his trousers down.

Second stop in Oslo for the team, therefore, was the head office of expedition sponsors Helly Hansen, who were providing the essential items of kit. 'The people at HH,' wrote Ed, 'were enthused by what we are doing and spent a lot of time going through what clothing was available to us and how we could best maximise its use. Obviously because our team has unusual physical needs, it is vital that we have clothing which works. It was fascinating to see how the boys' injuries can be approached and how we can adapt kit to their specific requirements.'

'Helly Hansen trialled some of the standard kit,' says Marcus Chidgey, 'and realised they needed to go to another level to cater for what the guys actually needed. They did a lot of experimental testing of bits and pieces to make sure that, for example, Martin Hewitt's arm was going to be insulated properly. Obviously they wanted to be part of it, but also raise awareness for their brand.' In due course, Helly Hansen would create a micro site on their main website, dedicated to the expedition; this included footage of modifications being made in the company's stitching rooms, as well as cinematic sequences of the team out on the snow. Inge Solheim was naturally enough the focus, talking about everything from big zips for the one-armed guys to what had inspired him to become a polar guide.

After their productive session in Oslo, Helly Hansen reps accompanied the team on the drive to Geilo, a ski resort north-west of the capital in the mountainous Buskerud region. 'Spending eight hours on a bus with the guys,' says Marcus, 'we got to know them all pretty well. There were of course rivalries between the Paras and the Welsh Guards, but they were all in agreement about the level of care they had got from Headley Court.' By Saturday morning the soldiers were out on the snow with their pulks (each laden with an extra 50 kg of salt to bring them closer to what they would weigh on the expedition itself). The Helly Hansen reps went with them to monitor how the new kit was performing and work with the team on ideas for improvements.

The Rhondda Valley is not noted for the excellence of its skiing. For Steve Young, this was the first time he had ever put on skis, let alone the long, narrow Nordic variety that had caused Rob Copsey so much trouble back in May. 'Saturday morning provided potential entertainment for the rest of the team,' Ed wrote, 'as Steve donned skis for the first time. Sadly the result did not lead to hilarity, as he turned out to be almost a natural, although none of us told him so!'

'The boys were all laughing at me as I fell over,' Steve says. 'But the whole process of Nordic skiing is such a gentle, flowing movement that there is no impact whatsoever.' With his damaged back, though, Steve had to be careful how he loaded up his kit. 'When we first started pulling the pulks,' he says, 'I initially had a day sack over my shoulders.

138

But that was causing me a lot of pain. So I reverted to one of the belts around my waist. That way there was no pressure on my spine whatsoever.'

However flippant he was in his diary, Ed was keeping a careful eye on his newest charge. 'His is the injury I can't see,' he said. 'So I have to trust him.' Steve had told Ed about his one-to-ten scale of pain, so Ed asked him to use that as a way of keeping him informed. 'He tells me he is never less than a five. When he gets up to eight I start getting worried.' At one point, when Steve stopped skiing to go to the loo, his back seized up, and Ed was on the point of pulling him off the exercise. Instead, Steve skied without a pulk for two hours, and slowly loosened up again.

Nor was Steve the only team member Ed was monitoring closely. 'It was interesting to discover,' he wrote, 'that Jaco's arm got cold very quickly and then took a long time to re-warm. Guy was rather worried about it for Jaco (who was being a little too stoic in his silence), but I think it was more a question of Jaco not managing his clothing properly. He needs to learn to take things off when he gets too hot and immediately put more on when we stop.'

'It's difficult,' said Inge, 'to keep Jaco's stump and Martin's arm warm enough, because the two limbs are passive. The only way to get warm at the Pole is either to dress with more clothes, increase your activity level, which is difficult with a paralysed limb, or to have an external heat source.' Inge and Henry were now thinking about adding electric or chemical heat pads to the insulation around the wounded men's non-functioning arms.

As this Norwegian weekend was more of a kit

trial than a full-blown rehearsal, the team weren't spending the night in tents, but in a ski resort hotel. Here the group banter rose to a new intensity, focussing in particular on a squat, ginger-haired staff member whom Martin had nicknamed Nik Nak, after the orange-coloured corn snacks. Dags meanwhile had assumed the name referred to Nick Nack, the diminutive villain in the James Bond film *The Man with the Golden Gun*. Not that this misunderstanding stopped the gag running . . . and running. 'We decided,' says Martin with a chuckle, 'that Nik Nak was something between a human and a god. He morphed in and out of the room as and when he saw fit. We were threatening each other that if any of us didn't come up to scratch on the snow we'd invite Nik Nak into their room at night to give them a good kicking.'

'The joke then developed,' said Dags. 'Nick Nack appeared in many guises. Anyone who was short and squat became Nick Nack. He was everywhere.'

On Sunday the hyped-up group trailed two and a half miles uphill to the flat Geilo plateau, which more closely mimicked the conditions they would find next year on the ice. 'I found myself leading the team through this soft snow,' wrote Ed, 'blazing the trail. It was incredibly hard work, while all the others behind me found it relatively easy as the track had been prepared. Talking to Inge he said this was quite normal up in the Pole where there is obviously unprepared snow in whichever direction you go. We pulled from 10.30 to 17.00 hrs, so it was a decent session. Encouragingly all the boys' injuries held up well.'

Coming back downhill, the team again encountered the problem they had come across in Svalbard: that of pulks running wildly out of control. 'We started off by sitting on the pulks,' says Martin, 'and letting the skis come down with us, which was good fun, but with big hills it was quite dangerous and we fell quite a lot. Then Inge showed us how to ski standing up, holding the pulk alongside you almost like a dog on a lead. You just push it to left and right with your arms to steer it. I started trying that, but most of the others carried on with the sitting technique.'

On the last night the guys relaxed back in the hotel with a few drinks. Nik Nak hovered in the background as they were joined by Inge's wife and a friend, who took an instant shine to Jaco. 'As a lot of the ladies seem to,' says Martin. 'This Swedish girl was all over him, which was very entertaining.'

Nicknames for all the team members were falling into place. Henry Cookson was Mudge, because the soldiers had decided that the bearded guide looked like a member of the Mujahideen; Steve was Welsh Wales, for obvious reasons; and the charming and handsome Jaco had now become Jaco van Rat. 'Because he's a rat with the ladies,' said an obviously unenvious Martin.

*   *   *

Back in the UK, there was a welcome letter waiting for Ed. Sent by the general who had headed the Army's panel of experts, it was thoroughly upbeat in tone. 'The team here has analysed your excellent presentation and consider that you are taking all of our concerns into account and that I can have confidence that the expedition has a good chance of success and that the risks are being managed.'

141

Two small undertakings were requested: that the expedition leaders should keep the Army updated about the results of further planned cold chamber trials, 'as this might limit participation by some of the wounded, depending upon the results'; and that they should consider increasing January's planned cold weather training in Norway from five to ten days. But otherwise it was a clear green light. 'I think your vision with regard to this expedition is fantastic,' the general went on. 'We are here to assist you in this endeavour wherever possible.' Ed was delighted to see that Colonel Porridge was copied in.

With sponsorship now confirmed by Artemis, Carillion and Lloyds Development Capital, among others, the costs of the expedition were fully covered. Helly Hansen were providing kit free of charge and other sponsors were being sought for everything from rehydrated food to satellite communications. All of which meant that every penny now raised from the general public would go directly to the retraining and reskilling of wounded servicemen who had left the armed forces.

At the end of November, three of the soldiers attended a fund-raising evening at Holkham Hall, just along the coast from Ed's north Norfolk home. 'Tom Coke,' Ed wrote, 'whose family owns Holkham, was a Scots Guard, and generously agreed to allow us to hold an event at the Hall. Harriet put together a small committee of lovely ladies earlier this year and has gone about organising the evening with her usual energy. The plan was to hold a champagne reception followed by a presentation by the team and we would all be on our way by 9 p.m. Jaco and Steve came up for the evening, and for Guy it was easy as his regiment is based half an hour away.'

Martin was away training with the GB Paralympic Team in Austria, but his place was taken by Henry Cookson. Ed's nephew Harry also put in an appearance. 'Harriet and her ladies had managed to get about 150 people to come, despite the snow, and there was a great buzz about the place. The team mingled with the guests and I think it was their presence which made the real difference. The boys were brilliant about talking to people with great humility and confidence and the presentation seemed to have a very positive impact. While many of these people have been generously giving to military charities for years, most of them had never met a wounded soldier before and so it had a profound effect on them.'

After the presentation there was an auction of lots ranging from a day's sailing on the Artemis yacht in the Solent to an original cartoon by Annie Tempest, which raised a total of £13,000 for the charity. A great result, Ed thought, and hopefully a foretaste of the grand Ice and Diamonds ball planned for March at Battersea Power Station.

One other issue had cropped up, which nobody could have foreseen: 'The small matter of a royal wedding,' wrote Ed. 'It has been suggested to us prior to the official announcement of the date that our timings might now be a little tight. With the wedding on 29 April, Prince Harry has to be in the UK for the rehearsal on the 28th, and working this back, he will need to be off the ice by the 24th. This probably means we'll have to bring everything forward by a couple of days. Also, and this is a slightly selfish thought, I do hope that the wedding doesn't take anything away from what we are trying to achieve. Arriving at the Pole is designed to have quite a media impact. I want the papers carrying pictures of wounded soldiers on the Pole and making people realise how amazing they are. Hopefully both can be fitted in!'

*　　　*　　　*

By early December, Jaco had joined Martin at Neustift in Austria, to train with the Combined Services Disabled Team. It seemed like a good plan for Steve and Guy to meet up with them for a few days of practice and general team bonding. It would also give Guy a chance to try out the new prosthetic leg that Jamie Gillespie had designed specially for him, and on which he had recently completed work. 'There are two main aims of the week,' Guy explained. 'The first is to improve our skiing ability—having seen the Norwegians on skis the previous month it very quickly became clear that the more proficient we are at Nordic skiing the more energy we will save on the exped itself. The second is to see how our injuries cope with prolonged periods on skis.'

The four of them soon established a good working routine. While Martin and Jaco were out training with their teams each morning, Guy and Steve followed the cross-country skiing route at the base of the huge U-shaped Neustift valley. The snow was fresh and thick and on the first day the pair managed eleven miles, skiing for two hours at a time before taking a break, essential for Steve's back. 'That was when I realised,' says Steve, 'that I can get through the day by stretching every two

144

hours and being very disciplined. Even if I'm not hurting, I get down on the ground and loosen up. I've got to make sure I do it, otherwise the cold just seems to penetrate me and stiffen me up.' On the second day, having searched every shop in town for a proper exercise roll mat, Guy and Steve bought a rubber doormat, which they took out with them on the snow from now on.

In the afternoons Martin and Jaco joined them on the slopes. 'This was the first time,' Martin explains, 'that they had been on these long thin Nordic skis without a pulk. It's massively different, because you pick up speed on them.' There was a nice variety of terrain to practise on: up the main valley or through the forests, where there were streams and other natural obstacles to contend with. In the evening all four had a big meal, chilled out for a while, then moved on to the gym, for cardiovascular fitness training and a session with the weights. They were nothing if not dedicated.

On the third day they gave themselves a shock. Guy and Steve had managed to cover seventeen miles in the morning and were feeling rather pleased with themselves. They met up with Martin and Jaco as usual for the return journey. But on the way back a clip on one of Jaco's skis broke, and he could no longer keep his boot on the ski. So the two novices left him and Martin where they were while they skied the last kilometre or so to fetch the car; it was, they thought, five minutes or so further down the track. 'They thought they were closer than they actually were,' says Martin. 'The ten minutes they were supposed to take turned into forty minutes. Waiting all that time in that temperature was a big wake-up call. It was probably minus twenty, and both of us only had limited insulation kit with us. For me, a real intense nerve pain kicked off in my arm, while Jaco's stump got seriously cold.'

'It got to the point,' says Jaco, 'where I couldn't even move the muscle because it was so cold. Even giving it the slightest touch was painful.'

'By the time we got back to them,' explained Guy, 'they were both shivering and finding it hard to talk, on the point of going down with hypothermia. A valuable lesson was learnt about wearing the right kit and keeping moving.'

Back at their hotel, Jaco jumped straight in the shower to try and warm up his stump: 'The feeling slowly came back, but my actual arm was still freezing for ages.'

All was well. Neither Martin nor Jaco suffered even a touch of frost nip. But they had all realised that they couldn't afford to be the slightest bit complacent about the cold and its power to harm. If this could happen to them in just over half an hour at −20°C, what might go wrong over twenty-five days at −40 to −50°C?

The next day Martin took them touring up a glacier, in temperatures that dropped to −25°C; −35°C, Guy reckoned, if you took wind chill into account. This time they made sure they took the full Helly Hansen kit, which 'more than did the job', Guy was happy to report. Then, on the last day, Steve and Guy went out on their own, and covered an impressive twenty-two miles. 'A perfect culmination to our week,' observed Guy. 'Our technique on the skis was massively improved. We had stopped falling over, were steady on the skis and managing to stay upright on good steep inclines. You watch Norwegians ski and they

146

are just so efficient in the way they do it; they save energy with every step. Trying not to be a floundering Englishman is a good thing.'

Guy was also more than happy with his new leg. He'd had a few blisters, but had got through the week without a single 'rub'; this remained his worst fear, because if a rub became infected at the Pole, his expedition would be over. Back in the UK, he wrote an upbeat thank-you letter to Jamie Gillespie. There were three minor issues to be sorted out, to do with the locking mechanism, a catch on the back of the leg, and the bolts within the leg shrinking in the extreme cold, 'but all in all it fits fantastically'. Guy took his Nordic skis home with him and in the UK's newly icy climate managed five days' skiing in Norfolk over Christmas.

*   *   *

Back home Ed was busy with the seasonal demands of his day job, though the continuing bad weather had made 2010 a business Christmas to forget. Lead sponsor Artemis, however, had invited the whole team for a Christmas lunch at its offices in London. 'In the morning,' Ed wrote, 'the MD's assistant called to ask me whether we were all still coming, fearing that the snow might have caused us difficulties getting to London. It seemed a little wrong that she was worried about a team which they have generously sponsored to get to the North Pole having problems with a little English snow. I was delighted to be able to tell her that we would be there on time, and even Inge made it in from Oslo while Heathrow was pretty much closed. We had a very delicious lunch which went on into the evening, and then conveniently became dinner! It was great to see all the team together, and the excitement is beginning to build.'

13

DRESS REHEARSAL

On a drizzly grey Wednesday at the start of January the four wounded soldiers posed in the middle of Trafalgar Square against a huge photo backdrop of ice and snow. They were dressed in their full branded crimson expedition kit, tailored by Helly Hansen with a prominent Artemis logo, their Alpha Modre boots positioned on top of one of the (rolled-up) tents they would be sleeping in on the ice. In front of them stood a barrage of cameramen. This was Walking With The Wounded's second official press launch, but the first with the final team. 'I think the first launch was to announce the whole concept,' says Marcus Chidgey. 'The second was a countdown towards the expedition, but also a chance to give the sponsors some value back as well.'

'It was another day,' says Alex Rayner, 'when the media interest just seemed to take off. You can feel it the day before, because broadcasters are asking for permission to park up satellite trucks and so on. When ITV, the BBC and Sky are going live from the square, you know it's going to be big.'

'Encouragingly,' wrote Ed, 'there were plenty of journos who turned up from the print media,

148

so hopefully we will start seeing more about the expedition in the press. There still seems to be plenty of interest in what we are doing. The boys did brilliantly when they were interviewed and were a credit to the whole project. We never considered their "media ability" when we selected them, but they all come across very well, and maintain a healthy dollop of humility when they are talking. None of them have let the attention go to their heads.'

Perhaps this was because at least one of the soldiers was genuinely uninterested in having a high profile in the media. For Guy Disney, subjecting himself to interviews and having his name in the papers was something that had to be done for the good of the charity—nothing more. 'I'm a captain in the Army,' he says, 'I'm not anything special. I actually think privacy is one of the greatest things in the world. To suddenly get thrust into the limelight I find quite odd.' Nonetheless, quizzed by the BBC's Frank Gardner inside one of the tents, Guy acquitted himself well, talking Gardner through the team's kit and training sessions to date. Martin deftly answered a question about whether he might throw a snowball at Prince Harry by saying that the Prince would more likely be the one doing the throwing. And Jaco and Steve said all the right things about challenges.

Gardner had of course been out with the original line-up in Spitsbergen the previous May. At that time Inge Solheim had told him bluntly that the team weren't yet up to the harsh realities of the Pole. Now the Norwegian was more optimistic. 'They have been training individually for many months and they are getting there,' he said to camera.

In addition to Gardner's item on the BBC News, there was good coverage in the print media, though inevitably perhaps the newspapers' main focus was the royal angle (even though the Prince hadn't been present in person). PRINCE HARRY TO JOIN SOLDIERS FOR GRUELLING ARCTIC TREK was the headline of a double-page spread in that afternoon's London *Evening Standard*. The next day's *Daily Telegraph* had ARMY AMPUTEES TO EMBARK ON RECORD TREK TO NORTH POLE WITH PRINCE HARRY. As the newspaper subs were finding, this was a story with almost too many buzzwords to include. Not that this troubled BBC South East Wales, which had its priorities admirably clear: TONYPANDY SOLDIER BEATS INJURY FOR NORTH POLE TREK.

As it happened, the story the media were being given was slightly behind the curve. Two days before, Ed had attended a meeting at Clarence House, where he and the charity's PR agency had been presented with 'a slight bombshell'. Owing to the royal wedding, Prince Harry would not, after all, be allowed to join them at the Pole. Even with an adjusted timetable, the royal advisers weren't prepared to take any chances with William's best man. 'I hope,' wrote Ed, 'that we are now going to stand on the Pole on 23 April, but they weren't willing to risk even six days of leeway before the wedding.' Instead, the Prince would accompany the expedition for a few days at the start; and then, in lieu of a Polar media moment, he would be on hand to greet them when they got back. 'We were able to agree that Harry would come to Gatwick to meet us on our return to the UK on 26 or 27 April, at a

150

time when there will be thousands of journalists in London trying to justify their existence ahead of the big day.'

The team were now on a publicity roll. The next day they headed down to a disused aircraft hangar in Wiltshire to be photographed by David Bailey for *GQ*. Prince Harry was to join them for the shoot and would grace the cover of the May edition of the magazine, with photos and profiles of the soldiers inside. 'Again, we were stepping way out of our comfort zone,' wrote Ed. 'I think we were all very apprehensive, but it ended up being huge fun. David Bailey immediately put us at our ease with a wicked sense of humour. It is clear he is a big fan of the armed forces and he treated the boys brilliantly.'

'It was cool to meet him,' said Guy. 'His face is incredibly animated. He smiles at you and makes you smile. He was quite jittery around the room, but very entertaining.' The only person who might have disagreed with these upbeat assessments was TwoFour director Alexis Girardet, who was attempting to film the occasion for his documentary. 'Alexis took his camera out,' says Dags, 'and David Bailey said, "If you poke that fucking thing in my face, I'll stick it up your arse." Alexis is quite mild mannered. I think he was rather taken aback.'

Prince Harry joined them at the end of the session. 'It was very informal and relaxed,' Ed wrote. 'Bearing in mind that he will be with us on the ice, there will be no difference between any of us there and it is so important we all know and trust one another.'

'It was a bit old world meets new world,' says

151

Alex Rayner. 'Bailey was literally having a fag outside on the wall. Inside you had your stylists. *GQ* had earlier said to us, "So styling, hair and make-up, who does Harry use?" I rang Clarence House to ask. There was this slightly condescending tone down the phone: "Harry has never used a stylist or make-up person in his life and he's not going to start now." But Harry met the boys for the first time there. He was very keen to meet them on his tod, so all the rest of us were told to sod off. It was raining, and dark, and Harry went in and had a good twenty minutes hob-nobbing with them, having a cup of tea and chatting.'

'I thought it was a nice touch,' says Marcus Chidgey, 'that he took the time to go out and meet the local kids at the airfield before he went in to do the shoot. These kids had been waiting patiently since ten o'clock in the morning and he went over and said hello. One of them then used a little photo of Harry in his school assembly that week. And that school went on to raise £300 for the charity as a result. It was all a bit like that at the time. Once the awareness was going, we were getting a lot of emails in the office, saying things like "Hello, I'm Tom, I'm twelve, I'm from such and such a school, I'm going to be doing an auction or a tombola." We'd then get a T-shirt or a cap, package it up with a nice brochure and some kit and send it off.'

When the shoot was over, the entire party headed off to a local pub for supper. Being close to the Prince's barracks, it was a place where the staff already knew him well, so there were no deference or celebrity issues to worry about. Dags had met Harry several times. 'I couldn't claim to be best buddies with him,' he said, 'but I know him well enough for him to know my name. I've been on a stag night with him, I've been to rugby with him, the odd party, that sort of thing. Ed and I tried to point out the boys' frailties to Harry, so he could join in the ribbing of them. Harry is a really nice guy and I think anyone who meets him is instantly at ease. He probably has his mother's genes in that respect. I don't think any of the boys felt intimidated or in any way out of place with him being there. That's why having him on the ice is going to be great, because he will just fit in.'

'You could see them all instantly hitting it off,' says Alex Rayner. 'There was a lot of military chat; a lot of acronyms.'

*   *   *

A week later, the team were well away from the fripperies of the media world; back in Norway again, this time in Beitostølen, in the county of Oppland, where there were snow-covered frozen lakes that offered a fair approximation of the polar terrain, even though none of this ice was moving, and there was no danger of either open water leads or pressure ridges. They were there for ten days, eight of which would be spent out in the cold.

Ed and Simon had intended this final session of cold weather training very much as a practice run for the main event, but things didn't start well. Checking over their kit in the hotel on the Monday before they set off, the organisers were seriously disappointed with what Inge had provided. Much of the adapted gear they had asked for wasn't there; nor, even, some of the basic items. 'The bloody gloves hadn't turned up,' says Simon. 'Eventually they arrived a day late and were all the wrong sizes. Ed and I were furious. It was a repeat of a pattern we'd seen before. The kit wasn't there when we'd been adamant it had to be. We took Inge aside for a quiet word. Within about two sentences Ed had lost it. He really went for him.'

Henry Cookson wasn't happy either. 'The whole idea of Beitostølen,' he says, 'was that it was going to be a total dress rehearsal. All the kit, everything as it should be, so if there was anything wrong we could change it. But nothing was ready. There were bits missing and it wasn't right. Inge is very efficient out on the ice, but when he makes up a kit list, it's literally just a list. It doesn't specify size, colour, brand. We need roll mats, we need bottles, we need this, we need that.'

'There were two main problems,' Inge explains. 'One was a misunderstanding, because Ed thought the down jackets were for walking. He saw a long arm on Jaco's jacket and thought they were supposed to be adapted as well. So I explained to him that the down jackets were a new thing, they're to put on outside when you're stopping for breaks, or sitting down, you don't walk in them.' There had also been a mix-up with the gloves, which had only come in two sizes, rather than the necessary three (Ed's were supposed to be extra large); and some Helly Hansen kit had also been delayed at the factory. 'So we only got it the day before we started the training. It was in time, but they would have liked it two days earlier. I understand that people get anxious when things are not there in time. But that's good. It proves that they're paying attention, that they want to have it right.'

With all the bother over the kit, the team didn't

154

finally leave base till early afternoon on Tuesday. They only had an hour or two's skiing before the light started to fade. 'Are we going to camp in the dark?' Simon shouted out, as they skied along the edge of a rounded hillside.

'We can camp whenever you guys want,' Inge replied. 'We have our torches, so we can put up a tent wherever we want.'

'I think I'd rather camp in the light if I'm honest.'

They agreed to stop where they were. For Inge, putting up a tent in almost any circumstances wasn't a problem. The rest of the team were less practised, and it soon showed, as they struggled in the dusk with unfamiliar tents, poles that seemed much stiffer in the cold, and uncompacted snow four feet deep.

'We can't actually see what we're doing,' said Henry, 'which is causing a certain amount of consternation.'

'We haven't made our life any easier doing this in the dark,' said Ed, 'but you've got to start somewhere—I suppose today is that somewhere.'

In the chaos Jaco was learning fast: 'This was my first time out with the tents and only now did I realise how difficult it is to have one arm in the cold. When we were setting up, I was in the way. Because the amount of help I can give with one hand, trying to pitch a tent, is nothing.' After his experience in Svalbard, Martin already knew his limitations. 'The greatest frustration,' he said, 'for me with my injury is the tent routine, because I'm not as efficient as the other guys are. You feel, as we say in the military, jack. Which means you're not pitching in, not doing your job properly.'

Ed and Steve, and Guy and Dags, however, were

155

more than happy to put the tents up for the others. Perhaps the trickiest issue was one of tact, as Guy knew only too well: 'The thing I've found most frustrating since being injured is when people have tried to help me do something that I can already do perfectly well. I don't want to be mollycoddled. I'm a young man who has commanded men on operations. So I've been very wary with Jaco and Martin, not to try and do too much for them. If I've noticed Dog doing something, and he's cracking on with it, I'll let him do it. But if he looks like he needs a bit of help, I'll offer it. Most of the time anyway now he'll ask.'

Eventually the camp was pitched, though Henry had managed to fall over and imprint his body shape in the snow beneath the Officers' Mess. 'I'm lying on a pothole which is mega,' said Martin, 'so tonight's sleep is not going to be the best.'

The new tents could each hold three men; after Svalbard, the organisers had realised that two sets of two arms per tent was the optimum arrangement. But this meant that the old line-up of Officers' Mess, Other Ranks and Care Home was restructured, as the organisers joined the wounded. Dags was sharing with Martin and Guy, Ed with Jaco and Steve, and Inge with Henry. Considerable thought had gone into these arrangements. 'You've got Martin and Guy,' says Dags, 'who have become very close friends now. They're quite noisy and gobby, particularly Dog. He'll talk for an hour and a half. Then you have Jaco and Steve, who are quieter. Given that Ed is gobbier than me, we decided to switch Ed and me to rebalance the tents. Otherwise I think you would have had a tent that was gobby, gobby, gobby and another that could, on the ice, have withdrawn into themselves. That is a disaster when that happens, because then you've got a split.'

Snow was now melted on the little petrol-burning heaters to make the necessary water. This was a long slow process, taking an hour at least. In the reconstituted Officers' Mess, Dags was doing the cooking.

'Dags is our new bat boy,' said Martin.

'That is *bat* boy,' said Dags, laughing.

Martin cackled. 'So tonight he's going to cook us up a particularly fine cuisine. What is it, Dags? Lancashire hot pot?'

'No, chilli con carne.'

'How wonderful. And what's for dessert?'

'Dessert is muesli, with sultanas. And cinnamon just sprinkled along the top for you, sir.'

'I'm very excited.'

'Or it could be chilli powder, as it's so dark we can't see.'

And so they bantered on, as they prepared their rehydrated meals. Over in the less gobby tent, there was a choice of Game Casserole, Stroganoff Beef Stew or Greek Feast. Jaco was fantasising about the South African *biltong* he was going to bring on the expedition proper and Ed was asking Steve about Afghanistan.

'How did you cook in the FOBs? Did you have a rota?'

'It depended. Sometimes we'd have a curry night, you'd get chicken from a local village or whatever. But it was just so hot out there, you didn't always want to eat. You'd have to force yourselves sometimes . . .'

As they settled in for the night, they took a while

157

to get used to the cramped conditions, particularly Martin. 'I tend to move my body around more,' he said, 'because I can't use one limb to rest and the other to do things with.'

'When he's in a confined space,' Dags observed, 'he has to swing himself round rather than use his hands to manoeuvre himself, and as a result there's arms and legs going everywhere. With the cooker boiling away, that's all a bit dangerous.'

'The water sits in a metal Tupperware container on a petrol burner,' said Guy. 'If that gets knocked over in the tent, it'll be disastrous.'

While the heater remained on, it was surprisingly cosy. Martin's arm had been rather cold earlier, but with the warmth of the tent and a couple of chemical compound heat pads provided by Henry, it was now much better. Most importantly, thanks to the work of his doctors, he had enough nerve regeneration to feel the temperature change. 'So I can deal with it if it cools down too much.'

Dags, with his South Pole experience, had opted to sleep between the two others. 'He knew that was the warmest place to be,' said Martin, 'so he had a very pleasant night's sleep, snoring away like a hog. At one point, I was dreaming about being on a beach, lying next to a beautiful woman. I woke up and saw Dags's face. I can't tell you how disappointed I was.'

As soon as the heaters were switched off, they were surprised by how quickly it got cold. Ice rapidly formed on the inside of the tents and the sleeping bags weren't so much wet as frozen. Here was another lesson they needed to learn: to bring the very least amount of snow possible into the tents when they removed their kit, while somehow managing the cooking to minimise the damp. 'As the steam comes up,' said Martin, 'the more moisture you get on the roof. When we woke up in the morning it was caked in ice everywhere.'

The next day the temperature had dropped in any case. The previous afternoon Martin had been saying how much milder it was than he'd imagined it would be; now they were all feeling the chill. 'This is as cold as I can remember,' said Dags. 'Take your hands out of your gloves for more than five minutes—phew. It's just reminded me of why I said I'd never go to a Pole again.' He grinned. 'And here I am.'

Ed's gloves were a continual reminder of the screw-up over the kit. The inners were too small, so he had no dexterity and couldn't help Jaco do up his bootlaces without taking them off. When he did, he found it wasn't a good idea. 'I got cold very, very, very quickly indeed,' he said.

All packed up, they headed off, initially over rather hilly ground. Their routine was as it would be at the Pole: two hours skiing, then a five-minute stop for rapid calorie intake: nuts, flapjacks, Twix snack bars, Rolos, wine gums, all washed down with water or hot soup from a flask. Even wearing the thick down outer jackets they put on for the duration of each break, in this temperature none of them wanted to hang around for longer.

At their first stop Guy added an extra layer of thermals. 'If I'm honest I've got a slightly cold John Thomas at the moment,' he admitted. Cue Steve with a story about a horrific picture he had back home of a polar explorer whose genitals had frozen.

'I don't want to see it,' laughed Guy.

'He just forgot to do his flies up and froze the

159

last inch of his cock. And when he tried to go for a pee, nothing came out. It was solid.'

As they came down off the mountains, Guy was struggling a little with his balance, as he always did going downhill. Then, as they ventured out on to the snow-covered ice of the first of a string of spectacular frozen lakes, things became easier again; he was always happier on the flat.

Out on the lake the wind picked up and it grew even colder. 'When it's still,' said Ed, 'it's a piece of cake. You just put your clothes on and you're warm. But with the slightest breath of wind it becomes a different beast altogether. That's when you feel the frost nip on your cheeks and fingertips. The other thing is that it never, ever goes away.'

'Your nasal hairs stick together,' said Martin. 'That's a good indication of the kind of temperature we're getting into. Anything that's exposed very quickly begins to sting.'

Jaco in particular was suffering with his damaged arm. 'It starts off as a tingly feeling, then as I contract my biceps and triceps I can feel it, they're really hard to move, it's very painful.' Hardest of all was getting his layering right; after skiing for a couple of hours, the rest of his body might be boiling, but his unexercised stump would still be cold. He was planning to experiment with the heat pads that Henry had brought along, which they were going to try and embed in the insulation fabric he already had on.

The snow on the lake wasn't easy to pull through either. It was deep and sticky; like porridge, Guy thought. Dags was soon out of breath. More worryingly, Steve was in pain with his back; his scale, he told Ed, was now fluctuating between five

160

and seven. Around one o'clock, reluctantly, he gave in and took painkillers.

After the chaos of the previous night, the team pitched camp while it was still light, on a little plateau Inge had chosen for them up above the lake. Inge pointed out to Martin that in order to avoid finding a Henry-shaped hole under his sleeping bag, it was best to stamp down the snow where the tent was to be pitched, a job that Martin now decided to make his own. After that, while Simon and Guy were sorting out poles and pegs, he used his good arm to dig a hole where the front porch area of the tent would go, so that his tent-mates could sit and brush the excess snow off themselves with their backsides comfortably sheltered. This would reduce the moisture inside the tent.

Drills were becoming noticeably slicker, down to fifteen minutes now, though Dags felt it needed to be five. 'We've got a very strong team, physically,' he said. 'Take their disabilities out, they could do the North Pole, the South Pole, Everest, any damn thing you put in front of them. Put the disabilities in, it becomes something quite different. And what we're all realising is, how difficult it is for someone with one arm. The administration round the camp, they can do very little; everything's very slow, and they have to use their teeth as a second arm. Holding on to zips, undoing packets and so on. At home, that's fine. Out here, in the minus thirties, using your teeth is not such a great idea. So we're gradually working it out, getting a system which allows them to do as much as they can, but at the same time, we're able to do everything at the speed we need to. Mentally, our wounded guys are

161

learning a lot about themselves. It's the first time they've been tested in a harsh environment since they were wounded. It'll be interesting to see how that goes. Martin was angry this evening, definitely.'

* * *

Back on the lake the next morning Inge was happy. His home village of Otta was just the other side of the mountain, so as a kid he had spent all his time out in this beautiful empty country: 'Fridtjof Nansen, a very famous Norwegian polar explorer, once said, "I'd rather be skiing and thinking of God, than being in church and thinking of skiing." I'm not religious, so for me I guess that means I'd rather be out here than at home thinking about it.'

Guy was loving it too; the stunning scenery, the fact that they hadn't seen a single other human since they set out. Steve kept going, managing his pain, trying not to succumb to the pills, zoning out to the music on his iPod—a mixture of his own favourites and music his fiancée Emma had put on for him (including the 2010 *X Factor* finalists' cover of David Bowie's 'Heroes', recorded in aid of Help for Heroes). Jaco now had two electrical heat pads on his stump under the main insulation; they were keeping it nicely warm and he was starting to hope he might have cracked his problem. Martin was wrestling with a similar issue: trying to insulate his useless right arm while not getting so warm elsewhere that he was sweating: 'What I need to do is cut off some of my merino wool tops and tailor them. Another day, another lesson learned.'

Ed, however, had lost his fizz. He knew he was sweating too much and he suddenly wondered what

162

he was doing, at the age of forty-five, out here in this bitter cold, struggling to pull his heavy pulk through this dreadful thick snow, which seemed to get more like glue with every step. Every jolt was an effort. Could he even make it to the next break, he wondered, let alone do the full day? And if he was having problems here, now, on this relatively simple trip, what would it be like at the Pole, day in, day out, in temperatures twenty degrees colder than this? Perhaps he just wasn't up to it. But he couldn't pull out now, could he, because the whole thing had been his idea. Walking With The Wounded had become a monster with its own momentum and its own rules. Sponsors, PR agencies, royal involvement, TV companies, it had all gone so much better than he or Dags could ever have imagined. So now he had to do it, come what may. Even if part of him would rather have packed it in, gone back home to Norfolk and Harriet and the family and accepted that he was a middle-aged wine merchant who should be taking things a bit easier, not some mad adventurous spirit who was trying to break records in one of the most inhospitable environments known to humankind.

Somehow he made it. He drew deep on his resources, remembered endurance techniques from his days in the jungle in Borneo. Count to a hundred and keep going. Do the next hundred yards and that bit at least is behind you. He had one energy gel left, which he saved as a talisman to see him through the last couple of hours of this awful day. On the final break he downed that and a blackcurrant energy drink. Almost instantly he started to feel better.

When they stopped for the night and Ed went

163

for a pee his urine was dark yellow. His problem was clear: he was simply very dehydrated. As soon as he and Steve had put the tent up he started melting snow. He was gulping it thirstily out of the pot before they had even started cooking. He drank two litres in half an hour. Then, when the food was ready, he ate and ate and started to feel better and to look forward to a good night's sleep.

As Inge knew all too well, the team's greatest challenge would be managing their individual body temperatures and fluid intake. 'Half of them are still either too hot or too cold,' he said. 'We have to find the right balance and stress the fact that if you're sweating too much it's dangerous. Because either you lose too much fluid and then you'll lose energy and crash at the end of the day, or you might freeze and become hypothermic.' Getting it wrong was OK here, in relatively high temperatures, but up at the Pole, in –50°C, it would be dangerous. 'If you get too cold out there, the consequences are really bad. It is the most hostile place on earth.

'So I want everybody to be confident they are well adjusted, so they don't get the fear. The famous North Pole fear when they land in the helicopter and see the vast ice cover. You're suddenly out there in minus forty-five and it can take your breath away. Scare you. You know there's no escape from this cold for three, four weeks. Every time I go there, at least once on the trip I'll say to myself, "I am never going to go to this shitty place ever, ever again."'

Over in the Officers' Mess they were discussing what luxuries they might take with them. After his South Pole experience, Dags found a bottle of Tabasco absolutely vital on an expedition. 'Stuff

164

the weight,' he said. 'This makes any meal taste good. It's a deal breaker, to be honest.' It was just a shame that the bottle he had brought with him to Beitostølen had frozen solid.

Martin, meanwhile, was preparing dessert. Which tonight was sweets accompanied by a hot coffee mixture. 'And the Officers' Mess has, of course,' he added, breaking for a moment into song, 'al—co—ho—ol, which nobody else knows about yet.'

'No,' agreed Dags, turning the fine bottle of Glenfiddich slowly in his hands.

'Especially Inge.'

'It's a need to know basis.'

'Yes.'

'And Inge doesn't need to know.'

That night the wind got up. Ed could hear it howling across the slopes outside, the heavy gusts whipping and snapping the tent flaps. Next to him on the roll mat Welsh Guardsman Steve was oblivious, snoring away noisily as usual. Ed wished he still slept like that, without a care in the world.

Over in the Officers' Mess, Guy was woken by the wind. He opened his sleeping bag to look up at the roof of the tent and was showered with ice crystals. It wasn't the nicest sensation he'd ever experienced. Martin, too, hadn't slept well. 'It's as if the Philharmonic Orchestra's out there,' he said, 'playing some mad symphony outside your tent, on your tent. I didn't bring any earplugs either. Another lesson learnt.'

When the light finally came up in the morning, Inge had his head inside the other tents early. It was too windy to strike camp, he said, so they would stay put for the time being. Have breakfast and see where they stood. It gave Martin plenty of time to put his boots on properly. The elastic laces he had been experimenting with had frozen overnight, making things even harder for a one-handed man. When he got back home he was going to have his boots specially adapted: Velcro straps over the top would work better, he reckoned. He really didn't want to be hassling Dags or Disco every morning to give him a hand.

By half ten the wind had eased slightly and Inge reckoned they were good to go. Tents down, camp struck, they pushed on across the lake. The wind was still blowing a good thirty miles an hour or so, but the sky was clear, and snow rippled across the ice. All around them were the slopes of steep white mountains. The whole scene was like something on a magnificent Christmas card.

Jaco and Ed had swapped pulks and Ed was enjoying the lighter load; Jaco, meantime, felt happy that he was useful. With one arm there were so many things he couldn't do around the tents, but out here he came into his own. He could carry his weight in the team, show he was here for a reason; he was strong and he could pull.

Martin was actually enjoying the wind on his face. He would almost go so far as to say it made him feel at one with nature: 'If I was a more artistic man, that's the phrase I would use.' Guy had a slight problem with the moulding in his boot, which had started to come unstuck, so his prosthetic leg was at an awkward angle for a while; but with some help from Henry and Inge, and a section or two of Simon's roll mat, that was soon fixed. More important was that the other end, where the prosthetic linked to his stump, was working well.

He had no blisters and, as yet, fingers crossed, no hint of a rub. He was glad he'd done all that impact training back in the UK, hardening up his stump with regular games of squash.

Steve was faring well too; managing the pain in his back by making sure he lay down on his mat in the breaks and had a really good stretch. He was trying to get through the first four hours of the day without painkillers, reserving them for use only after the second break. The main thing he had learned was how important it was to wear the right layers of clothing; so that you didn't get too hot and sweat too much, and then find when you stopped that the moisture froze and formed ice in your clothing.

In the afternoon they reached the end of the lake. The mountain towered above them. It was time to turn round and head for home. Even that made Ed feel better. By the time they stopped to camp again he felt two hours closer to civilisation. The task no longer seemed endless. Three days' pulling back and then beer and a comfortable bed.

They set up camp that evening in the middle of the lake. After their windy departure in the morning, the guy ropes of the Officers' Mess were a little tangled. Dags and Guy set about sorting them out while Martin headed off to attend a call of nature. While he was squatting in the snow a few yards away, Sergeant Steve Young thought it would be amusing to sneak up behind him and throw a cup of snow on to his naked backside. 'Which froze pretty quickly,' said Martin. 'And I don't mind saying was rather uncomfortable. I think you might call it the early onset of frost nip down there. I will get him back for that, don't worry. But revenge is a dish best served cold. Very cold in this case.'

It was hard enough anyway, doing your number twos in sub-zero temperatures, with the wind blowing into your underpants and the cold stinging your exposed flesh. Having one arm just made it all the worse. 'You dig a hole and squat and you need to keep your balance,' said Jaco, 'which is hard in a strong wind. Then when it comes to wiping, it's really difficult, because you have to take a bit of paper off the roll and not let it blow away. You can't even put the roll down on the snow, because that will make it wet.'

Inge, observing the two one-armed men, had been trying to come up with a system to make things easier for them. He suggested having the toilet paper parcelled up and ready to use, easily available in a pocket or inside a shoe. Or else they could wait until the tent was about to come down in the morning and be the last person to leave, having done their business in a hole in the vestibule. Like everything else on this extraordinary expedition, it was a matter of experimentation.

The wind blew stronger and stronger during the night and none of the team—bar the snoring Steve—slept well. In Ed's tent the problem was compounded when the air vent became blocked with spindrift. It was no longer very cold, a mere −10°C or so, and without air moving through, the atmosphere soon became damp. Even as they lay awake in the howling, flap-slapping wind, condensation dripped down on them from the tent walls.

In the morning Inge decided it was again too windy to strike camp. So they were tentbound for the time being, three men in a space four and a half

168

feet by six and a half. The heaters went off after breakfast, so the temperature soon dropped and the guys got back inside their sleeping bags.

In the Officers' Mess they were regretting not bringing some distractions.

'We had a last-minute shop in Longyearbyen and Disco and I thought it might be an idea to bring some playing cards,' said Martin. 'At which point, Dags, with his wealth of polar experience, told us we wouldn't have time for cards.'

Dags cut into the laughter of the younger men. 'I think my point was that the only game these guys play is Snap and I didn't think I could play Snap for that long.'

'So anyway, that's the last time we'll listen to Dags about kit preparation or what to take. We should have brought Monopoly. Or chess. Oh no, Dags can't play chess, because it requires strategic thinking!'

Over in Ed's tent they were better organised. Both Ed and Steve had brought books with them. But it was still a long day with nothing else to do but sleep, eat and chat.

Outside the blizzard howled on. At one point, on Inge's instructions, the soldiers emerged from their tents for ten minutes to clear the snow that had piled up on their pulks. Darkness came, dinner, sleep—or at least the attempt to sleep. At 5 a.m., finally, the storm blew itself out. But when the guys emerged in the morning light the tents were half-buried in snow.

As they readied themselves for the off, Steve headed to the dirty area for a poo. But as he was squatting, trying to clean his freezing naked arse with toilet paper, he felt a massive shooting pain up

169

his back. It had locked and he couldn't straighten himself up. He stumbled back to the tent, grabbed some painkillers and threw himself down on a roll mat. He was in agony, and it wasn't at all clear how he was going to pull his pulk.

Ed and Simon were seriously concerned. 'He's being a typical man,' said Ed, 'and saying it's fine, but I think he's in a great deal of pain. Dags and I have said from the off that we have a duty of care to these guys. We know they're never going to say "Stop", so it might be one of us that has to say it.'

A Skidoo snowmobile was coming out to meet the TV crew that morning and Ed was thinking that maybe Steve should get on it too, go back to Beitostølen and see a doctor. 'I should think that will go down very badly with him indeed, because he'll start thinking that it's the end of the road for him, but the bottom line is that his back is far more important than the expedition.'

Steve was ordered to have no part in the taking down of the camp, and for the first two hours of the day Jaco pulled Steve's pulk as well as his own. At the first break, Steve insisted he was OK to pull his own pulk again. By the time the Skidoo arrived an hour later he was allowed to stay off it.

With Steve's drama over, or at least on hold, it was Simon's turn to have a bad day. He was pissed off in particular with his fellow tent members, the Morecambe and Wise team of Disco and Dog. 'I don't mean to be miserable and serious all the time,' he said, 'but please, guys, look after your kit. Know where your gloves and boots are, know where every single bit of kit is.' He had wanted to go to the loo earlier, only to find one of the pair had gone off to the other tent and taken his gloves with them. 'They had lost theirs and so they thought they would use mine. So I couldn't get out of the tent. It's OK out here, but you do that in the North Pole and you'll cause real issues. Sorry, there's no sharing of kit because it ends in disaster.' With all his experience of previous expeditions Simon curbed his anger for the time being. 'It's not the right time out here,' he said. 'We can address it when we get back. In a jokey fashion I just said, "Give me back my ruddy gloves, you stupid Dog."'

But he was still peed off and the long day pulling his pulk seemed harder than ever.

It was, in any case, for all of them, something to get used to, hour upon hour with nothing but the swish of the sledge in the snow and the view of the backs of the men in front of you. 'Polar travel,' says Henry Cookson, 'is mindless, mundane and boring. It's not for nothing they call it the polar plod.'

'It is boring,' says Martin, 'but it gives you time to think about everything you can imagine: things you've done, things you want to do. It's not too dissimilar to doing long marches when you're working in a military context. For me in particular, now I'm getting discharged from the Army, it gives me time to plan what I'm going to do next.'

Guy found it harder to switch off and let his mind wander. 'During the two hours between breaks, if the weather is clear and you can see for miles, you can look at a point in the distance and then estimate the time until you ski right up to it. The stupid thing to do then is look at your watch. Because you can think, *Right, I've been skiing for about an hour now, I'll just check my watch.* Then you discover it's only been five minutes. That's potentially dangerous. You could drive yourself

171

mad like that.'

By the time they came to camp that evening, on a different lake, the wind was up again. It howled through another long night and in the morning the tents were covered even deeper in snow. Ed had to dig through a drift just to get out of the front door flap. Inge now had a hard choice. The blizzard hadn't let up, but if the team didn't move soon, they would be buried in snow. After waiting out the morning, he decided at one o'clock that they should be up and off. 'Be very careful how you take the tents down,' he told his charges. 'We can't afford to break them. And make sure you don't lose anything. Keep checking where all your equipment is at all times.'

Despite this warning, as the team dug the tents out in the whiteout, then struggled to dismantle them without losing them in the sudden gusts, two skis went missing, buried somewhere in the snow. The flakes were whirling in so fast that anything left on the ground vanished within seconds. Pulks finally packed, they hunted for the skis for an hour and a half, but to no avail. They were all getting too cold. It was time to cut their losses, learn their lesson and go.

They pressed on across the lake, leaning into the wind, eight individuals in bright red thermal gear skiing in single file, pulks swishing along behind them. Ed was relieved that Steve's back had recovered. 'I want to take all four of them,' he said, 'and I know they all passionately want to go, but if there is an element of doubt with any of them, as we had in Svalbard, we will just have to say no. Hopefully this won't be the case, this will just be a little glitch from which we can learn.'

The snow was blowing in long white trails off the lake and as the sun sank lower the sky was criss-crossed with swathes of deep purple and a brilliant Arctic yellow. 'It was the most beautiful afternoon ever,' said Jaco. 'This incredible sky and then the massive snow-covered mountains on either side of us. We were the only people out in this place for miles and miles. That was when I realised I love this stuff, that I will somehow try and do more of it when I leave the Army.'

The surreal atmosphere had affected the entire group. When they stopped to camp in a more sheltered spot at the edge of the lake, they were all in high spirits. 'Wow!' 'Great!' 'Unbelievable!' they said to each other. The wind had dropped. Setting up camp and cooking their evening meal their routines were slicker than ever. They all slept better than they had done in days.

They woke to a beautiful, still, clear morning and headed back to a lake near their starting point at Beitostølen, where they set up camp. Here they were scheduled to meet representatives of the world's press, who would trek out through the snow to meet them, help them strike camp, then ski with them for a mile to a yurt where they would have a hot lunch of reindeer stew, organised by Captive Minds. 'I really wanted the media to feel how hard it was going to be for the team,' says Alex Rayner, 'so I made anybody who could, get on to skis and ski out to meet them. All credit to Danielle from the office here who led them all the way. She had never skied before, but she was going, "If I can do it, you can do it." It was quite a long way from the hotel to this camp. A couple of the guys got there and they were really huffing and puffing. They got there and sort of collapsed.'

Meanwhile the PR man himself had led an advance party. 'I did feel rather bad getting on top of a Skidoo and going out, though I have to say a Skidoo is a very uncomfortable mode of transport; you don't sit on a seat, you sit on a sledge.' Once there, though, he was glad he had reached the camp ahead of the pack. 'I'll never forget unzipping their tent. They were sitting there inside all toasty. It was the last day, so the burners were on full. I opened the zip and there were three sets of feet and it stank. Really reeked. As I jogged the tent this condensation fell on my face and I gagged.' Despite the media training the soldiers had been given by Captive Minds, they hadn't yet fully understood how carefully the press needed to be handled.

Guy in particular was still learning to adjust to the attention. 'I think all of us soldiers find it quite surreal,' he said. 'Being asked to expose everything about yourself. But we've all realised it's part of it and we've got to open up to the cameras a bit.' For Guy, the two most irritating questions were: 'How has your life changed since you lost a leg?' and 'What will you feel like when you get to the North Pole?'

There was another wake-up call when one of the photographers managed to get frostbite. 'He was just taking photographs for too long without his glove on,' said Martin. 'It was horrendous. I couldn't believe it when I saw it—massive blisters on his hands. I think he's probably kept his hand, but the nails will all have gone. The tips of his fingers, too.' It was Martin's main worry about the upcoming expedition. 'I go into this with the knowledge that I've already got a paralysed right arm. For anything to happen to the left would be most unwelcome.'

Back in the hotel the team gathered in private for a lengthy debrief. Inge had plenty to say, about managing their body heat, looking after their kit, making sure they kept the moisture in the tent to a minimum, and of course having a shit in −30°C.

'I get this every time I do a talk,' he said, 'it's always one of the top three questions, "How do you go to the toilet?" And the answer is: it's the same way you do it at home, it's just that you do it faster. If you do it right it's a really quick and easy process. But I found out yesterday that some of you didn't even realise that you now have zippers on the side of your pants, so you can just pull them to one side. Sit down and it reveals everything. Quick on, quick off. With one arm I can see it's harder. But what I need to stress again is, structure. Plan your toilet visit. Do it as regular as you can. A quarter to eight every morning, if you can.'

As for the shambles of striking camp yesterday in the whiteout: 'The first thing I said before taking down those tents was, "Please, be very very careful you don't break them. That you don't lose anything. Look where your skis are, your equipment, your gloves." But then, despite all that, we lost two skis, we ripped two tents, and we nearly broke one tent completely and lost it. We have to sort this out, because we looked like amateurs yesterday morning and that's not acceptable. So we all have to look at ourselves and how we can improve our admin and work better as a team. Think in front of a situation, *What can happen if I lose this? If I take out these anchor points, is the tent supported? Is somebody else holding the tent now? Can I let go?* These things are so important because if we lose a tent up there at the Pole and our house is gone, we're more or less f.u.c.k.e.d.'

When he had finished, he received support from a surprising quarter. For all his normal joviality, Dags was deadly serious now. 'I don't think we've quite accepted that we need to be much, much more organised than we are out on the ice. When I trained for the South Pole, by this stage of the game we had military discipline, we were boxed away. But we haven't even started that process yet, I don't think. And it worries me. We have to know when we go in our tents where every single piece of equipment is. And here's an example, and I only use this, Dog, because it's relevant. You nicked my gloves. Had the tent gone down at that point, I would have been fucked.'

On they went, detailing the lessons they had learnt from the week. Henry, in particular, had a long list of points to share: better 'stuff sacks' to hold their kit; tent trousers and booties to wear inside the tent; tent seats for Steve 'and the old men'; more cookers for greater warmth and to speed up the snow melting process; an internal washing line to dry clothes; nose guards to sew on to goggles; and if they each marked all their kit with different coloured tape, that would cut down on the chaos in the tents. 'Get your mother, girlfriend, whoever, to sew on to each sock a colour, so you don't get them all mixed up. Because if the shit hits the fan, in a storm, you want to be quick. At the moment it's like, "Is that my glove, or your glove? Is that a large one?" It's not good.'

The list went on. But at the end of the meeting, Inge's summary was upbeat. 'The most important

176

thing,' he said, 'is I feel that it was a successful training. I'm very confident that we will be one of the best prepared expeditions to the North Pole ever. I don't say that,' he added, 'to suck up to you. Because I don't suck up to people.'

'Yeah, we noticed,' said Dags.

14

SEND-OFF

On the evening of 3 March 2011, the decommissioned hulk of Europe's largest brick building, Battersea Power Station, stood brilliantly floodlit above the high tide on Chelsea Reach. Beneath the four iconic chimneys the Walking With The Wounded logo—a bent figure pulling a pulk, designed by Harry Parker—was projected on to bare exterior walls. Smart cars and taxis approached gingerly down the bumpy track that led across the surrounding wasteland.

Men in black tie and women in elegant evening wear were disgorged and made their way through an entrance tunnel of mock icebergs, which gave way to white canvas walls hung with framed photographs of polar explorers of yesteryear. Inside the huge marquee at the far end of the tunnel there were chairs in transparent Perspex; long chandeliers that looked like icicles; a roving light show in chilly whites and blues and greens; and an ice luge from which vodka could be drunk. Looking up through a transparent section of ceiling, guests could see the derelict inner walls of the old boiler

177

house looming spookily above them. Below, on a terrace, stood a hooped white tent and two unlikely Arctic trees, liberally covered in stage snow.

The Ice and Diamonds Ball, which Ed and a committee had been planning for almost a year, was now finally taking place. Champagne and cocktails were followed by a three-course meal at tables for ten which had been sold for £6500 apiece. The starter was a celeriac and truffle velouté containing an individual poached egg. 'A very very posh soup,' says Harriet Parker, who had thought it the most delicious thing she had ever eaten when she'd been to the pre-dinner tasting. 'I don't know what it is,' said Steve Young, who was seated next to her, 'but I don't think I like it.' As themed puddings of cloved Arctic roll and cinnamon baked Alaska arrived, ex-World Cup rugby player Martin Bayfield (all 6ft 10in of him) took to the stage to host the evening's entertainment. After an amusing speech in which he was a bit rude about the velouté but very welcoming to the soldiers, he introduced the first musical performer of the evening, 2009 *X Factor* runner-up Olly Murs, who soon had the more lively of the guests up and dancing, before he was co-opted to help hand out prizes for the raffle.

'Is it the earrings or Olly who's made you breathless?' asked Bayfield of the fortunate female who scooped the second prize. The winner of the first prize £20,000 diamond gave it to his girlfriend on stage; from the tears in her eyes it seemed there might be more at stake than just a precious stone. 'It looked like an unmistakable proposal,' said Alex Rayner.

Then Ed and Dags were up to outline the purpose of the new charity. There was an audible

178

gasp at the statistic that more veterans had committed suicide after the Falklands War than had died on the battlefield. The presentation concluded with Harry Parker, steel legs on show under shorts, telling the audience that as he had no toes left to lose to frostbite, he had decided not to go on the expedition. But the burden of his speech was serious enough. It wasn't officers like him who needed help, he said; they would probably be fine. It was the soldiers from less fortunate backgrounds, with fewer resources, who needed to be shown a way forward.

After the raffle came the auction, with lots ranging from a day with Zara Phillips at her yard, through various exotic holiday opportunities, to the chance to name individual sledges or fly out to meet the team at the North Pole. The bids were in thousands, rather than hundreds of pounds, pushed ever higher by the skilful encouragement of Christie's senior director James Bruce-Gardyne.

'Two thousand five hundred I have! It's here at table twenty-five. Three thousand I have!'

And after that, a secret gig by Duran Duran, whose songs got almost everyone to their feet, even if the band weren't that familiar to some. 'They're not really my era,' said Jaco, who nonetheless enjoyed meeting the musicians backstage, as they all posed for a group photo in which Steve Young had his arm round John Taylor. Out front, the dinner-jacketed crowd bobbed and swayed, mobiles held high in the air, flashing away. To one side, dancing with his Sony 900 Hi Def camera, was the quietly smiling figure of Alexis Girardet, catching the moment as ever.

'I'm not sure I really enjoyed myself,' Ed wrote

in his diary, 'as I spent the whole evening worrying that everyone was having fun. But the party was brilliantly organised, delicious food and wine, great venue and great entertainment, although Duran Duran were outshone by Olly Murs in my opinion.' By the end of the night the charity had raised nearly £150,000. A decent sum, Ed thought, 'though I did feel there was the potential for more.'

With that big hurdle out of the way he sneaked off on the Eurostar to Paris for four days of R & R with his wife Harriet. 'That week,' she recalls, 'I said to him he could have half an hour on his Blackberry. Each call was five minutes, so I said, "If you have more than six calls I'm throwing it in the Seine." He said, "That would really annoy me." I said, "That's the deal. We are going away. We are not going to talk about Walking With The Wounded. We are not going to think about it, we're going to enjoy Paris and chill out." He got to his six calls and I was counting. Of course I wouldn't have thrown his phone in the Seine, but I would have told him I had. Then turned it off and hidden it till we got back.'

*   *   *

Back in London, the day after the ball, Martin, Jaco and Guy paid a visit to the special school attended by Simon's son Felix. 'The children loved it,' says Dags, 'and Felix thought it was wonderful. He adores the boys. Primarily because they are soldiers and they've killed people. In a nine-year-old's mind death isn't death as you and I envisage it. Also, for him, he is severely disabled and they are marginally disabled. He can see that his heroes, these people who have fought great battles, are a bit like him. I think he relates to that. He has a particularly good relationship with Jaco; Jaco's very good at communicating with children.

'In fact none of this would have happened without Felix. He has been the inspiration for all the trips I've done in one fashion or another. The original row that I did was about raising money for the charity, Tommy's, that would have prevented Felix being born prematurely. When we went to the South Pole that was about raising more. And now it's about raising money for a different sort of disabled person.

'There's an interesting thing about looking at a child who was born with a disability and lived with it all his life, and then at those who have become disabled later in life. Felix will often say to me, "Daddy, I wish I could run" or "I wish I could play football." But he's quadriplegic, so he never will. Lots of people say, "If he's never known it he'll never miss not having it." But that's rubbish, because he does. All the children do. He said to me the other day, "I want to join the Army." I said, "You can't mate, because you can't walk." He said, "Jaco can push me." I said, "Jaco has only got one arm, so he wouldn't be very good at pushing, but I see your logic."

'But these guys who've come into disability . . . how do they handle not being able to do the things they previously could have done? The frustrations are the same.'

*   *   *

The day after the ball, it properly hit Jaco that he

181

would soon be out on the ice, attempting to walk with one arm across the frozen ice cap to the North Pole. 'Everything kind of led up to the ball. We knew that was where we said goodbye. After that, I was suddenly realising that we set off in three weeks' time. *Have I done enough?* I was thinking. *Am I prepared?*'

In answer to Jaco's question, there was still plenty to do. First off, the final medical at the Institute of Naval Medicine in Gosport. 'Ever since the first time,' Ed wrote, 'there has been a dispute between Martin and me about who was top in the VO_2 Max test. Being six foot five and fairly fit and strong does help, and obviously able-bodied, but I am forty-five and Martin has been training for this expedition all through the winter—and he is only thirty! During the medical Martin made the schoolboy error of going first, so he had to set the benchmark. I left it until the end so I knew exactly what I had to do on the exercise bike. As it turned out, I was able to exceed Martin's time— the dispute was over. I also lifted the heaviest deadweight they have on record at the INM, which was a bit of a thrill, although I would have been pushing my luck a little to compete with Martin on that with his one arm.'

Overall, the Institute's medics were pleased with the team's progress. Steve was able to deadweight lift 45 kg more than on his previous visit, a clear measure of how his back strength had improved. Martin had a thermograph test to check the blood flow in his paralysed arm—there was a significant improvement. Guy scored lowest on the bike, as was only to be expected with his leg; but his body weight was well up (as a glance at his chubbier face

182

could have told you). Jaco's fitness level was the same as before, but he too had managed to increase his body fat, in his case from 5 per cent to 12 per cent.

Paradoxically, for gym enthusiasts like Martin and Jaco, achieving this result had been hard work. To put the weight on, they had had to adapt their normal routines, slackening off their fat-burning cardiovascular exercise and concentrating instead on building up endurance capability and muscle strength. For Jaco, this meant dropping his thrice-weekly run and his daily cycle ride and sticking to tyre-dragging walks, followed by long sessions of weight lifting to build up the strength in his right side (for he would not only be pulling his pulk with one arm, but also attempting to lift it over the slippery walls of broken ice that are Arctic pressure ridges). Martin's training underwent a similar change of emphasis: 'The key for me,' he says, 'was to work on my core stability and fitness. For the final three months I didn't do running of any kind. Instead I started dragging tyres with a rucksack on; and did weight lifting in the gym to strengthen my legs and back.'

Getting fatter also meant eating—with the stress on all those things most people spend their lives trying to avoid. Pizzas, burgers, steaks, chips, ice cream, chocolate brownies, beer—this was the diet the soldiers were encouraged to stick to. 'A fat person's dream,' as Guy put it.

'It was an awesome period in my life,' says Steve, 'because I could eat what I wanted. For breakfast I'd have a couple of boiled eggs, bacon, mackerel on toast, beans on toast. I'd snack constantly throughout the day, then my evening meal would be massive. I was told I had to be a fit fat man.'

'It was all about taking in more calories,' says Martin, 'so I used a skimmed milk product in hot drinks in addition to milk, then I started actively going to takeaways as well as having normal meals.' Jaco was also gorging, though he did his best to distinguish between good and bad fat: cream, butter, mayonnaise and nuts were fats that would last longer and do him good; Macdonald's and other takeaways were 'basically just blubber'.

Four days after being passed fit for purpose by the INM, the team met up for a last big day in London. First, a meeting at the offices of their head sponsors, Artemis, where the group was given a special gold sovereign to take to the Pole as a good luck charm. After saying their goodbyes, they hopped in a couple of cabs and drove round to 10 Downing Street for a meeting with Prime Minister David Cameron. On this very special occasion, Ed had persuaded his nephew Harry to go with them.

Once through the famous door, Jaco was surprised by how big the building was inside: 'When you see it on the TV it doesn't look spacious at all.' Cell phones were handed in and the team were taken down to the Cabinet Room. Seated with teas and coffees around the oval table, Simon couldn't resist the opportunity to sit in the PM's chair. Opening up the leather-bound folder before him he wrote on the uppermost piece of paper, *Invade China*. There was further laughter when Steve was told in prime ministerial tones that Wales was shortly to be removed from the United Kingdom. 'We were behaving like excited schoolchildren,' Ed wrote.

After ten minutes the door opened and the real

PM was shown in. All rose to their feet and lined up to be introduced by Ed. 'He was very well briefed and easy and natural with them,' Ed wrote, 'and seemed genuinely interested in the care they had all received when they returned from Afghanistan. We then went outside for a photo with him on the front door step before coming back inside to chat for a further ten minutes or so. His time is obviously very precious and it was hugely generous of him to meet us and wish us good luck.'

'He knew what he was talking about,' says Jaco. 'He knew about the ice rubble, pressure ridges and open leads. He asked questions and got us to explain certain things. He was really interested— not just seeing us to get a tick in the box. He'd done a bit of homework on it.'

'He sat back with his hands in his pockets,' says Alex Rayner, who had accompanied the team, 'and his first question was, "How has your care been since you've been hurt?" The boys couldn't say enough good stuff about what had happened to them up to that time. Finally, having signed a Union Jack for them to take to the Pole, he said, "I've got to go now because I've got a phone call with the Queen and it's something you will quite enjoy." Later that day he announced that Wootton Bassett was becoming Royal Wootton Bassett.'

And that was their final engagement before they flew off the following Thursday. 'The last few days have been a bit peculiar,' wrote Ed on Sunday evening, 'and the bed in the spare room is now laden with everything I need to pack before we go. Harriet and I went to the village church this morning and the vicar very kindly said a brief prayer for the team. It is that sort of thing which

185

makes it all seem a bit more real and as I sat in church the adrenalin started flowing.'

* * *

The team met at Gatwick at noon. Captive Minds had sent out a press release and as a result, a couple of photographers had arrived to take pictures of the guys lined up with their enormous pile of baggage, topped with a wooden box containing a Jeroboam of champagne sent by Pol Roger; the London *Evening Standard* later ran the photo on page three. Harriet was there to see Ed off, and she was accompanied by Steve's fiancée Emma and Guy's mother Fiona. 'Not as painful as I feared,' Ed wrote later, 'but with most of the rest of the team there, there was a lot of banter and excitement ahead of the adventure. The longest I have been away from my family is two weeks since I have been married. In the morning I had dropped my two girls off at school which had been agony. Olivia was very upset, while Kitty was incredibly brave. Not a moment I relished.'

The guys had a long and wearying day ahead of them, with a flight to Oslo, another to Tromsø, then another to Longyearbyen, rechecking their huge pile of baggage each time. 'It was quite a rush,' says Jaco, 'getting everything out and making sure we had all the luggage, putting new tags on and getting it booked in, then on through customs and security.'

They finally arrived in Longyearbyen at 1.30 a.m., having picked up Inge and Martin and yet more luggage in Oslo. Getting off the plane they were wearing no more than their expedition T-shirts and fleeces. Outside it was −20°C. 'Loading up the van with all the kit,' Ed wrote, 'my ears and fingers

186

started hurting within no time—it was freezing. A rude awakening—and a harsh reminder of what was to come.'

*　　　*　　　*

On Friday morning they were back in the warehouse they had used in May 2010 on the very first selection weekend. Their first task was one which Martin and Inge had already started in Oslo, stripping the foil vacuum packaging from their rations and sorting the freezedried food into zip-locked freezer bags. This cut down on weight and bulk and meant that there would be less to carry onward with them (because of course no litter may be left out on the polar ice). They planned for a maximum twenty-five days on the ice, which meant organising twenty-five breakfasts and evening meals, along with twenty-five daily snack bags for the two-hourly breaks. In order to reach the required daily calorie count of 6500, the guys were doubling up meals, two packs per dinner.

It was noticeable that Martin was packing far more food than the others; by the end he had over 60 kg of provisions in his pulk. 'As long as we're getting over six thousand calories a day,' he said, 'we'll be OK. Otherwise you lose fat and muscle degradation becomes a problem. Ultimately you'd become so drained that you wouldn't be efficient. In endurance events I've done in the past there comes a point where you hit a wall. The mind can do so much to help you over that, your training kicks in too, but you've also got to have the energy inside you.'

'Martin is a knob,' says Dags. 'I said to him,

187

"Inge and Henry will tell you to do this, but you'll probably only be able to eat three or four thousand calories, so pack for that. Otherwise you're carrying a mass of dead weight." But he packed so much food that frankly he could have fed us all.'

The meals all had exotic-sounding titles: Beef Stroganoff, Chicken with Herbal Sauce, Chilli con Carne, Greek Feast, Peach and Pineapple Dessert. In reality, rehydrated with boiled melted snow at the end of a hard day, they tasted much the same. But the guys were still making sure that Steve got all the Wolf Fish Casserole, which no one else liked; although Martin, ever the jester, was packing a couple as a little surprise for a friend. 'We're gonna sneak some into Dags at some point. When he's really low and pissed off, we'll whack a bit of fish in his main course.' To add to the fun he had also bought a pack of the hottest curry powder he could find. 'I'm going to wait for him to have a really, really bad day,' he said, 'and then I'm going to put the whole damn thing into one meal. So when he's really depressed he's then forced to go out and attend a call of nature when he doesn't want to.'

But the team member getting the rawest deal on the food front was the one currently absent: His Royal Highness Prince Harry of Wales. Henry Cookson was packing up his food for him. 'Not that he's lazy or anything,' he said, 'it's just that he's coming in late in the day, so we've got to have everything ready. The trouble is, the vultures have had first pickings, so he's getting whatever's left. So, uh, soup and spam. He's going to be a happy boy.' The plan was for the Prince to spend five days on the ice with the team, but Henry was packing for eight, just in case anything went wrong, or for any reason Harry was stuck out there.

Little extras were sneaked in too. Ed had Cadbury's Fruit and Nut bars, macadamia nuts, and three tins of foie gras he'd brought from Paris, 'which I'm taking for those particularly bad days, just to melt into my stew.' Guy had chilli powder, to spice the meals up a bit. Dags had his favourite Green and Black's chocolate. All of them except teetotal Inge had whisky. 'I do think luxury items help with morale,' Guy said.

Just making a start on sorting out their food had taken the team a good six hours. 'We had all thought,' wrote Ed, 'that arriving a week before we departed was overkill. After this first long afternoon in the warehouse we realised this was not going to be the case.'

Saturday morning brought more of the same. With the main meals organised, the team moved on to preparing the snack nosebags for their two-hourly breaks. It was similar high-calorie stuff to what they'd had at Beitostølen: mixed nuts, Boost and Twix chocolate bars, high energy Mule bars, wine gums and M&Ms. Henry had also arranged for some healthier options to come from small UK suppliers, who had generously donated to the cause: nut balls from Upcakes, flapjacks in various flavours from TV chef Gerard Baker. Martin's mum and sister had baked tiffin, a scrumptious melange of chocolate biscuits, sugar and raisins. All together, they provided the extra 3000 calories to bring the daily intake up to 6500.

Once their nourishment had been squared off, the team moved on to preparing their kit. Despite the fuss Ed and Simon had made at Beitostølen, there were still problems. 'That afternoon,' wrote Ed, 'we were back in the sports shop buying more kit, much to my frustration. This time face masks and gloves—and we still don't seem to have the right combinations. It should not be at this stage that we are finalising our equipment. It remains a bugbear of mine that we are having to spend money on kit we could have got sponsored if we had been more organised at an earlier stage. It is a key element of the expedition and we had too many chiefs.'

Whatever else was true, it was certain that the two chiefs in question thought very differently about what was necessary for an expedition such as this. 'When you're in the tent in the evening,' says Henry, 'you don't want to be wearing your Gore-tex outer shell. It's not wet but it gets cold very quickly and it's not nice against the skin. So you have these insulated trousers that are like duvet trousers, really comfortable, nice warm things to have on in the tent. It's worth it for another five hundred grams.'

'Totally unnecessary!' says Inge. 'Tent trousers are like a luxury item you can have when you've paid to be on an expedition led by someone who's just strolling along. Are you focussed on doing the expedition efficiently or are you there for a holiday? Every little thing you add is complicating the picture. So people would ask Henry, "What do you do about keeping your neck warm?" His answer would be: "I always wear a neck gaiter." Neck gaiters! We don't need neck gaiters! That is just one example. My kit list was the need-to-have list. Not all the nice things that the guys may have talked to Sir Expedition-Leader in England about, that he always uses this and he always uses that. If I gave in to everything they thought they needed their pulks would have been twice as heavy.

'Every little thing you add is complicating the picture. How many times do you really need to change pants on an expedition like this? It's comfortable to change four times, but it also means an extra weight of three hundred grams and that much more luggage volume than if you just change twice.'

In any case, this was not a normal expedition: 'With so many people involved it was a very special project. They weren't like paying clients who had signed up for a trip and wanted the package, they were in every way involved. We had emails going around about food and recipes, for example, and after about fifty-six I had to say, this is irrelevant, we can't be focussing on desserts here, we have to focus on the expedition.'

For Inge, veteran of ten previous North Pole expeditions, last-minute worries about kit and supplies were only to be expected. 'If I get twenty emails about something totally irrelevant, it is sometimes a symptom of fear. It is a natural thing for anybody who goes to a hostile place like the North Pole to be worried about it.'

'It's been a very interesting cultural journey for me,' says Henry. 'Having dealt a lot with Norwegians over the last year and having spoken to other guys who have dealt with them, they are a very direct people. They don't accommodate for other people's ignorance or weaknesses. Which doesn't necessarily work that well if you're taking the people you're guiding out of their comfort zone. I very much deferred to Inge, having brought him in and because he was leading on the ice, but we did have our disagreements.'

* * *

Each of the four wounded participants had meanwhile been fine-tuning the adaptations that would help safeguard their particular injury. Guy had his new, improved prosthetic leg from PACE Rehabilitation. Martin had three specially tailored merino wool sleeves to insulate his paralysed arm, with tailored sockets for chemical heat pads, one on the forearm, one on the bicep. Jaco, likewise, had heat pads in special Velcro-sealed pockets. Steve had his roll mat and a hefty collection of painkillers.

For everyone, getting the kit sorted out and packed was part of the pre-expedition ritual. 'I suspect,' said Simon, 'between now and Friday, when we go, we'll probably unpack it all, lay it out again, check it, pack it again, then get worried we've left something behind or haven't put something in, take it out again. And we'll do that about five times, until you realise you've actually got everything.'

'You tweak the kit,' said Guy, 'just like you do in the Army. And then you get the fear, if someone else has done anything. You think: *Has it been done in the wrong way?*'

Martin's gear was arranged in colour-coordinated compression sacks: 'I've got purple for food, green for clothing, red for gloves and yellow for socks—and orange for toiletries. So I can reach in, grab one bag for meals, one for night-time kit and so on. It speeds things up on the ice, though it takes a lot of time prepping now.'

Jaco was doing something similar, marking each

192

bag with a pen: 'It's my own little personal system. Otherwise you forget where things are.' Like all the others, his pulk was methodically arranged. At the back, 'the dirty end', he carried two big cans of fuel, padded out with roll mats, behind a plywood divider that he'd customised himself. The rest of the heavy stuff was at the bottom of the pulk, to keep it grounded. Then came his food, in the new zip-locked bags inside a big cooler bag. On top of that, his five layers of clothing, with spares; and then, accessible near the front, his tent bag, containing everything he would need for the night. Right at the top was the big orange down jacket which they all wore when they stopped. The whole lot was held in with one big central zip, and over that three horizontal straps with plastic clips.

Each participant was taking essential team gear as well as his own kit. Guy carried cooking pots, fuel bottles and half the fuel for his tent. Jaco had all the fuel for his tent, while Martin carried both tents and all the roll mats, as well as the satellite phones and batteries, in a pulk that was longer than the others. If he only had one arm, he nonetheless had strong legs, so this was his contribution to the team.

Guy had a fine range of medical supplies for general use: Compeed and Granuflex for blisters; Imodium for diarrhoea; painkillers; zinc oxide tape; alcohol gel wipes. 'My father's a GP, so I got him to sort it out for me. That's why your taxes are so high, because you're paying for people like me and Martin.'

There were other items, too, which were not strictly essential. Jaco had a collapsible dart board, because he wanted to play darts at the Pole. Then there were sentimental items, which had come courtesy of loved ones. Martin's family had given him photos of them all, including dogs Mel and Mojo. 'And then my stupid sister has put pictures of random flowers in there, I've got absolutely no idea why. Together with little one-liners to keep me going when I'm tired. She's basically given me abuse, that's what she does. Well, that's what I've done to her for God knows how many years.' There was a card too. 'Which I'll probably open later. Which will no doubt be another combination of good luck messages, don't quit messages, and abuse, primarily from my mother and sister, because they've got the same warped sense of humour as me.'

Jaco's sister had put together a photo album for him, with pictures of family and friends from home. 'I guess through the long and hard days ahead, I'll just have a look at it, remember why I'm doing this and all the support my family's given me and then, yeah, just crack on.' One picture was of his ex-girlfriend, still out in South Africa. 'She stood by me through Afghanistan and during my injury, but it's hard keeping a relationship going long distance. It's kind of heartbreaking, I do care a lot about her and we're still very good friends.' Underneath the photo was a little message in Afrikaans. 'Basically saying this is a once in a lifetime opportunity, she's very proud of me for where I am today and she'll be thinking of me every day, lots of love, and their prayers are with us.'

Nothing for Guy, though. 'The others have got letters from home that they'll open every five days or so, but that's not for me. I personally just like to put my head down and go. My dog can't write so

194

I haven't asked her for a letter. Perhaps I should have got a paw print or something.'

Were the soldiers and ex-soldiers in any way apprehensive about the upcoming challenge? 'I'm not really nervous yet,' said Guy. 'I think there's a real sense about everybody now that we just want to crack on with it.' Having said that, he added: 'I'm probably a bit more nervous than when we went to Afghan, which is wrong, because when we got back from Afghan I had a blown-off leg.

'But it does make the challenge more appealing, the risk side makes it more desirable to achieve it. It's why people join the Army. We live in a society which is quite risk-averse these days, and I think risk is healthy. We bumped into someone yesterday who did the South Pole a few years ago and he's got some kids he's brought out here now. Four teens who were apparently a bit naughty at school. And that's brilliant. That's exactly what kids should be doing.'

If Martin wasn't exactly nervous, he certainly didn't want anything to happen to his good arm: 'I don't want to get any more injuries, that's for sure. The threat of losing my left arm to frostbite is a concern, because it would have a serious impact on my day to day life. But it's not something that's going to stop me doing this.'

'If I was feeling vulnerable,' said Steve, 'I don't think I'd admit it. But I'm the sort of person who's got to prepare. I've got to check and check and check and recheck, make sure my kit's there, so I know in my head I'm confident in myself, my own abilities and the blokes I'm going up there with. At the end of the day we're facing challenges, but it's against Nature. It's not like out in Afghanistan, where it was us against other men.'

'During the day you don't really think about it,' said Jaco, 'you're too busy doing bits and bobs, but just before I go to bed I start thinking about it a bit more: have I done this, have I done that? Wondering what to expect.'

Ed, older, wiser, in charge, was 'very nervous'. 'We're sitting here in Spitsbergen,' he said, 'and you look outside and it's stunningly beautiful and then you walk outside and it's stunningly cold, but we know that where we're going is another twenty degrees below this. The one thing that's preying on my mind is just constantly, constantly, constantly having the cold there. Never being able to get away from it.'

On Saturday night they went out on the town, for a meal at Kroa, the wood-panelled, candlelit restaurant that was fast becoming the expedition's watering hole of choice. Then on to Longyearbyen's only nightclub, Huset. 'Which was surreal,' said Martin. 'It was about fifteen metres long and ten metres wide, with a DJ booth in the corner. The only women in there were aggressive cougars, who wanted to spread the Longyearbyen gene pool by taking someone new into it, which we managed to avoid.'

'Ed and I being the old gentlemen went home,' said Dags, 'and they carried on. Martin had two or three tequilas whilst trying to dance with one of the locals, thinking that perhaps this was his moment for a last love before he went to the North Pole.'

'Strangely he didn't have any success,' said Ed.

'Again.'

'It's like taking a group of school children away for the weekend. Quite tiring.'

'Very tiring.'

*   *   *

After all that, Sunday was a quiet day. Ed spent the morning in his room, fine-tuning and adapting his personal kit. 'We've sewn Polytek material on to the bottom of our goggles and sunglasses,' he wrote, 'to protect our noses and faces from the wind and frost nip and frostbite. A significant test of my sewing skills—not sure if I passed! Then I spent a lot of time working out what was really necessary. In Norway in January my tent bag was huge and full of clutter which I never used. Steve slightly despaired about my admin. Hopefully he might notice a slight improvement this time.'

In the evening, spruced up and recovered from various mighty hangovers, the team went to the Basecamp Hotel to meet the world's press. The promised presence of Prince Harry had brought reporters to Norway in droves—and, in this royal wedding season, not only from the UK. 'Encouragingly,' Ed wrote, 'NBC and ABC, the American networks, had sent teams. It was fascinating to meet Bob Woodruff, the anchor for ABC. Bob was blown up by an IED in Iraq when covering the US forces, so he has a strong empathy with the wounded.'

There was more press interaction the following day over lunch. 'We all realise the importance the media has for our project,' Ed wrote, 'so we must get on with it. After lunch Inge took us outside behind the hotel for interviews. It was around minus twenty and we weren't that well dressed. Most of us were wearing jeans—hardly the well-prepared Arctic explorers. After twenty minutes we were all very cold, and we haven't even started—not good.'

Otherwise it was another day of preparation, packing and repacking the pulks, checking that they were all set for departure on Friday. 'It's beginning to get to us a little,' Ed wrote. 'While it's all below the surface, it's clear that there is a bit of tension beginning to build. It's not personal tensions between the team members, but we all know the start time is getting closer and the fear is getting to us in different ways. When I woke this morning the enormity of what we are doing really hit home. I lay in bed for ten minutes really missing home and wondering what on earth I was doing here.'

15

ONE OF THE LADS

HARRY: I sometimes feel as though my role is a little bit of a spare part. You know these guys have been bonding for the last year now. As a team they're completely solid, they've gelled together perfectly. So my role I would see as basically trying to come in and help out as much as I can and try and be a bit of a boost to the team. Hopefully I've managed to lift the guys and bring something different to the party.

I've met Dags a few times and Ed as well—and actually I'd met a couple of the other guys too before they started this trip. Obviously once I was asked it was a very, very easy thing to say, 'Yes, I'd love to join in on this.' It's an opportunity I couldn't let go, the chance to be with these guys out in this environment. Even if I had the chance to chill out with them for a week in the pub I'd do that—because once all the boys are together, it's good banter, it's just like being back in the regiment.

Myself and my brother and I suppose a huge majority of the British public support these guys in everything they do. For me, after doing a very small stint in Afghanistan, I like to think I've got a rough idea of what goes on out there and how they feel. Obviously I haven't been through the same things as them, I was only there for ten weeks, but to be able to say I've been there and experienced similar things to them—though not, of course, the injury itself—then it's nice to be able to sit down and have a conversation about that. And I like to think they can open up to me and that I can ask questions that maybe other people wouldn't be comfortable asking.

The expression that's used the whole time is 'brotherhood'. And it's true, because everyone looks after each other out there. It's a feeling which is very hard to explain unless you go out and do it, but it's very different when you've got a weapon of your own and you're next to guys who are shooting past your ears and all that sort of thing.

If I'd been hit there would definitely be some stories to share. Obviously that never happened to me and I'm very lucky it didn't. But after seeing these guys and the way they've dealt with it all, if I did ever go back I wouldn't have as much fear as I did the first time.

No one wants to get injured, but these guys have accepted what's happened to them. They look at their mates who've lost a leg or an arm or both and they think, 'You know what, you've served your country, you've done well and your life's not over. It's not come to an end. There's other things you can do.' Even walk to the North Pole. The inspiration that these guys give to everyone else is unbelievable. This expedition is going to be seriously nails for them and nobody should underestimate what they are putting themselves through, not just for themselves, but for everyone else who's been injured. They're proving a point: that no matter what happens to you, you don't need to give up on life. You can achieve whatever you want to if you put your mind to it.

My father obviously knew I was coming out here and so did my brother, but otherwise I kept it quiet until it happened. My grandparents and the rest of my family have probably just found out about it. They probably think I'm completely mad. My father was very nervous about it because of the lack of training that I've done—and rightly so, because he's got a lot of friends who have done this. But I am only here for a very short space of time.

I have to accept the fact that me coming here is bringing more limelight to them—and if that's the case, then brilliant. I'm just happy to be here and give them as much support as I can and have a laugh with them, because I like to think I'm one of the lads. Whether I am or not!

16

ON HOLD

This period—the end of March and the start of April—was Longyearbyen's high season, and the remote settlement was full of adventurers getting ready to hit the polar ice cap. Most expeditions involved only the 'last degree' or 'ten day trip', as Henry Cookson puts it. But not all. Buying gloves in one of the stores, Guy and Martin ran into two explorers from Belgium, who the previous year had skied from the Siberian land mass to Barneo, from there to the North Pole and then on to Greenland in one go. 'Which is astonishing,' said Guy. 'Suddenly you start to feel pretty insignificant. You realise what you're doing is not that special.' Another guy the team ran into was preparing to be flown straight to the Pole. From there he was going to walk to Greenland, on to Newfoundland, then work his way down through the United States and South America, doing two marathons a day, before skiing the last degree to the South Pole.

As well as extraordinary characters like this, there were others who were somewhat less inspiring. Some even cast aspersions on Walking With The Wounded's chances of being successful at all. 'It was all in the third person,' says Guy. '"So-and-so says you're not going to make it."'

In one bar they met the very explorer who had been critical of them to the Marines back in the UK, and had indirectly been responsible for Matt Kingston's removal from the expedition. 'He was quite sheepish,' says Guy. 'He was with somebody else we knew who had done other expeditions, so we went over and had a chat. I couldn't understand why this one chap was looking down at the floor and wouldn't really talk to us. I thought that maybe that was just a polar explorer type personality. But at the end of it, we were told his name, and it suddenly dawned on us it was this chap.'

'As we were walking away,' says Dags, 'Parker said, "Who was that?" When we told him, he said, "That's the bloody Marine who said you wouldn't be able to do the trip." After that he became a hate figure—our own personal hate figure, we never talked to anybody else about him.'

'When I was up there,' says Guy, 'and having a time when I was feeling particularly cold or miserable, I would just think, *Bugger that! X thinks we're not going to get there.* That drove me on. It's typically British. When somebody says you can't, you come back with the attitude that you can.'

*   *   *

Prince Harry flew in that night at 1 a.m. 'I think,' said Ed, 'it will be quite an eye-opener for him. He's coming out to an environment which we're quite practised in now, so I think it'll be quite a shock to his system. But he'll have a far lighter pulk than us, so he should have no problem keeping up. The four boys are absolutely chuffed he's coming. It means a huge amount to them. And for us it's great because just by coming here there's more attention to what we're doing. The wounded of our services matter a hell of a lot to him. But it'll be good crack. It's not often you go for a walk with the third in line to the

202

throne.'

'Speak for yourself,' said Dags.

The organisers, along with Alex Rayner and Henry Cookson, were at the airport to meet the Prince as he emerged from the plane in a black beanie hat, in the company of two close protection officers and his press secretary, Jamie Lowther-Pinkerton. Back at the hotel they all decided to go out for a welcoming nightcap at Kroa.

It was late and the place was quiet. As Harry and the group walked up to the bar, the barman jumped back and started swearing at him. 'Quite violently,' says Henry Cookson. 'Harry stopped in his tracks and you could see the security guards wondering what the hell was going on. It turned out that the barman had a severe allergy to apples. And Harry had walked into the bar chewing on an apple. We all cracked up. Harry was saying, "Normally it's people running towards me, not telling me to get away." I was laughing so much I set fire to myself. I was wearing a rather poncy yellow down jacket and I put the sleeve in a candle that was on the bar.'

In the morning the Prince met the rest of the team, went through his kit, checked that it fitted, and was shown what was in his pulk and how it was arranged. 'We were all quite unsure what to call him,' Guy admits. 'You don't want to just say, "All right, Harry." At the end of the day he is part of our royal family. So I said, "Hello, your Royal Highness" to start with. He called me a dick and said, "Call me Spike or H." He was very relaxed.'

The team spent a couple of hours putting sponsors' stickers on their pulks, as well as attaching the names for each sledge, which had been auctioned off individually at the Ice and

Diamonds Ball. Martin's, for example, was called 'William Horlick', Jaco's 'The Commander' and Steve's 'Ged's sledge'. Ed and Dags then had to pick up one more key element of kit: a hundred supermarket shopping bags which would act as vapour barriers inside their boots, preventing their socks from getting damp with sweat which would then freeze. 'We were very generously given these,' Ed wrote.

After lunch, H and the team put on their expedition kit and went for a practice ski, without pulks for this initial session. It was Harry's first time on Nordic skis and he took to them straight away. 'He listened well,' says Inge. 'When we told him to have lazy strides and to glide a bit more on every stride, he picked that up really easily. He has been very active in his life, so he has what I would call a motoric—a muscle intelligence. If you've done a lot of different sports you can learn things really easily because your body is smart, it understands new movements.'

At the top of the valley Harry needed more than mere motoric intelligence: the world's press were waiting for him. NBC anchor Bob Woodruff was quickly in there, wanting to know if Harry was going to be writing his best man's speech for the upcoming royal wedding while he was out on the ice.

Harry's look was patience personified. 'Writing a speech while I'm stuck in a tent in minus forty?' he answered. 'Well, if there's time I might give it some thought. But I think pens and paper are probably going to be safe until I get back home. I'm here for these guys and these guys alone. So that part of my life will be kept separate, probably.'

'He turns it on and off brilliantly,' says Ed. 'One minute he was there with us as a team member, the next he was speaking to the press very much as Prince Harry, with his responsibility as patron of Walking With The Wounded.'

'I was so impressed by his patience with the press,' says Inge. 'I would never have had it. But it's probably the wisest approach.'

'For us it was great,' says Guy. 'Because it went from them wanting to speak to us to them suddenly wanting to speak to him.'

Alfresco conference over, the team skied back, climbing a steep hill on their way.

On the last leg, Steve fell over and for a long minute or two lay prone in the snow. 'I had an awful feeling,' Ed wrote, 'that he had knackered his back completely. After walking a short way he seemed all right, but it had given me a fright.' Being a man down before they had even set off was not part of the plan.

Safely back at base, the team headed out to Kroa for dinner, followed by a few beers. 'Harry was probably quite relieved to be able to let his hair down,' says Alex Rayner. 'He's a member of the Army who had just done a lot of intensive training. I think he was gagging for a pint.'

*   *   *

Wednesday brought an experience Ed had been quietly dreading. Up on the ice, they were going to encounter open water leads, and if they couldn't jump over or walk round these, they would have to swim over them—temperatures of –45°C notwithstanding. In preparation for this troubling

205

eventuality, the team would be taking immersion suits, all-in-one waterproof survival outfits which are worn dry over existing clothing. Rune Malterud and Petter Nyquist, the two guides from Inge's Storm Adventures who would be accompanying the TV crew in a separate party behind the main expedition, had found a nice little patch of water in front of Longyearbyen airport, so the entire team, Alexis and Rob included, headed out to test the suits and learn the basics of wearing them.

'Guy and Steve went in first to much hilarity,' wrote Ed. 'Because the suits are so full of air which can't escape, the wearer bobs like a cork when in the water and it's difficult to manoeuvre. The key is to lie on one's back and do backstroke to move. With the water temperature being −1.5°C and the air temperature being −25°C, lying in the water was actually much warmer than standing on the ice—a strange sensation. Harry and I went in together after Guy and Steve. Harry managed to push me while I was plucking up courage to leap in! It was an extraordinary sensation. I felt so buoyant and it was hugely easy to get out. In fact all my fears were completely unfounded and it was a piece of cake. This gave me huge confidence should we need to use them next week.'

'It went up my nose,' Harry gasped to Ed, as he rolled around in the icy water. 'But it had to be done. Quite tight on the balls,' he added, audibly.

The press, needless to say, were on hand throughout, and pictures of Harry grinning as he bobbed around in his orange suit made the pages of most of the tabloids the next day. MIND MY CROWN JEWELS read the headline in the *Daily Mail*, making the most of the Prince's off-the-cuff comment.

206

ABC's Bob Woodruff was right behind the team, leaping in himself to get the feel of what it was like. 'Hey, Prince!' he shouted after Harry. 'Was I insane to do that?'

'You tell me,' replied His Royal Highness.

After their swim the soldiers were driven up to the Governor of Longyearbyen's rifle range for a briefing from the local police about the threat of polar bears. There followed a practice session with the flare guns and rifles they would be taking with them on the expedition. 'If we encounter polar bears,' said Ed, 'they're likely to be very hungry. If so, maybe the first thing they'll go for is the food in our pulks, but we really don't want to be messing around.'

'Especially the ones from eighty-nine degrees northward,' said Steve. 'There's not a lot of food up there and they've got an awesome sense of smell. They can smell us from three or four miles away. Obviously they're natural hunters, so they're going to come looking for food.'

Guy, as always, was practical: 'There's definitely a risk, otherwise we wouldn't be here doing this. But I think if we saw a bear it would be more excitement than fear, because we've got the means to deal with it. Interestingly, chatting to the guys here, they're saying that of the three incidents they had last year, two could have been prevented by people using their flares properly.'

That night the Prince and his close protection officers spent a night in a tent on the snow, in order to experience a little of what he would be going into. Henry Cookson shared a tent with the officers while Inge was in with Harry, as he would be once they were out on the ice. 'We went through the tent routines,' says Inge. 'I explained to him how the stove worked. We cut off some pieces of the sleeping mattress and he insulated the eating bowl which he used.' Then they wrote their names and drew pictures on the tent roof, something which Inge often did on expeditions. 'In Norway,' says Inge, 'with our social democracy we are all so equal that nobody thinks twice about somebody being royal. Harry was just one of the guys, though sometimes he had to play a role. He is born into something really big.'

As they melted snow for water and cooked and ate their rehydrated meal, they chatted; in particular about any worries Harry might have about the upcoming ordeal. 'The main concern I raised,' Harry says, 'was about the mentality within the British forces: that when, if you're tabbing, you feel yourself becoming man down, then you don't say anything, you truck on, because you don't want to slow anyone else down. Eventually you drop and that happens a lot during training. But obviously in an environment like this you've got to be honest with yourself and honest with the group. Inge has apparently spoken to all the guys and said, "Look, gone are the days of trying to be Mr Tough Guy. If you have a problem, or even a niggle, you talk about and share the pain because otherwise you're not going to survive." So that put my mind at rest. Because my only fear, apart obviously from parts of my body dropping off from frostbite, is that I don't want to slow them down. So long as I don't get in the way, and I muck in and do my bit for the team, then it's job well done as far as I'm concerned.'

At 8 a.m. Alex Rayner was on hand with the press pack, who were inevitably eager to see how the royal camping night had gone. But as they arrived there was no sign of movement, just two zipped-up tents, side by side. 'I went up to the tent,' said Alex, and I could hear them all gossiping and chatting inside. I said, "Harry, we're here."

'"Who's that?" he said.

'"It's Alex."

'"God, are you here with the press already?"

'"Yeah. Sorry."

'The little zip opened a fraction and an eye appeared. Then it zipped shut again and we all stood in the cold for about half an hour. It was pretty chilly. Ben Fogle was reporting for one of the American networks and he was going, "This is frostbite weather."

'Finally Harry came out with Inge. He was wearing this flappy, dog-eared hat and they asked him how his night had been, what he'd had for breakfast, that kind of thing.

'"Does he snore?" one journalist asked Inge. Harry's head jerked up under these flappy ears as he waited for the answer.

'"No," said Inge, "it's more of a mewling sound."'

There was laughter all round.

* * *

It was now Thursday 31 March, a day away from their scheduled departure. The pulks had been packed and unpacked to exhaustion point, each individual's kit had been tailored and adapted, the boys were more than ready for the off. Inge had managed to book them on to the first possible flight of the polar expeditioning season. But then came disappointing news. Their departure time had slipped by twenty-four hours, to Saturday 2 April. 'Hopefully this won't happen again,' wrote Ed. 'We understand that the site for the runway at Barneo has been identified and the Russians are starting to prepare it. We hope to be on the second flight in—the first technical flight checks that the runway is OK for landing! It's beginning to get boring here. Today has been very slow with little to do apart from checking kit again and adapting things further. Time to go!'

With no immediate departure to look forward to, the boys went out on the town again. Jaco had picked up a cold from Steve and peeled off to bed early, but the rest carried on in the hotel lobby, having a merry time into the small hours—at one point, vodka was drunk from Guy's prosthetic leg. Barriers were breaking down.

*　　　*　　　*

Friday 1 April. Instead of flying north on a plane, the boys—and Harry—went for an awesome ride around Spitsbergen on a rescue helicopter, at one point swooping down low above some real live polar bears. If the others were feeling a little fragile after the previous night, Jaco was genuinely unwell. The cold he had caught from Steve was more like flu, and he now had a sore throat, a splitting headache, and was coughing continuously. He felt, he said, 'like the back end of a dog', but his main worry was that Ed might question whether he should still be on the trip. However dreadful he felt, Jaco was determined to go.

'Jaco is not feeling well,' wrote Ed. 'Seems to be

just a cold but he is looking pretty rough and we don't want him to spread it round the team. We are all starting to get cabin fever and need to get going. I feel the longer we stay here the more we lose our edge. After all the talk over the last few months, we do need to deliver. I just want to feel the weight of my pulk in my harness and to know the work has finally begun.'

That evening Inge arranged for the team to be given a briefing by Viktor Boyarsky, the Russian who ran Barneo. His assessment wasn't encouraging. The tractors which were used to clear the runway in the first place hadn't yet made it out of Murmansk, owing to poor weather. Even if they were landed on Barneo first thing, the earliest the expedition could now fly would be Sunday evening. None of this was good news. Prince Harry only had limited time. And with each day that passed, the team's task was growing harder because, come what may, they had to be off the ice by 25 April, the last day the helicopter would be allowed to land at Barneo before the camp packed up for the season.

Back in London, at the offices of Captive Minds (now dubbed 'Expedition HQ' by Alex Rayner), the staff were doing their best to field the numerous press calls. 'We created a dedicated expedition news wire,' says Marcus Chidgey. 'Thank God we did, because each time they were delayed, we were getting messages left, right and centre. "Has Harry gone yet?" "When's he going?" "Is it going wrong?" So we were able to send out images, videos and emails in one fell swoop rather than having to send them out bespoke. At the same time we were having to manage all the logistics of the delay. Rebooking hotel rooms, flights, shipping bits of kit around.'

'I asked the question,' says Alex, '"What if it all gets too late?" But the Clarence House people were clear. "Harry is adamant he's going out on the ice cap, whether it be for one night or five." There was no way he wasn't going to support his soldier mates in doing this.'

*   *   *

'It seems difficult at the moment to get into the right mindset,' Ed wrote on Saturday evening. 'I am apprehensive and want to get going. I am worried about being able to manage the constant cold (it's only −5° here today, almost shirtsleeve weather, the acclimatisation is working) and I still have concerns regarding the boys' injuries. But these can't be answered until we start. So let's crack on.'

Ed was particularly worried about Steve's injury, the one he couldn't see. 'We've got to trust him,' he said, 'to tell us when his back hurts. I can feel Martin's arm when it's cold. And Jaco's. We can see if Guy's stump's got any abrasions on it. But Steve's got to be honest with us. He's as determined as any of us to get to the Pole. I just hope he doesn't kid himself that his back is OK because he wants to get there and then he pushes it too far. Because obviously it will be not just to his own detriment but that of the team. We're not doing this as individuals—it's Walking With The Wounded getting to the North Pole. He's a fantastic guy, I only hope there isn't that little switch that could tick over and say, "I can make it" when he can't.'

Ed instincts were spot on, because Steve was in considerable pain that day: 'I think really

212

because we've been getting delayed day after day. We haven't been doing any physical activity, so the whole lack of movement and the lack of keeping my back supple has caught up with me. So today it's sore and very stiff.' Luckily, as Steve had discovered, Rune Malterud was a trained physiotherapist. 'So he's kindly agreed to do some stretching with me and hopefully that will square me away for tonight. It's just unfortunate he won't be able to do it when we're up on the ice. But if we want to keep the unsupported tag he can't help.'

Sunday brought another delay. 'The runway has yet to be finished,' wrote Ed. 'Nothing to do except read and eat. We watched a movie. Very bored and frustrated.'

'A big concern for me,' said Martin, 'is the fact that it's essential for us to get a good distance covered, in order to prove that we did a full-length expedition and overcame the criticisms that certain people have of us.' Because of the Barneo end-of-season deadline, the planned length of the walk was having to be reduced with every day they waited.

Guy was in his room, about to sign an insurance disclaimer. 'It's quite funny,' he said. 'It goes along the lines of, "The Arctic Ocean is one of the most inhospitable regions of our planet . . . logistical problems are enormous . . . the weather ferocious and unpredictable, ice conditions are unstable, distances are immense, facilities scarce, safety and self-sufficiency are the paramount rules . . . we acknowledge and respect this . . . it is our obligation to warn all our clients that they, like us, and everyone else attempting to function in this extreme environment, are at the mercy of forces

213

more powerful than any of us."' He smiled. 'That's rather reassuring.'

The only member of the team who didn't object to the hold-up was Jaco, still coughing and spluttering with flu: 'We were all frustrated about the delay, we all wanted to get out there, but in a way it played to my advantage as well. It gave me a couple of days to recover a bit. It was literally the night before we set off that I finally had a decent night's sleep again.'

*   *   *

On Sunday evening there was a glimmer of hope, as the soldiers were instructed to deliver their pulks to Longyearbyen airport to be weighed.

'Then all these Russians appeared,' said Dags. 'With big smiles. "We have banquet for you," they were saying. "Please to come upstairs and watch lovely video." So we sat down in a room above the main hangar and they brought in plastic cups of tea, chocolate biscuits and tinned salami. It was revolting.

'"Lovely banquet," they kept saying, "Eat! Eat!"

'"I'm not that hungry, sorry."

'Then the owner of the airline came in and they put on a video of the Barneo Ice Camp. They presented Harry with a watch and insisted on kissing and hugging him. Poor Harry was looking more and more out of place. We were all going, "Kiss him! Kiss him!" It was great fun.'

Finally, on Monday morning, the team were given the green light. Barneo's ice runway was ready and they were to depart that afternoon, as soon as the six-hour round trip test flight returned.

A real danger: polar bear warning sign in Spitsbergen

Fully laden: Martin with his much heavier pulk (note the sponsor's sticker down left)

Royal duties: Prince Harry faces the Press on the Svalbard snow

The team test immersion suits in Svalbard

Prince Harry and the team pay careful attention to a briefing from Inge at the Basecamp Hotel in Longyearbyen

Final leg: the team with Prince Harry on the helicopter out from Barneo

Serious struggle: Jaco
negotiates a pressure
ridge with one pole

Getting the rhythm:
Prince Harry with his
pulk on the polar ice

Petter Nyquist/www.flashstudio.no

'We haven't trained for this': Martin pulls his pulk across a fiendish pressure ridge

Day 7: crossing a lead using a pulk as a bridge

Petter Nyquist/www.flashstudio.no

Dags enjoys a private message hidden in his Horlicks sachet

Inge Solheim

Robert Leveritt

Crimson hoops against the snow:
the camp at night

Pit stop: the team on one of their regular two-hourly
food breaks, Steve in foreground

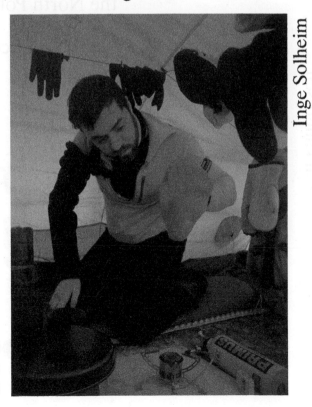

Martin tries to dry his
hat over one of the
Primus stoves

'It just happened': the team line up to advance on
the North Pole

'We've done it!': a new world record is set at the Pole

'We are flying out tonight,' wrote a relieved Ed. 'In the morning I made my final call to Harriet to say goodbye. It was horrid and very painful and we both found it difficult. After hanging up I needed five minutes to sort myself out before going back into the room with the boys.'

'Hello, Harry here,' said the Prince on the audio blog that went out every day on the Walking With The Wounded website. 'All the boys are really excited to finally be going. We've been sitting around here for far too long now. Blue sky outside here at Svalbard, can't wait to get on the ice with the boys, shame I will now only be able to spend about two and a half days with them, but they are all really excited. The miles may have to be minimised by a little bit, but it's not going to make a difference to what these guys are doing, it's truly inspirational, so let's keep the support going.'

The afternoon and evening passed slowly. A 4 p.m. departure was delayed till 6 p.m. Finally, at 9 p.m., the team drove out to the little airport and put themselves through security, which, under EU rules, was as stringent on this final flight to the ice cap as anywhere else in Europe. No liquids, no sharp objects, even if all the luggage was going to be in the same place as the seats and they were already carrying rifles and flare guns for the polar bears.

At 11.35 p.m. they boarded. The Antonov AN-47 was a short, squat aircraft with wings and jets mounted high on the fuselage. Inside it was considerably more basic than the average plane. There was just one window in the cramped passenger section, and the twenty or so seats wouldn't stay upright, tilting back to squash the legs

215

of the person behind. Some passengers had no seats at all, and squatted at the back next to the luggage and cargo, which was piled haphazardly to the roof, held in by precarious-looking webbing. 'The safety aspect,' Ed wrote, 'made me smile quietly to myself, as well as saying a short prayer. Our safety briefing was the loadmaster turning around as the engines fired up, smiling broadly and shouting "Take off" over the noise. Oh God!'

It was warm inside the plane and the three Norwegian guides fell asleep almost as soon as they were in the air. Flu-bound Jaco made a cushion with his down jacket and had soon nodded off too. The rest of the team made some attempt at dozing. After an hour or so an in-flight meal of sorts was handed out. 'Our air hostess was called Sergei and he had a moustache,' says Guy. 'He gave us a disgusting Russian sandwich.'

'I had very much the same feeling,' he adds, 'as when we last went from Brize Norton into Afghan: that sense of flying into the unknown. You're thinking, *What's it going to be like? Have I prepared enough?* Actually I was probably more nervous this time, because expectations were higher. Once Harry was on board, the whole expedition had a lot more exposure than we thought it would, which put the pressure on massively. There's nothing like setting yourself up for a fall. I suppose it's vanity slightly, not wanting to fail in public. We suddenly had a lot of people watching, whereas with operations in the past it had just been a few friends and family.'

For Martin and Steve, sitting by the single bubble-shaped window, there was a good view out over the polar terrain: a vast sheet of whiteness, broken here and there by the snaking black lines of open water leads. After two and a half hours they were there, the whine of the engines changing pitch dramatically as they circled in to land. Down on the ice there was thick fog. The plane didn't make it first time, rising sharply up and round for a second pass. This wasn't successful either, and the engine screamed as the plane rose in the air again. Steve, who was not a fan of enclosed vehicles at the best of times, clenched his fists till his knuckles were white.

On the third attempt they did hit the runway—hard, the port wing inches from the ice. 'As we landed,' says Steve, 'I could see the tip of the wing probably a metre off the ground.' The plane bounced ten feet into the air before thumping back down again, the engines exerting massive thrust. Up front in the cockpit, filming, Alexis Girardet watched as the pilot wiped his brow with his hand and muttered a Russian expletive. Inside the main cabin the Russians cheered. 'It wasn't hairy at all,' says Inge. 'A totally normal flight. No problem. The runway was smooth.'

'And here we were,' wrote Ed, 'finally standing on the Arctic Ocean, surrounded by chattering Russians at two in the morning. We were all wrapped up in our big down jackets, but the temperature had clearly dropped.'

'It's the same feeling,' says Dags, 'as when you leave the UK and arrive somewhere hot on holiday. When you step off the plane you suddenly feel that heat hit you. It was like that here, only in reverse, with the cold. You get off and think, *Whoah, flaming hell! This is going to be my home for the next twenty-five days.* We were suddenly flooded with Russians taking photos. One chap had a full set of

217

gold teeth. And they're so hardy. We were in our big down jackets, face masks and gloves. This guy was standing there in a pair of combat trousers, no gloves.'

As the Barneo baggage handlers hurried to unload the plane, the soldiers moved in. 'They wanted to get the plane off again,' says Jaco, 'and everything ready to go, so they were throwing stuff around, dropping it all. It was some of their equipment first, but once it came to the pulks we didn't want any damage, so we had to slow them down. We stepped in and unloaded our stuff ourselves.'

They then dragged their equipment over to the helicopters and collected the final necessary ingredient: fuel, in five-litre containers, which went in the back of the relevant pulks. There was a little kerfuffle over how many helicopters would be needed to take them out to their starting point at 87° 44', a degree and a fraction further away from the Pole than Barneo. Originally the plan had been to walk three degrees; with the delay that had now been changed to 2.2 degrees, or around 165 miles.

After a few firm words from Inge, extraneous Russians and royal bodyguards were left behind at Barneo, while the core team took to the air in a Hip Mi-8 helicopter. 'I lay on top of one of the pulks,' wrote Ed, 'and tried to sleep. Even though it was broad daylight outside, it was the middle of the night and I was feeling very tired. After about an hour I sat up and looked out of the window. The cloud had cleared and there below us was the sea ice, stretching as far as the eye could see. It was a breathtakingly beautiful sight. From our lofty position, it looked fairly flat too. I was to

218

learn shortly that this elevated view did not entirely reflect the nature of the ice.'

The helicopter finally landed at 4.30 a.m. Pulks were pulled out and at last they had arrived, standing in their orange down jackets in the middle of nowhere. 'When I first got off the helicopter,' said Guy, 'the feeling was a bit like when I got hit in Afghan. That sense of, *Christ, where am I?*'

'OK. Good luck, guys!' shouted the Russian pilot, running for the chopper. Up in the air he circled once over the team and then made a beeline back for Barneo, an ever-smaller dot above the vast empty whiteness.

'Watching the helicopter disappear over the horizon was a strange sensation,' wrote Ed. 'I felt very small and very alone.'

'I didn't feel alone at all,' says Dags. 'I had Dog chirping in my ear.'

17

'WE HAVEN'T TRAINED FOR THIS'

Originally the plan had been to ski for a couple of hours before pitching camp. But everyone was tired, so it was agreed they would get the tents up straight away, melt some snow for a brew, then snatch a couple of hours' sleep before cracking on at 10 a.m.

'You see that elevation where you have a little bit thicker snow,' Inge told them. 'That's the easy place to put up camp because we can put our skis down for tent pegs, OK?' He looked down. 'This is good old ice, very solid, probably one and a half, two metres thick.'

The team hadn't put up tents since Beitostølen in January, so they struggled with the task. 'It took us a while to get settled in,' says Jaco. 'It was a skill fade. If you don't do something every day, you lose the skill.'

It was 5 a.m. and the sun was shining brightly. Once the Officers' Mess had got their tent up, Guy, Dags and Martin felt almost warm in their down jackets.

'Shall we leave the end of our tent open?' Guy said, 'because it'll probably get too hot tonight...'

So the end-flap was left undone; and an hour later Guy woke frozen to the marrow. 'We got it so wrong. It was incredibly cold. I was thinking, *If it's this bad now, what's it going to be like five days in?*' Guy lay tense and shivering in his bag, snatching five minutes' sleep here and there.

DAY 1. Tuesday 5 April. 87° 49' 54"— evening position. Temperature –22°C still air –35°C with wind chill. Distance covered 6½ miles—1½ miles SE drift.

The rest of the team were woken at 10 a.m. by a shout from Inge. In Ed's tent, now known informally as the Sergeants' Mess, Steve was the first to get going. The inside of the tent was covered with white frost, but somehow he made it out of his sleeping bag and fired up the cooker. Then, even as the moisture from a night spent inside a plastic vapour barrier steamed off his T-shirt and long johns in the icy cold air, he hurried to pull on his other layers. By the time he had been outside, collected some snow on the shovel and boiled it up in the pan to make tea, he was starting to feel human again. 'It's all excitement now,' he said, 'the anxiety's gone. I can't wait to get the first day done.'

Ed was next. 'How to describe the place we found ourselves waking up in?' he wrote later. 'The bright white of the snow and ice blinds one, but within the white there are a plethora of colours: aquamarine, yellow, lime, light brown. It's a quite extraordinary place, an icy desert, I would think something like the surface of the moon. Imagine somewhere completely barren, with boulders strewn all over the place.'

'The view was breathtaking,' says Jaco. 'The sheer vastness of it all. I just stood there looking. For the first time seeing these blocks of ice: the colours in them, the blues and the greens. A video can't capture them, it's only what the eye can see. The shapes and sizes as well. Some of the blocks look as if they must have been cut by someone, because they are perfectly squared. Others are triangular.'

Impressed though they all were by the stark beauty of the place, once the team had taken their GPS reading, they realised the news wasn't good. During their short sleep, they had drifted a mile and a half south-east, taking them away from the Pole. This was not what Inge had planned—or expected. At this time of year, the predominant ice drift was east–west, so he had deliberately arranged for the helicopter to land them on the Siberian side of the polar cap, to make the most of the prevailing conditions. 'I wasn't worried,' he says. 'More curious. We had a time buffer. If that negative drift had continued all week we would just have had to work two more hours every day and use the whole

221

of our time.' For now there was nothing to be done except set off and see how much ground they could cover in what was left of the day.

They were finally on the move at noon, some time after Inge would have liked. For a few minutes progress seemed easy. 'My friend Mr Captain Guy Disney here and I,' said Dags, 'are just discussing the fact that the sleds are gliding really well. On the Arctic snow. If it's like this the whole way it'll be brilliant.'

But after half an hour they encountered their first pressure ridge. As they contemplated the wall of ice boulders created by the collision of two ice floes, the true nature of their challenge started to become clear. 'You are presented with a pile of rubble that's like an old-fashioned rampart,' says Ed. 'Broken, higgledy-piggledy blocks of various sizes, some the size of a semi-detached house, all at different angles. At some points it may be fifteen to twenty feet high, at others only five, but then it might be thirty feet deep.' Sometimes these ridges conceal thin ice or even open water within; they can run for miles, so there is no easy way round them. They have to be climbed over, and of course the 70–100 kg pulk has to go with you. 'So,' says Guy, 'you are suddenly having to lug something that weighs more than yourself up and over this huge pile of ice.'

The two men who had lost an arm had extra problems. 'The other guys,' says Jaco, 'had the ability to balance themselves and use both ski poles. But me and Martin really had to jiggle our bodies around to balance ourselves—and to get the pulk over some of the rubble.'

'Without a pole on my right hand side,' says

Martin, 'I couldn't stabilise myself. You can use your core to some degree, and your leg strength too, but some of the blocks are at such an angle and you've got so little hold on them, especially if they're pure ice, that if you start going to the right, you reach a point of no return. And that's it. You know it's coming. You've just got to accept your fate. Down you go—*bang*. There's a half-second when you know you're falling, and then you have to prepare for impact.'

'In the beginning,' says Inge, 'I found the routes over the ridges and they followed. Then I stopped and gave them some little hints: "Here, it's easier to do it like this." I think some of them wanted me to explain more, but I wanted them to help each other and find out how to do it themselves. I was surprised at how long it took some of them to learn from their mistakes. Not having an arm is a factor they know about, so after a while you should learn a particular way is not good for you—you have to do it another way.'

Jaco had other problems too. He found his warm breath was rising up to fog his sunglasses, and the neoprene nose cover he had sewn on beneath wasn't working well either; he kept having to pause to adjust his face covering. Before they had even stopped for the day's first break, Inge came over to him to point out the early signs of frost nip on his cheek: 'I was like, oh my God, how can I?' says Jaco. 'I've only started this trek an hour and a half ago.' Inge blew warm air on to his skin to get the blood flowing back into it, then made sure Jaco wore a Skidoo mask over his face and a hood over his head. But even though he was now adequately protected, the shock stayed with him: 'It plays on your subconscious. I could feel my balance and my technique going too. I was thinking, *Bloody hell, I've still got twenty odd days of this to go.*'

Jaco wasn't the only one having problems keeping his face effectively covered against the cold. 'I tried goggles the first day,' says Steve, 'with a neoprene wind stop. That didn't work too well. I had imagined it would be a big gale of a wind, but it was only a small breeze. But it was so cold, it bit into you. It came consistently from the right hand side, so I found that side of my face was stinging constantly. In the end I found the best thing was to pull up the tube of elasticated cloth I had round my neck. I pulled it up my face and cut a hole in it for my mouth.'

Guy had a rabbit-skin hat, which at least kept his ears and head warm. But he found his neoprene face mask restrictive. 'It was slightly too tight and not comfy. It would slip and you would breathe into it and the whole of your mouth would freeze up, which was pretty miserable.' His goggles were steaming up too, and he soon sacked them, to use Army terminology.

'I hold my breath when I put my sunglasses on,' says Inge, 'and then I breathe out against the wind. When I walk my goggles are clear, because I have been keeping the moist air away. I told them how they could do it, and they tried but they couldn't get it to work. It's all about experience and accepting the cold.'

'I spent most of the day,' wrote Ed, 'trying to get the right combination of gloves, working out what hats or head bands to wear, whether I needed a face mask, trying to stop my goggles freezing over from the condensation of my sweat . . . in fact it was just like the first day at school when everything is alien. I found the environment harsher than I had imagined, and my initial thoughts were that this was going to be far harder than expected.'

As pressure ridge followed pressure ridge, and with no let-up in the bitter cold, the seriousness of what they had let themselves in for was coming home to each member of the team. When they finally stopped to camp that evening they were all demoralised. 'I think everyone's had a bit of a shock to the system,' said Martin, 'with the temperature and the difficulty of pulling the kit over this type of terrain. Everything Inge's had us training on to date has been nothing like as challenging as this.' From noon to 6 p.m. they had covered only six and a half miles. Taking into account the previous night's negative drift they had moved just five miles closer to the Pole. They had a hundred and sixty miles to walk. It wasn't looking good.

Tired, and still out of practice with their routines, they were slower than they should have been setting up camp. Then, just as Ed and Steve had got their tent in position, a pole snapped. One of the aluminium sockets that held the sections together had split. Back in Longyearbyen, Ed had asked Henry for a spare set of poles, but they had never materialised. Now he cursed both Henry and himself for not chasing the matter up. Here they were on the first night, with no spare poles and possibly no tent.

Fortunately Inge had a set of spares in his pulk. One was the perfect size. The drama was over, for the time being. Fumbling in their big gloves, Ed and Steve were able to undo the length of elastic that ran down the centre of the pole, thread in the new pole and get their tent up.

Over in the Officers' Mess the tent had gone up fine, but once they'd started heating their meal, the guys were worried.

'Dags,' Martin said, 'we haven't trained for this. If it's going to be as bad as this every day we're not going to make it.'

Looking at it baldly, Simon had to agree. 'I did the maths in my head,' he says, 'Guy and Martin did it too, and we thought, *Shit, if this is what we're doing each day we're not going to get there.* At that point there was a sort of panic.'

DAY 2. Wednesday 6 April. 88° 01' 34".
Distance covered 12 miles. Nearly 3 miles
N drift overnight. Temperature –22°C still
air, –35°C wind chill. Sunny to start, cloudy
middle of day, very low contrast.

'First thing,' wrote Ed, 'Dags came into our tent concerned about the small distance we had covered yesterday. He and Guy and Dog were worried that we had bitten off more than we could chew. He wondered if we should look to using the helicopter that was coming in to collect PH to put us a little nearer to the Pole, so that we had a better chance of success. If we only cover six and a half miles a day, he is right, we are not going to succeed, but I felt we just needed to settle down and see how we get on over the next couple of days before we make any decision like that.'

Unbeknown to Ed, the situation had in any case changed a little since the previous evening. Overnight they had drifted almost three miles, but this time in a northerly direction, just as Inge had

226

planned. Add to that the six and a half miles they had covered and things were looking up.

Inge had woken the camp at 7 a.m., but they weren't on their way, much to his frustration, until 9.30. 'The first day you can test out,' he says, 'how fast can I do this or that, and if you're fifteen minutes over, it's OK. But if you're fifteen minutes over the next day, you should have woken up fifteen minutes earlier. It's not right and it's not nice and it's not part of the plan that we prepared for that some people finish and are ready half an hour earlier than others. That means that someone will have to wait in the cold. I have no sympathy or tolerance for that, and I let them know that.'

Despite not having trained anything like as hard as the others, Prince Harry seemed in an upbeat mood this morning. 'I'm starting to get into a rhythm now,' he said, 'so hopefully today will just come naturally. The sun is shining from a clear blue sky, there's a strong westerly wind, it's a good time to be on the frozen sea. I've got some sweet tunes in my ear, so excuse me if I start hopping. I'm about twenty yards behind Stephen, we're all in a single line, all wearing red jackets, black trousers, all for one good cause.

'I'll tell you what, the persistence and determination of these guys is absolutely astonishing. That's the only thing that will keep them going, driving across this incessant, continuous ice field. When I took my clothes off last night I was completely soaking wet, I'd been sweating so much. I was lying there listening to music, trying to dry out, thinking to myself, *If I had a choice, would I want to be here any longer?* I can't really answer that question until the end of today, I don't think. Part of me says yes, part of me says no.

'To summarise, it's very cold and very white. Inge and I were talking about it last night in the tent. There are elements of walking across the moon. Then Stephen said to me this morning, "Look up in the sky, you could be anywhere." I disagree, there's only one place you could be—that's on a floating ocean. Now I can see what looks like the iceberg that sunk the *Titanic* up ahead. One, two, three of them. Huge.'

Five minutes later the team had skied up to their biggest pressure ridge yet, a mass of boulders several metres high.

'This one is quite fresh,' said Inge. 'It probably only formed yesterday and it still hasn't frozen up properly, so we have to avoid an open lead in the middle. It's quite challenging. Slow and steady is best in every way, because you can easily get your foot trapped and then the pulk could run over you and break your legs. So please, don't try and take it too fast.' Following instructions the team took their skis off, strapped them on top of their pulks and clambered over the ice rubble in their boots, helping each other to pull their sledges as they went.

'Every time you try and get into a rhythm,' said Harry, 'you come up against another pressure ridge.'

After two hours it was time for their first break, and now that they were starting to settle into a routine, it was painfully clear that Jaco was struggling. The normal procedure for each team member at a break was to stop, unzip the front of his pulk, take out his down jacket to keep his body temperature up, then sort out his flask of hot drink and his snack bag and start on the important business of getting some calories in. But for one-armed Jaco, this was all taking too long. By the time he'd taken off his face mask and unzipped his pulk to find his down jacket, put it on and located his snack bag, the others were ready to move off again. 'I find it a massive struggle,' he said. 'It's so much more difficult doing everything with one arm in this temperature. Especially when the wind's blowing. Especially trying to do something with a glove on.' It had become apparent that he would need some help, which tent mates Ed and Steve were more than happy to provide. 'Me and Ed quickly worked out a system,' says Steve, 'where he would do one stop, I would do the next, and so on. Unzip Jaco's pulk for him while he's doing his harness, get his warm jacket out, put it on. Then he would sit down and get his food out of his bag and unscrew his flask with one hand.'

'Steve and Ed are absolute heroes,' said Jaco. 'They're helping me a lot. At the breaks one of them will come over to me, help me out, help me get my kit on, get everything ready to go and then we'll just crack on.'

During breaks the team downed coffee, hot soup and a high calorie drink called Mountain Fuel, which came in blackcurrant or tropical flavours. Some of the snacks they had brought, though, were not quite so enjoyable in these low temperatures. 'Jelly beans taste like little pebbles because they're so frozen,' said Steve. 'They pretty much take your teeth out.' Even Dags's favourite Green and Black's wasn't what it should be. 'In UK temperatures it's absolutely the best chocolate you can imagine, but when you go to minus thirty the cocoa gets really dry—it's like eating mud.'

Henry Cookson's carefully-sourced nut balls were also causing problems. 'They were quite tasty,' says Jaco, 'but what we soon found is that they made your stomach work a bit too much, which obviously wasn't so good. In the end everybody was just chucking them around. There was a Hansel and Gretel trail to the North Pole of nut balls.'

'They became missiles,' says Dags. 'You would sit down to have your break and a nut ball would go *Froo-o-o-o-o-m*, whizzing right past you.'

After the first monster pressure ridge, things became easier; the terrain was flatter today and the team sped along. Guy was settling into a routine between the two-hourly breaks. 'It's amazing when you stop for a bite to eat, you have half an hour or so when you're absolutely flying along. Then you have a bit of a lull again, then you go into the last half-hour and you pick up again, because you know you're about to get a break, which helps a lot.' The extreme temperature, however, was taking its toll on his leg. 'In this cold, I'm getting more phantom pain than I've ever had in the past. Sensations that feel like electric shocks. There's no rhyme or reason why they happen, they just suddenly kick off.'

During their third session the soldiers crossed the eighty-eighth degree, meaning that they now had only two degrees left to walk. This was more like it! If they continued at this pace the Pole was well within their grasp. By the end of the day, they had covered twelve miles. The team felt recharged and upbeat and the mood was celebratory. 'It's been a cracking day,' Dags reported on the blog. 'I don't think we could have asked for more. Lots of miles covered and spirits are high. Captain Guy

Disney, bless his cotton socks, has just produced a single malt to go with our delicious supper.'

'I think we all felt a bit despondent this morning,' Ed told the outside world, 'because we had a disappointing day yesterday, but we're right back on course—a mile or two ahead of target, in fact, which is fantastic.'

There was one notable exception. Despite his flying start, Harry was, he admitted to Jaco, 'absolutely knackered'. 'He came up to me,' Jaco says, 'and said, "I just haven't done the training you guys have done." It was so great of him to openly admit that.'

Not that it should have mattered. A helicopter was due to fly in that very evening to pick Harry up for the transfer to Barneo, Spitsbergen and then home, in plenty of time for his brother's wedding. But when Inge called Barneo on the satellite phone, the news came through that the runway at the temporary ice camp had developed a crack, so no planes were going in or out at all. Even the Prince would have to wait another twenty-four hours. 'I had to tell him he wasn't going home that night,' said Dags. 'He didn't look best chuffed.'

Back in the real world, meanwhile, all hell was kicking off. 'I got the nod that night,' says Alex Rayner, 'that there was a problem at Barneo. So I spoke immediately to Clarence House, who were fully in the loop with us. In the morning we were told it was going to take twenty-four to twenty-eight hours to repair. So I issued a statement to the media saying there was a crack in the runway and Harry would be spending more time on the ground with the team. Then I obviously contacted my man at the *Evening Standard*, who stuck it on the front

231

page. But the story ran everywhere. I had an email from an old colleague of ours in Australia saying it was all over the papers there.

'There are certain expeditions where you're struggling for something to say. That wasn't an issue here. Rather than dramatising anything we just had to put across the facts. Actually the news had already leaked out, because there was supposed to be a flight over the Pole that morning for the North Pole Marathon and it hadn't gone, so the phone was already going hot.

'All the time we were dealing with it I had Jamie Lowther-Pinkerton's words ringing in my ear. "What happens if something goes wrong and you don't get him back for the royal wedding?" Had we gone for the royal wedding week, which we very nearly did, it would have been an extremely close call.'

DAY 3. Thursday 7 April. 88° 14' 12". Distance covered 12 miles + 2 miles N drift overnight. Temperature –23°C still air, –35°C wind chill. Clear sunny day.

Ed woke at 4.45 a.m. to hear 'a rather strange noise, like two pieces of polystyrene being rubbed together'. He rolled over sleepily and ignored it, but once they were up and about, two hours later, he and Guy found a long crack in the ice. 'It goes through the corner of our tent,' said Guy, 'which is quite worrying, because you can see it's split these tents apart. It's definitely getting wider because it was only a couple of millimetres when we first saw it. Now it's half a centimetre. It makes you realise nowhere is completely safe, because Inge has told us this is good old sea ice, as thick as it gets, and it's still splitting.'

Inge inspected the crack and was able to reassure the team. 'If you look across this ice field,' he said, there are probably fifty cracks like this. It happens all the time. Sometimes it's pressure from the sides and sometimes the ice is just stretched. It's only if they get a lot bigger that it's an issue. There's no drama with this one.'

Ed had in any case endured a bad night. 'Coughing all the time,' he wrote in his diary. 'I think I have brought Jaco's lurgy with me. Only had three to four hours' sleep and started the day feeling rotten and running a temperature.' Jaco had slept badly too, still suffering from the symptoms of flu, and 'really, really cold'. 'When we stopped last night,' he said, 'it took me an hour just to warm up. I had to get some warm food into me, and some warm drink, and then I got straight into my doss bag.'

Out on the ice, there were more pressure ridges. During a break Guy was asked by Alexis how many he thought they had crossed: 'I said I thought about thirty. He said, "I've been counting and it's more like two hundred."' Martin was still struggling with each and every one, falling repeatedly as he tried to negotiate his way across the slippery surfaces with a single ski pole. At one point, as he slammed down face first on to a block of ice, he heard a crack and thought for a moment his expedition was over. But he managed to right himself again and realised he was OK. 'Most of the time when I fell I laughed,' he says, 'but when you've fallen five or six times in a day it stops being funny and becomes quite annoying and painful. But you just have to suck it up and crack on.'

'The ice is like concrete,' says Ed. 'It's not lovely soft snow. If you smack into it, it bloody hurts. So it was tough on Jaco and Martin. But you have to let them get on with it. You couldn't spend all your time saying, "Are you all right?" Because that would have pissed them off.'

Just before the third break of the day, they were crossing a ridge when Jaco fell hard to his left side. 'I was trying to protect my stump and I fell straight on to my elbow and shoulder on the other side. I hurt it badly. I rotated my shoulder around throughout the whole day, because it started stiffening up a bit. That evening in the tent I was getting pins and needles in my right hand—that numb, dead effect. But I didn't tell anybody about it because I didn't want anyone else to worry about it.'

'I can tell Jaco's struggling at the minute,' said Martin. 'He's a hard boy, a tough soldier, and he's gone quiet. He's done that because something's wrong.'

'The first couple of sessions pulling were ghastly,' Ed wrote, 'and I felt terrible, but by 1 p.m. I started feeling much better. The walking is the best bit of the day. You get warm and start eating up the miles, with the Pole getting ever closer, and I was beginning to enjoy the opportunity to spend the day with my own thoughts and very few interruptions.' Of all the team, he was the only one without an iPod. 'I didn't want it to get in the way,' he says. 'I loved the silence. I spent a lot of time thinking about things you wouldn't normally get time to think about: children's first days at school, holidays we've had. I went right back to my first day at prep school. I was a bit anal, probably. I woke up in the morning and I thought, "I'm going to think about this and this today." And by and large I did. It made the time fly by.

'I also thought a huge amount about my family. That was an added dynamic I hadn't been anticipating. We were away from home for four and a half weeks, but I really missed them. On the ice, in the lower moments, it would slightly compound all that. Simon had warned me. He said it was something the boys wouldn't experience and we would.'

By the end of the day they had covered another twelve miles. Once again, they were two miles ahead of schedule. 'But I'm under no illusions,' said Guy. 'This is just going to get harder and harder. The injuries are going to start taking a toll on us. Without injury you can grizz it through to some extent. But if something goes, it'll be game over.'

*   *   *

The crack in Barneo's runway had been sorted out and, a day late, a helicopter arrived to pick up Prince Harry. On board were Viktor Boyarsky, Harry's two close protection officers, and Jon Haldorsen, another of Inge's guides, who was staying at Barneo to act as a facilitator in case of emergency. 'Harry said "Good luck!"' says Ed, 'and gave me a hug. He gave all the boys a hug. I said, "Thank you very much for joining us." He said, "Thank you very much for asking me." I thought that showed he was a humble chap.'

'We all said our goodbyes,' says Jaco, 'which was quite sad. Harry was part of the team by this stage.

It was great to see the guys on the chopper, some other people, after a few days. They were all so proud of us, telling us how well we were doing, that everyone was following us now. It raised the bar a little bit, made us realise how important it was for us to reach the Pole. Then they were gone and that was us alone for the next seventeen days.'

Once in the helicopter, Viktor had a little surprise for the Prince. In the 24-hour daylight they sped on over the ice cap and dropped down to land for a few minutes at ninety degrees north. 'Sadly I think it was covered with fog when he got there,' says Ed. 'But at least he stood on the Pole.'

Ever happy to play the role of reliable, normal bloke, Harry now acted as the team's courier, taking with him the memory cards from Alexis's camera containing the TV material shot so far. When he arrived back in London, they were picked up by bike and delivered to TwoFour. Over at Expedition HQ, Alex Rayner was a little disappointed that Alexis and Rob hadn't sent more stills. 'We were saying, "I wish the guys had sent us some pictures." Then I got a phone call from Clarence House. "Oh, by the way, Harry has found another card in his washing." Brilliant! They were all there.'

*   *   *

Back on the ice, after three days of hard walking the team were all suffering from blisters. Steve's and Jaco's feet were particularly bad. That night they went into Inge's tent to have the blisters treated. 'They were quite painful and sore,' says Jaco, 'but still manageable.' He cut some of them with one of

236

the sharp blades on his Gerber multiple penknife and left others as they were. Then he applied Compeed blister plasters, which contain antiseptic gel and are specially shaped so they fit snugly round the toes.

In the Officers' Mess, meanwhile, Dags had been doing the cooking, and had made a right mess. 'The food went everywhere,' said Guy. 'The tent was in a shit state. The way he was cooking just wasn't working. The moment you lift the lid off the boiling water, steam comes into the tent, which then freezes. Martin and I looked at each other and said, "It can't work like this."'

'All that happened that night,' said Dags, 'was that I took the pot off the cooker and accidentally put it on a chocolate chip snack that was in the vestibule. Which meant that the ice melted and the pot got chocolate chip on the bottom of it, and when I put it back on the cooker the whole place smelt of chocolate chip. Then I leant over the cooker and my coat caught fire. It really wasn't that exciting.'

Careful not to offend Dags, Guy quietly took over the cooking. He and Martin worked out a routine whereby, having boiled the water in the pot, they would take it outside into the tent porch to pour it into their flasks, which would then go back into the tent. 'So you've only got a small aperture letting out steam instead of a much bigger pot.'

'This is how you work out your different duties in the tent,' says Dags. 'My view is that if you see someone is a particular stickler for something, you let them do it, and you go and do something else. I was quite happy to hand over the duty of cooking, because it was a miserable task.'

237

In Ed's tent, by contrast, admin was shaping up nicely under the efficient leadership of Sergeant Steve Young; and that evening their rehydrated meal was properly hot for the first time. But they too were grappling with the moisture that rose from the boiling water, then froze inside the tent overnight. There was an extra problem: Ed's clothes, which he was trying to dry over the cooker. 'Ed's a very, very sweaty man,' said Steve, 'so we've got a lot of kit to dry out.'

'What I find at the end of the day,' said Ed, 'is within my middle and outer layer I have a thin crust of ice. And I haven't seen any book that says it's good to have a thin crust of ice in your clothing.'

'It's very humorous for the rest of us,' said Steve. 'After a day's walk Ed looks like Frosty the Snowman.'

Before he rolled over that night, Ed took a couple of sleeping pills, in the hope of a decent night's sleep, something which had eluded him since Longyearbyen.

DAY 4. Friday 8 April. 88° 24' 73". Distance covered 12 miles + 1 mile N drift overnight. Temperature –24°C still air, –28°C wind chill. Clear blue all day, little wind.

It was not to be. Both Ed and Jaco had another dreadful night, constantly bumping into each other in the tiny space, coughing, lying awake and listening to Steve's powerful Welsh snore. Ed now definitely had Jaco's flu; he was running a temperature and was full of phlegm. Jaco, meanwhile, was suffering secretly with his bruised elbow. Every time any of them shifted, a shower of frost fell on their heads.

'The worst part of the whole thing,' wrote Ed in his diary, 'is the black vapour barriers that we sleep inside to stop moisture getting into the sleeping bags and freezing. As a result we all get wet during the night from our body's moisture and getting up in the morning becomes even more unpleasant as you are not warm and dry when you get out of your bag, but damp and cold.'

Says Dags, 'Oh God, those bloody vapour barriers! They're like giant shopping bags which you have to wear to stop the sweat coming off you into the sleeping bag and compromising the heat retention. So in the morning you wake up wet. Outside this sweaty, hot thing you're in you know it's minus fifteen, minus twenty, which you've got to get out into, staying in your thermals without putting anything else on until you've got rid of the moisture. You know that the top of the tent is frozen with snow and it's going to fall on you. You know that breakfast is going to be disgusting. And to cap it all, I had Martin's socks, right in my face. Which really stank. I did think, every single morning, *This whole thing is a stupid, stupid idea.*'

This first dash to get up and put the heater on was the worst part of the day. 'It was something we were unanimous on,' says Guy. 'The low point of the day was the beginning. Waking up in the morning to a horrid smell, which is the smell of people not washing for several days, plus urine, of course, because people are peeing in Nalgene bottles. You're feeling sweaty and cold, you've got to get out of your sleeping bag into your long johns in minus twenty-five and light the pressure cooker, when touching the metal surface with bare skin gives you a freeze burn instantly. You are shaking

239

with cold until that fuel is burning.'

'There is no comfortable way to do an expedition like this,' says Inge. 'You have to accept that it is cold sometimes, and you have to expect to be wet and uncomfortable sometimes too. We could wake up dry every morning if we didn't use the vapour barriers, but then the sleeping bag would accumulate ice. That would be very heavy to carry and uncomfortable to defrost every night with your body heat. You would be wet and it would turn into a cooler bag rather than a sleeping bag.

'So instead, while I am getting up and melting water and tidying up around me, I stay damp and let myself dry in the air, because my body is still warm. I accept that my skin is cold because of the damp clothes, but my core temperature is warm. If you're not born and raised in a cold climate, having cold skin is like being cold. But it's really just superficial. If you can accept that little bit of discomfort and pain, you will dry out very fast.'

It was doubly grim for those with only one arm. 'As we were getting up,' wrote Ed, 'Jaco was very frustrated by his inability to help and the trouble he has getting dressed and putting on his boots. I find it extraordinary how patient they all are with the difficulties they have due to their injuries and it's so understandable when they get pissed off. We can only offer support. Generally tempers were all a little stretched this morning.'

One major improvement, though, for the one-armed guys, had been made since the training week in Beitostølen: the toilet facilities, for which Ed had invented what he called Parker's Polar Loo. 'You know those fishing stools you see people sitting on. I had one at home for some reason. We

240

cut out the middle of the canvas and while we were in Longyearbyen the sewing lady who made the ruffs for our hoods stitched leather on the inside to reinforce the hole. We also had a windbreak that we took with us. Every night it was Dags's and my job to put up the loo—complete with windbreak. We would all crap through the stool, then pick up a shovel and bury the poo. For Martin and Jaco, squatting, balancing, and wiping their bottoms with one hand in the freezing cold had been very difficult. This way they had support.'

Inge thought they were all crazy. Quite apart from anything else, these unorthodox methods meant that the guys had no clean shovels with which to collect snow for drinking water. They had used not just one but both of the dedicated snow shovels to dispose of their poo, so now they had to keep borrowing his to sort out their daily ration of fresh water. Meanwhile Inge and his fellow Norwegians continued to do their business as they always had: make a neat hole in the snow with your boot, then lower your trousers and squat, before covering the evidence with a fresh layer of snow. Simple.

*   *   *

Jaco was feeling so tired this morning that he asked Guy to take a little of his weight: a pack full of heat pads. 'They only weigh about two to three kilograms,' he said. 'But it's unbelievable how, mentally, not having that weight in your pulk makes it feel so much easier. We're not here to be heroes or to outdo each other. There was no point in keeping quiet and struggling and getting frustrated and possibly injuring yourself. It is more about pride, and there's no point being proud. That day I said, "Listen guys, I'm struggling." Guy said, "Mate, I had a good night's sleep, I'll take them." And I felt a massive difference from that moment on. I got a bit of a stride in. The day seemed better.'

Outside, in any case, conditions were improving. The wind had dropped, and the surrounding air was correspondingly less cold. 'While the going's good and the weather's favourable,' said Martin, 'we've got to push the miles out. Yes, it's difficult terrain, yes, it's an uncomfortable environment, but all we're doing is walking. No one's shooting at us. No one's trying to blow us up. I'm not in fear of my life. So in comparison to some of the things I've done in my past, it's nothing. It's not like the first tour I did in Afghan, where you're fighting for your life every day, and you're genuinely worried whether you're going to stay alive or not.

'For me,' he reflected, 'this expedition is about sending out a message to the boys. A number of my mates, and a number of soldiers that I've had under my command, have got significantly worse injuries than me. Some of them are suffering at the minute, both physically and psychologically. If this gives them a bit of a boost, or encourages them to get back to being active again, that's what I'm hoping we'll achieve. We've taken a knock, but we're cracking on, we're keeping going. I can't do any more what I used to do in the Army. I'm never going to be as physically fit or able as I was before I lost the use of my right arm. There are lots of things out here I find hard because of that, but it hasn't stopped me from being here and doing this.'

After the first break, for a period of four hours

242

or so, Guy hit a massive high. 'I don't know what it was, something in the food maybe, but it suddenly felt really good to be out there. You're looking out at the landscape and you're thinking, *Wow! I can't believe I'm actually here.* It has been at the back of our minds for such a long time and now we're doing the trip. The light was amazing. The sun stays where it is, half way up the sky, and there's a real golden glow on the ice. Incredible shadows. And then you get to the pressure ridges, and where the light is shining through it's an amazing sort of ultramarine blue, almost fluorescent.

'The sense of freedom you have out there is almost like being in Afghan. That same feeling, where normal rules have gone out of the window. OK, in the Army you have a code of conduct to live by, but it's just you and the blokes and the job, and you get on with it. There's no niff-naff and trivia, no arseing around doing emails, no paying your council tax bill, no speed limit out in the desert. All the restrictions you have in the UK are gone and suddenly you're a young man doing a job. You're allowed to do things the way you would like to do things. It's almost a sense of, *This is what I'm meant to be doing in life.* It's very satisfying.'

Inge was enjoying himself too. 'Sometimes I think, *Why the hell do I do this?* Why do I come out here to freeze my fingers off and get frostbite in my face, eat boring dehydrated food and pull a pulk over ice rubble? But then, half an hour later, when I get into the zone, and I'm skiing through what I would describe as a huge art exhibition, with all the ice sculptures all around, I feel like the luckiest person on earth. But it's the hardship and the struggling that makes it so rewarding in the end.

There is no short cut to a place worth going.'

Having taken part in this kind of trip before, Dags was keeping the good weather in perspective: 'The thing about the Arctic,' he said, 'is you never know what it's going to throw at you next. So we have to lap up these good days, put them in the bank, with the knowledge that some other days coming up are going to be pretty dreadful.'

*   *   *

With more experience and practice, the soldiers were starting to find the pressure ridges a little easier to manage. 'At the beginning I was using my upper body a lot,' Guy said. 'But getting across them is more about technique than pure strength. It's knowing when to lean so that your pulk will come after you. Instead of trying to pull it up while you're climbing, it's best to drag it to the start of the ridge, then climb up on to the ice, because then you have some slack in your harness. When you get to the top, you then start leaning over the other side, and instead of having to physically hoist the pulk up, your body weight going over will start to move it. If it gets stuck, you give it a big yank with your arms.'

'I'm starting to take the ridges a bit more tactically now,' said Martin. 'Sometimes you just need brute strength and stubbornness to get over them. Other times you've got to approach them with a bit more tact and line things up properly.'

'What we got wrong to start with,' says Guy, 'was that people helped each other too soon. It's very hard watching someone with one arm trying to get over. You see them pulling and pulling and the sledge not moving at all. You're just behind them and you know that one shove will give them a help. But actually, you give that shove and they'll lose balance and fall over, flat on their face. Which is lethal, on that ice.'

'On the first day,' says Steve, 'when we were crossing pressure ridges, the whole team was waiting to help each other across. Within two or three days, what we realised we had to do—and Inge kept telling us this—was go straight over and carry on.'

'As the expedition went on,' Ed says, 'we all considered ourselves brilliant at picking routes. If the bloke at the front was struggling to find a route through, everyone would disperse to try and find another way. When I was leading I used to find that a bit irritating, because I would be there doing my best, and everyone would be saying, "Don't worry, we can do it." But then, when I was following, I would be behind the guy at the front, then out of the corner of my eye I might see a better route through and try and do it myself.'

'I wanted them to find their own way,' says Inge, 'so that we were moving like an organism over the ridges, instead of one at a time. Eventually it worked. You could see that the guys were reading the ridges, finding a perfect path over and laughing at us if we didn't find one. That is fantastic. I loved that.'

*   *   *

Ed led for the second session, but after the second break the sleepless nights caught up with him. 'At 1 p.m. I hit the wall,' he wrote, 'with waves of

245

tiredness washing through me. I really struggled for the rest of the day. Inge read the situation well, with a number of us feeling the pressure a bit. We ended up stopping at 5 p.m., not 6 p.m. as we normally aim to do.'

Ed had spoken to Inge about how neither he nor Jaco had been sleeping, and Inge suggested he take Jaco into his tent that night. With Harry gone, he had the room. Just before the day's final break Ed approached Jaco and passed on the suggestion, which was welcomed. 'Inge is like a Ninja,' Jaco says. 'He knows exactly what to do. Everything in his tent was warm and dry. Everything was spaced out properly. He had it all sorted out. But it was more about having the space. To move around, to do whatever you wanted in the tent around you.' Not for nothing had Inge's tent been nicknamed 'The Pleasure Dome' by a member of a previous expedition.

Inge cooked, and afterwards they had another good look at Jaco's feet. His blisters were cleaned and taped up again with Compeed, Granuflex and various other foot treatments Inge had in his supply. There was no sign of any infection. Jaco sought the expert's advice on his face covering too. He had been getting very sweaty and wet with his current arrangement, the Skidoo mask that Inge had recommended on the first day, which froze whenever he took it off. 'Then I have to put that freezing cold thing back on my face, which is not good.'

Inge suggested that he use the same Granuflex tape that he had used on his blisters. 'That's perfect for taping your nose as well. So every morning we can make some nose tape for you.' Inge hated wearing a face mask, he said; in fact, he would rather get frost nip now and then.

As they talked on together in the warm tent, Jaco confessed to Inge how tough he was finding the expedition. 'So far it's lived up to its name, it is really, really hard.'

'The good thing about the way we're doing it now,' said Inge, 'is that you're doing it yourself. You're not being carried to the North Pole. You're pulling your weight, you're doing your share of the job. This is not a typical handicap vacation, this is hardcore. And I'm not doing any more with you guys now than I would on any other expedition. Some people might think you should have had more help, but that would defeat the point of this expedition.'

This was Inge's eleventh trek to the North Pole. Many of the others had been last degree trips. But this wasn't, he told Jaco, the longest time he had spent in Arctic conditions. That had been three months, when he and some others had reconstructed the Scott–Amundsen relay race on Greenland, with all the old kit, wooden skis and sledges, and dogs too. 'Then you really get into the rhythm,' he said. 'It's very strange, you turn into—almost like an animal. You're feeling the environment so much, you become one with the environment.'

'Is there stuff that you used there,' Jaco asked, 'the old kit, that you think is better than the modern-day kit?'

'A lot of the old kit is more comfortable to wear. It's more natural and it works well. It's just that it's too heavy. The best sleeping bag I ever had was a caribou fur one. It weighed nine kilos. But it was the most comfortable ever.'

The two non-Brits chatted on, relaxed with each other in the warmth.

'What are you thinking about when you walk?' Inge asked, a little later.

'Terrific . . . everything.'

'Today, when you were walking in front, was that different to walking in line?'

'Yeah, it is,' Jaco replied. 'You obviously need to observe where you're going. You need to see a point, which you're looking at, so you can say, "OK, I'm heading towards that." And then you have to look at the ground, to make it easier for the other guys as well. So you're staying on track, making it possible for everyone to follow your route, yet keeping the pace. It's a lot to think about.'

'I think when you're distracted,' said Inge, 'when you occupy one part of your brain by navigation and route finding, you're able to start another, almost subconscious process in another part of the brain. So the really good thinking you do out here is when you're busy route finding and navigating. That's when I get into the zone. It's almost like meditation. You occupy one part of the brain with practicalities, then the other part can just wander off into the most amazing thoughts and fantasies and disappear into another world.'

'I do find that,' Jaco agreed. 'When I was more at the back it's more like you're thinking about daily stuff. Like ex-girlfriends. You sing a song in your head, you think, *When I go home next, what will I be doing, when we get back from the Pole?* All that kind of stuff.'

Over in Jaco's former tent, Ed and Steve were enjoying the space. With only two to heat water

248

and cook for, preparing supper had taken much less time. 'For us,' Ed said, 'to have a little break tonight, it's a bit of treat, to be honest. Also Jaco will learn a huge amount from spending a night with Inge, as far as tent admin goes. Funnily enough, Steve and I have been talking about how we could change things when Jaco comes back in, because this is the first time we've had the cooker in the middle, it's normally over in the corner. But actually we could put the cooker in the middle. It will be much more social, the three of us can get round it, and it will heat the centre of the tent more.'

Before they rolled over to sleep, both men had a hot drink. Horlicks was one of the expedition's sponsors, and the company had come up with a special calorie-rich brew for the soldiers. Encouraged by the folk at Captive Minds they had also had the idea of concealing inside each sachet a laminated message from the team members' loved ones. 'A little surprise we didn't know about,' said Steve. 'So it's obviously nice, each night when we're making a brew, to open it up and get a message from home. It makes a massive difference to morale. It's the same when you're away on operations and you get mail and parcels through. You're away from family, missing them, and it's a reminder that they're thinking about you. It brought a tear to Ed's eye tonight and I think he's feeling better for it.'

Tonight Steve had a message from his big sister: *Good luck for this challenge, Steve, my baby brother, my hero. So very proud for all you've overcome and achieved. Love you loads, my strong, brave, determined brother. Big hugs, your big sister. Kiss,*

kiss, kiss.

'I'd probably have the mick ripped out of me if the boys back in the regiment saw me with this,' he said. 'But they know what it's like. They've all been there and had messages from back home. It makes the world of difference.'

'Got into my sleeping bag feeling a new man,' Ed wrote in his diary. 'Looking forward to tomorrow. P.S. Here's to a good night's sleep . . . finally please.'

18

'GOING LIKE A STEAM TRAIN'

DAY 5. Saturday 9 April. 88° 37' 09". Distance covered 13½ miles. Temperature −28°C still air, −36°C wind chill. Clear blue, beautiful day.

Guy's stump had started to rub. This was something he had been dreading, always his greatest fear—the skin being rubbed off, exposing the flesh beneath. It wasn't as if he could even dress it, because if you put a dressing on one side it would increase the pressure elsewhere. 'You just have to grin and bear it,' he said, stoically.

As well as being sore, his stump would swell during the night, with the result that putting it back into his frozen prosthetic leg, first thing in the morning, was extremely painful. In normal temperatures, there was a bit of flexibility in the carbon fibre socket that the stump sat in; but

250

at −20°C, the socket was rigid: 'You have to really ram it to get it in,' he said. After that he would limp around for the first half-hour of the day, stiff and uncomfortable. Once he started skiing, though, the prosthesis would warm up and the pain would recede. On flat ground it was fine, as there was no pressure on either side of the stump. But over the ridges, Guy was having to lean in to his prosthesis to climb over, which was causing him agonising pain.

Being Guy, being a soldier, he didn't tell anyone. 'I was keeping it quiet, because there was nothing that could be changed. I couldn't dress it. I was buggered if I was going to give somebody else more weight, because the weight I was pulling was still manageable. I just thought, *Can I put up with this for another ten days or so? Yes, I probably can.*'

Only if the stump itself became infected would it be a serious problem for him. Not that this wasn't a worry: 'The rubs are under a neoprene liner, so they've seen no light, they've no oxygen going to them, it's a perfect environment for bacteria to get going. If an infection started, you haven't got long before it would be game over. The worst-case scenario would be that we'd have to chop off more, which would be disastrous, as bad as it gets.'

To add to the fun, he had been pulling shrapnel out of his stump. 'It sounds more dramatic than it is,' he said. 'It's just little bits of metal coming out, like splinters. Anything from the size of a pebble to the smallest bit of grit. It comes to the surface and you dig it out with a penknife.' Guy already knew that hot weather brought to the surface old fragments of the RPG that had hit him; now he had discovered that bitterly cold weather had the same effect.

In the Sergeants' Mess, things were looking up. With just two men in the space Ed had finally enjoyed a decent night's sleep. 'As a result,' he wrote, 'I felt totally different in the morning. Breakfast for two much easier and Steve and I found ourselves with time on our hands before we had to let the tent down, so we lay there with the cooker on just being warm! I have got a small blister forming on my left heel, but I covered it with Compeed and that lasted very well all day and it is giving me little trouble. So far the feet are holding up well and the boots are keeping them warm.'

Thoroughly refreshed, Ed had a great day. The sky was blue, the ice was relatively flat. After the first break he volunteered to lead, and did so for the next two sessions, doing basic navigation by the shadow from his ski pole. At 5 p.m. the sun would be dead ahead, due north, so they worked back from that, allowing 15 degrees from the full 360 for each hour of the day. At every break they would check their position on the GPS.

'Ed was amazing at navigating,' says Inge. 'He could keep a straight line for six hours. I never had to correct him. When the other guys were leading I would fall back two or three places. I would look at my shadow. If they diverted too much I would correct them. I would come up to them and say, "My shadow is now here. Follow that line." For Ed that was never necessary.'

After his dry night with Inge in the Pleasure Dome, Jaco too was in much better shape. 'I feel brilliant today,' he said, 'strong, everything is ready.' His nose and cheeks were taped up with Granuflex, just as Inge had suggested. 'I usually wear a face mask, but I sacked that today, so I'm looking like a twat with all this Compeed on my face. But who gives a shit, I don't want to get frost nip. My face is probably the only place on my body I haven't got a scar, so no need to get one there as well.'

Steve had slept fine as usual, because he had been on his back. 'For me, lying down flat is the best way to take the pain away. There's no pressure on the spine whatsoever. I can lie out and it's bliss.' Once he was up and pulling, though, even on a good day, his back would start to hurt by late morning. 'You're going along and you think you're doing fine. You forget about it totally, then it just starts up, to remind you it's still there.' At the 1 p.m. break he would take his first painkillers, Paracetamol and Ibuprofen, two of each. More on the second break, reserving the heavy guns—Tramadol—for the evening. 'That's a morphine-based painkiller, so it's quite strong; and it makes you tired, it mungs you a bit.'

Today, though, he was having a bad day. He would get through it as best as he could, with the painkillers and his iPod in his ears, listening to music he liked, such as Linkin Park, and tunes his fiancée Emma had put on for him, including some funnies: Shakin' Stevens and a lot of Christmas songs. 'That's her sense of humour.' The one thing he couldn't stand was David Gray. 'Very depressing music. You don't need that up here. Every time David Gray comes on I skip him.'

Otherwise he let his thoughts wander. 'Sometimes you go for a couple of hours without saying a word, so you have a lot of time to think. Your mind drifts back. You think about things that have happened in the past, how I got to where

253

I was. Afghanistan I'm thinking about quite a lot. The blokes I knew, my mates. The reasons why I'm doing the walk. I have a lot of good mates who were injured. Especially on the difficult days, that is predominantly what I'm thinking about. Just before Prince Harry left, I went across for a photo with him, just the two of us, and he said to me: "On the hard days, remember who you're doing it for."'

'It's starting to get to the point now,' said Guy, 'where during the day if you haven't got something to distract your mind it can get quite boring.' On his iPod he had audio books. Today he was listening to Khaled Hosseini's *A Thousand Splendid Suns*.

Like Steve, Guy often recalled his experiences in Afghan. 'I thought about RPGs and mines and what happened. I thought a hell of a lot about the lad who died in my vehicle, Robbie Laws. Partly I was thinking how lucky I was, to be out here doing this at all. For all the people who are injured, there are a lot of others who didn't make it. I had some nice text messages from Robbie's mum, before we left, saying best of luck. I think she sponsored a mile. It must be bloody hard. You just can't imagine what it's like for a parent to bury a child.

'I didn't get all het up about it, but I did play it through in my mind and think: *How would I have done it differently if I could?* There is a massive element of guilt. You think: *Had we done this, would he still be here? Should the RPG have killed me and not him?* All that sort of stuff. I don't think you can help thinking that way when things like that happen.'

For the first time on the expedition, Martin joined the others in listening to music. 'A lot of the boys have been using it since we got out here,

254

but I kept off it till today. The difference it makes is amazing. Early on, I put the tunes on and was looking around, snow everywhere, clear blue skies, a good pace. A bit of dance as I was going, a bit of bounce, the Scouse house on the go.'

Like the others, Martin had been thinking about the past; in Afghan and elsewhere. But he also spent a lot of time wondering about his future. 'I knew I was going to be medically discharged at the end of the summer,' he says, 'so I was thinking about what I was going to do next, what career I might try and have, how best to go about achieving that.

'I'm gutted about leaving the Army, but what I realised out there on the ice is that I can't go into anything else and compare it to being an officer in the Parachute Regiment, leading paratroopers in combat, because there is nothing I will ever do that will compare to that.

'Ever since I was injured, I've been doing competitive sport, which is great, but it's basically an individualistic activity. It's ruthless and a lot of the people involved in it are very selfish. They may be part of a team but they're not team players. Whereas this team I was in now was different; because I was with likeminded people who had a common goal and a common interest. It made me realise I wanted to be involved in something similar in the future, just like I was in the Paras.

'So rather than trying to compare things to my military experience, what I should take from this expedition was that the reason I got so much satisfaction from it was because of the service element of it, and the fact that I was working in a niche team with a certain mindset. That's what I want to move on to in my work in the future.'

Not only was the terrain today generally flatter, it was strewn with amazing ice formations. 'We saw the most beautiful features within the ice,' says Jaco. 'Shapes and forms that look like other things. Faces, heads, animals. At one point one of the bits of rubble looked exactly like a polar bear, with the sun in the background and the shade falling on it. Inge thought the same. He was leading, Guy was in front of me and I was the third man in the row. We saw it at the same time. We had to stand still for a few seconds to make sure it wasn't a bear. It was something we had to be constantly aware of, because the threat is real. It would be hard to spot one, too, because up north they're much whiter than closer to the coast. So I was always keeping an eye out.'

They finished the day at 6 p.m., having completed a triumphant thirteen and a half miles. 'Spirits were high,' wrote Ed, 'and everyone had had a good day. We are beginning to think that we are ahead of schedule and covering the distance quicker than we expected to. I think we might reach the Pole at this rate in nine more days, so three days early—hooray! In the evening our admin is getting much better and more efficient, and as a result we are able to look after ourselves better. Good day—best yet!'

Over in the Officers' Mess Guy was now firmly in charge of the cooking. Simon had Pasta Bolognese, Martin had Beef and Potato Casserole and Guy had Chilli con Carne. After that it was time for the team's nightly contact with the outside world. 'Hello once again from the Officers' Mess,' said Martin. 'This is Captain Hewitt of Her Majesty's

256

Parachute Regiment, Captain Disney from Her Majesty's Light Dragoons and Officer Cadet Retired Simon Daglish, from the Royal Military Academy, Sandhurst. Today was a cracking day, we couldn't have asked for better weather . . .'

Brief upbeat reports from all three men followed. 'These are the same phones we had in Afghan,' said Guy, looking thoughtfully at the satellite phone when they had finished. 'It's actually quite evocative holding it, because the last time I used one of these was probably about seven hours before I got blown up and brought home. Actually no, I called home the day after the operation. It was a Sunday morning and Mum answered the phone.

'"Oh hi, Guy," she said, "how are you?"

'"Yeah, good. But . . ."

'"Yes?"

'"I had my right leg blown off."

'"Right," she said. "Er, OK, I'll just tell your father."

'"Don't worry," I told her. "Everything else is as good as gold." So yes, it's quite evocative holding one of these.'

'We had them in Sangin,' said Martin. 'We were the first ones to get in there and for weeks it was just fighting. We weren't even getting half an hour a week to phone home, we were getting twenty minutes. I remember being in the back garden of a compound we'd just commandeered, phoning home. My dad picked up and I was just saying "Everything's going OK" and doing the usual chit-chat when suddenly it all kicked off again.

'So I was like, "OK, gotta go, Dad."

'"What's that noise?' he asked.

'"Oh, the boys are just firing some test weapons,

it's OK."

'"Sounds like grenades going off."

'"Yeah, the boys are just up on the range. I'm gonna have to go now anyway."

'Then for ten days, every day after that, it kicked off. So I couldn't phone home. And when I finally did, exactly the same thing happened again.'

'Your poor parents,' said Dags.

'Yeah, so having fun, we were, with that. I didn't phone them again till after we got back to Camp Bastion. Not good.'

DAY 6. Sunday 10 April. 88° 48' 30". Distance covered 12½ miles. Temperature −25°C still air, −35°C wind chill. Clear blue, SE wind.

In Ed's tent, things were now running like clockwork. Steve was up at 7 a.m., out of his sleeping bag and setting the cooker up. He was not, as he said, a great one for sweating, so even within the vapour barriers, he wouldn't get damp at night in the way the others did. Once outside, he would almost immediately put on his soft down tent trousers, his tent boots and his black shell jacket. He would roll up his sleeping bag, fold his inflatable roll mat in half, then put the cooker on the remaining foam roll mat. He would pump the cooker to build up the pressure, then release the valve and light it. By 7.20 a.m. he would be ready for the toilet. Leaving the cooker on to heat the tent, he would head out to Parker's Polar Loo and its surrounding windbreak, taking with him his sleeping bag and inflatable roll mat, which he would zip into his pulk. By the time he'd finished doing his business, Ed would be up, his own sleeping bag rolled and ready to pass out. Steve would put the sleeping bag in Ed's pulk, then go back into the tent to find that Ed had the first pan on the cooker to melt the water. 'We had a nice system going,' he says. 'Jaco didn't have to get out of his sleeping bag and get cold. He would just wait and have breakfast in his sleeping bag every morning.'

*   *   *

Out on the ice, the guys encountered their first open water lead, a giant crack in the huge white sheet, exposing the inky waters of the Arctic Ocean a couple of feet or so below. 'The sea is pitch black and rather ominous,' wrote Ed. 'Below the surface lies 4 km of dark nothingness—it is quite alarming. The best way to think of the leads is just as small streams and rivers which need crossing!'

The lead was only a metre and a half wide, but that, Inge thought, was too far to jump. 'You don't want to fall in,' he said. 'It's quite dangerous because it's very hard to get up and out again. There are no very solid edges here so you would be struggling. Obviously we would be helping each other, but it's still dramatic if it happens, very uncomfortable.'

'If your pulk goes in,' said Simon, 'it's going to pull you down. You're not going to get out of your harness and you're going to the bottom of the sea and that's that.'

On Inge's advice, they walked a few hundred metres to the east, crossing the lead at a point where it was narrow enough to push the pulks across. But this wasn't the end of the leads. As the morning continued, they encountered another, then another. 'We made a bit of a joke about crossing them,' says Ed, 'but it was definitely a bit hairy. It's like doing the long jump. You need a good twenty-yard run up, to get enough momentum going. Your boots are heavy and cumbersome, so it's harder to get up in the air. Then you leap, praying you've cleared it. But your trailing leg might easily hit the water, meaning you'd get a wet boot.' By the time they stopped for their second break, they had definitely earned their snacks.

They were going well, no doubt about that, but Ed and Simon were worried about their charges. Even though Guy had been keeping schtum, Simon was aware of the rub on his stump, and the pain it was causing him. Steve's back was an ongoing concern, and poor Jaco seemed continuously cold, particularly today in his hand. 'I have very, very cold fingers today,' he said. 'My right hand just does not want to warm up. Particularly my index finger and my thumb, they are absolutely freezing. No idea why. It's bad, though. No blood circulation in it at all. Perhaps I'm gripping the pole too hard, or maybe even the day sack around my shoulder is preventing some blood going down my arm.'

During that second break, Ed was so concerned about Jaco's arm that he gave him an extra chemical heat pad. 'My worry,' he says, 'was that if he got frostbite in that hand, he didn't have the left hand to fall back on if he started losing fingers. His right hand became for a while my reason for being. I hope I didn't badger him too much. But I was constantly saying, "Are you OK, Jaco? How's your right hand?" When I speak to my nephew Harry we play the let's lose a limb game. "Would you prefer to lose two legs or one hand?" He'll say, "Two

260

legs," every time.'

'We have a duty of care,' said Dags, 'to return these people in no worse condition than they were when they came out. That was our promise to the Army. Because their determination to achieve this goal is so great, we need to make sure that drive doesn't take over and leave them with permanent damage.'

As he skied along, Dags looked down at the names he'd written on his skis: those of his wife Emma, his children Oscar and Felix and his dog Womble. 'All of whom I miss a great deal. Those things are pretty important out here where there's nothing else except snow.'

*   *   *

The day ended, and once again they had covered twelve and a half miles in close to ideal conditions. 'We're going OK,' said Martin, 'we've had a bit of Lady Luck on our side. Good positive drift and good weather and the injuries are holding up OK. But we're by no means there yet.'

As if to remind them of the many disasters they could face, Ed then came close to setting his tent on fire. Having pumped up the cooker to get it started, he noticed there was a leak where the pump was attached to the gas bottle. 'There was a tiny pool of fuel at the bottom of the cooker,' he says, 'and I got a bit of loo paper just to dab up the fuel. As I was doing this, the whole lot caught light. Steve and I were in there together. I had the loo paper burning in my hands and I managed to get it out the front of the tent. We turned the cooker off. I think Steve smothered it.'

'Ed is quite clumsy,' says Steve. 'There was a leak in the fuel and he said, "Let's mop it with tissues, then light it up." So we mopped it up and lit the stove. Ed was still mopping away and he must have passed the tissue through the flame, because the fuel on the board that the cooker is on went into a big fireball with the other tissues there. I grabbed the lid of a saucepan and started dousing it, and Ed tried to put it out with a glove.'

Whatever the exact truth of the story, the conflagration might easily have ended with a tent fire. They had no replacement. 'Which would have been a shame,' says Ed, with classic understatement. In the end Inge explained why the pump had been dripping: they had been working it too hard.

With the fire out, and the cooker up and running normally again, Ed set to work once more drying out his damp kit. Socks, face masks, neck gaiters, gloves, all hung on a line strung down the middle of the tent. 'It's a bit like a Chinese laundry in here at the moment,' he reported on the daily blog.

Over in the Officers' Mess Guy was carrying out some crucial personal admin too, as he attended to his stump: removing the neoprene liner that covered it before it went into the prosthetic leg, cleaning that out with hot water left over from cooking. 'One of the big worries,' he said, 'when I was first selected, was that I'd get sweat between this liner and my stump and it would freeze. But touch wood, there haven't been any problems at all.' (The weeks when Jamie Gillespie had been fretting about Rob and Matt and Guy and thinking about a pop-up tent to dry out the expedition's prosthetic limbs now seemed almost to belong to

262

another era.)

That evening Simon was having supper with Inge in his tent, so the two younger men had been left to phone through the daily blog to Expedition HQ in the UK. That task done, Martin had the bright idea of ordering a pizza. 'These places maintain they can deliver anywhere in the world,' he said, 'and if they can't, that, in my opinion, is false marketing, and I will do everything I can to get them prosecuted under the Advertising Standards Authority. I'm not joking.'

Guy had now got through to Alex Rayner and was asking for the number of a Chinese takeaway. This was one request Expedition HQ had not anticipated. 'We really want to call one,' Guy was saying. 'Can you give us a London number? . . . Yeah, yeah, deadly serious. We want to try and order a takeaway that delivers.'

'You don't understand,' chipped in Martin. 'I've been eating dried food for weeks. I want a Chinese or a pizza.'

Two minutes later the pair had the number of a curry house in east London. 'That's brilliant, Alex, we'll call them now.'

Shortly after that Guy was ordering a chicken korma with pilau rice and a king prawn madras, with naan bread.

'Poppadoms, poppadoms,' chipped in Martin.

'D'you give poppadoms with orders over ten pounds?' Guy asked. Then it came to the question of getting the goods delivered. 'My address is Northing, north with ing on the end, eighty-eight degrees. Easting—that's E, A, S for Sierra, T for Tango . . . no, we haven't got a postcode, mate.'

Martin took over: 'If you just put these

263

co-ordinates into your satnav, you'll get to us that way. How? I suggest a moped probably wouldn't do it. I reckon you might need something like a helicopter.'

'What about a ship?'

'What about a ship. Have you got a ship?'

'You said you delivered,' said Guy.

'We're not far from a place called Barneo,' said Martin, 'it's an ice landing camp. But we're on sea ice and it's constantly moving, so you might drop it off and we're not here. Mate, you've got to do your best, because we're starving here, we're really hungry.'

'We're fed up of dried food.'

'We're fed up of dried food, mate. All we've eaten is sweets and dried food for the past ten days . . . He's hung up. Something tells me they're not going to make it.'

In the Sergeants' Mess, meanwhile, Jaco had opened his Horlicks and found a message from his mother, in Afrikaans. 'It was a really beautiful message, and it sunk in. It was just what she thought of me, where I have been and where I am now. It made me think about the fact that eighteen months ago I nearly lost my life, and now here I am on the way to the North Pole. It's been quite a remarkable recovery, I suppose, and she was saying, "Well done for that." But it took me back. I was thinking about what a mother would go through receiving the news that her son had been injured, with the limited information that they can pass over the phone. It must be so hard and horrible as a parent to receive news like that. That was the first night I started to think about home again. Family and friends.'

DAY 7. Monday 11 April. 89° 01' 80" 12 miles + 2 miles N drift overnight. –25°C. No wind.

Day seven, and the weather remained in the team's favour, as did the current. By merely sleeping on the ice in their tents they had moved two miles north. It could so easily have been very different. Many expeditions in the history of the North Pole had ended in defeat, thwarted by an ocean drift going in the wrong direction. 'How long will our luck last?' Ed wrote in his diary. 'Fingers crossed the Arctic doesn't come and bite us.'

Before the men set off this morning, team leader Inge had a few words for them: 'Apart from Ed,' he said, 'who sounds as if he's going to die, I hope you're all OK today. Now one thing I want you all to do in the next two hours, is agree on a schedule for when we wake up and when we go to bed. Because we can't let the last funny man at night and the first early bird in the morning decide how much sleep we get. Is that OK? So you have to decide. When is it quiet at night and when do we start to tell jokes in the morning?

'And the second thing is, I hope you can all manage your temperature and moisture better today, because every night people are complaining how wet it is in their tents. And it's up to you. If you know you're a sweaty bastard you have to ventilate a bit more, because you can't put it on other people to be living in a moisture hell.'

Who could he have been talking about? Ed was certainly aware that this was an area he needed to work on. 'I'm trying to keep my temperature as low as possible,' he said, 'so I don't sweat. Today I started wearing just a base layer and a windproof jacket and I got bloody cold and didn't sweat, that's for sure. But I was way too cold, so I've had to put my middle layer back on again and I'll try to keep venting as much as possible so I can keep the sweating to a minimum. It does make life a lot more complicated. But I'd rather be slightly warm than bloody freezing.'

'Ed and Dog were both sweating way too much,' says Inge. 'More than they needed to. I feared that they would get into a negative spiral where they were not rehydrated enough every day and that they would be constantly too cold. You might think they were warm because they were sweating, but when you sweat too much and then sit down during a break, you cool down three times as fast as if you're dry. So you have this constant up and down rather than an even temperature. Eventually Ed found a way to open up and ventilate through his head, so it got much better for him.'

As the morning went on, the guys encountered more open water. They were closing on the Pole, and as they did so the leads occurred with ever greater frequency. Most could be crossed by skiing east or west a little way, until the gap in the ice narrowed. But then they came to a lead with no clear crossing place in sight.

Inge was getting organised: 'So, I'm going to have two people in immersion suits, and I've found a good crossing point right over there.'

'I think swimming's great fun,' said Ed, 'but I think we want to try and keep the pace as much as we can.'

There was a short group discussion, before it was decided to walk down the lead for a while and see if there was an alternative. 'Alexis wanted

266

immersion suits,' says Inge, 'because it would be a new thing for him to film. I asked the guys and they said, "OK, let's do it." Everyone was enthusiastic apart from Ed. Then he convinced everyone it was unnecessary, so we agreed not to do it.'

Fortunately, as it turned out, there was a way over. After three hundred yards they came to a spot where the lead had been closed by a large block of ice. Inge led the way across and the others followed.

A little later they came to another lead. Though not wide enough to merit putting on immersion suits and swimming, it was too wide to jump. So Inge suggested another method of crossing: they would make a little pontoon bridge using the two longest pulks. Inge and Rune held the sledges steady while the others crawled over one by one, Petter and the TV crew included.

'Wouldn't fancy going in there, mate,' said Steve, looking down at the jet black water to either side. 'Bloody hell, it looks cold.'

'Youngy?' called Martin.

'Yep.'

'You stink anyway, so you need a wash.'

But Steve made it without incident. As did the others, even Ed. 'Nice to know that there's four thousand metres of nothingness down there,' he muttered as he went. Then the pulks were pulled over by their harnesses.

*   *   *

Shortly after the second break of the day the team crossed the eighty-ninth degree. Dags was leading and Inge had been checking their position from the back on the GPS. One more degree and they would have reached their destination. The entire team stopped for a minute and gave a big cheer.

'Sixty-seven miles left to go,' said Martin.

'We're going like a steam train,' said Dags.

'If we carry on with this pace we'll probably get there within six days. Maybe even faster than that.'

'That's an incredible thought.'

'North Pole,' Martin started chanting. 'Easy, easy, easy!'

'Don't ever, ever, ever, ever say that,' said Dags. ''Cos I tell you what. It's going to bite you in the arse.'

'It's easy,' Martin said with his trademark cackle. 'This is the easiest thing any of us have ever done.'

'Stupid boy.'

'You know what?' said Martin. 'I did harder walks than this when I was a child. Colder, harder, more dangerous.'

'Only five nights ago I had Martin in the tent going, "Oh, oh, I'm not sure about this. I don't know if my arm will hold out, oh dear, oh dear." And now it's the easiest thing in the world.'

*   *   *

As if to make the point that nothing on the expedition could be taken for granted, the same afternoon Steve's back was hurting worse than ever. He had taken painkillers but they hadn't helped. 'It seems every time I put a leg forward I get a throbbing pain down my back. This is one of those days when I feel like I've got the body of an eighty-year-old man. Of course I mentally prepared myself for days like this,' he said, 'so now I've just got to keep going, keep tripping. But it feels like I've got nothing left to give in my legs at all. Just got to keep in my head what we're doing it for. Every step you take is closer to the Pole and more money raised for the blokes.'

After the second break the others offered to take some of the weight from his pulk. That made things a little easier. In the last hour he had a second wind and somehow made it to camp.

As he plodded on, Steve was having the weirdest thoughts. One thing he seriously missed at the moment was crisps. 'Obviously all we eat during the day is chocolate and flapjacks. I'm a big chocoholic, so I thought I'd love it, but it's starting to drive me crazy. I just want savoury food—especially crisps, prawn cocktail flavour. When I get home I'm going to eat packet after packet of them.'

By the time they stopped that evening they had covered another twelve miles. Jaco was spending a second night in Inge's tent, which would, it was hoped, give him a chance to warm up a little. In comparison with his own tent, which he called 'the fridge', the Pleasure Dome was like a hotel. He had a big dinner and half of one of Inge's chocolate puddings and slept well.

*   *   *

In the Officers' Mess they were catching up on their diaries. These were brief and factual accounts, as the soldiers were well aware. 'I'm probably the least imaginative person in the world,' said Guy. 'I find it very hard to express myself. I don't tell people I love them, I don't write warming words in diaries.'

'You told me that you love me,' said Dags.

'Yeah, but that's you, Dags.'

'Good point.'

'No,' said Guy, 'I've been described by one girlfriend as emotionally numb. That isn't a good thing, is it? I don't think it was a compliment anyway. OK, I've just written *Quite a few open leads today*, which is pretty descriptive for me.'

'I've never had a girlfriend,' said Martin. 'I've never even been kissed, so no girls have ever told me anything about what I might or might not be.'

'That's not true, is it,' said Dags.

'Is that not true? No, I did have a girlfriend once ...'

'Was it a real girlfriend or one you blew up?' asked Guy.

'I think she was real.'

'Did she have real hair?'

'It was well, no, kind of stitched in, it was horse's hair.'

They bantered on, sipping their whisky and hot chocolate mix, a nightly tipple they looked forward to all day. 'In the tent we would sit and chat about all kinds of things,' says Guy. 'We would tell funny stories and fairly horrible stories. Stuff from the Army. Martin would chat a lot about his time in the Army. We would talk about Dags's disabled son, Felix. I think he was on Dags's mind quite a bit while we were up there.'

'For all of us it was an interesting point in our lives,' says Dags. 'From my perspective I was going back to a completely new job and life in London. Dog was being discharged from his last exercise in the Army. For Guy, he had made the decision to stay in the Army and go back to Afghanistan. We had the sense of it being a new beginning—or the end of the old.'

And at 11 p.m. sharp, as they had agreed with Inge during the first break, they all stopped talking; and stayed quiet till 7 a.m., so that everybody could at least try to get a decent night's sleep.

*　　　*　　　*

On the Walking With The Wounded web page that night polar explorer Tom Avery, the man who had once caused Harriet Parker to squeal with his line about facing death at the Pole every day, provided a professional assessment of the expedition's progress. 'The guys are doing incredibly well,' he wrote, 'but the hardest days lie ahead. They have been encountering dozens of pressure ridges a day, which can be as high as forty feet and guard the route to the Pole. They require physical strength and delicate balance to negotiate. During our expedition to the North Pole the pressure ridges were the bane of our lives, both physically draining and mentally demoralising. At times you feel as if you're making no progress at all. How the Walking With The Wounded team are tackling these unstable walls of ice with their injuries is beyond me.

'They will be increasingly wary of the weather conditions. Minus twenty-five might seem inhospitably cold, but the team won't want it to get much warmer as that increases the amount of open water they are likely to have to contend with. Channels of open water (known as leads) can open up in the blink of an eye and lead to soul-destroying detours, and even block you off altogether.'

271

DAY 8. Tuesday 12 April. 89° 1' 30". –25°C still air, –35°C wind chill. 13½ miles + 3 miles N drift overnight. Clear blue, light cloud midday, wind around to SW.

Day eight of the trek and Nature, it seemed, was still on the team's side. The sky remained blue and when they woke in the morning and consulted the GPS they discovered they had drifted north three miles as they slept.

Out on the ice there were more and more open leads to cross, though still none so wide that the team had been required to use immersion suits. One lead this morning was moving apart as they crossed it, which Ed found a little alarming. But they all made it safely to the other side.

Guy's leg was not getting any better, but as yet there was no sign of infection. Forcing the sore and swollen stump into his prosthesis every morning was the hardest part of his day; after that he just had to grin and bear it, because the pain wasn't about to go away. 'So far it hasn't actually stopped me, which is good. You really don't want to be the one to force the rest to stop.' Being with the others, too, made things easier; partly because the feeling of being in a team kept each individual going and partly because each man could see what the others were going through themselves. 'Some days, watching Steve suffering with his back inspires me to keep going. Then watching the guys who've only got one ski pole is good motivation, especially when they're crossing the pressure ridges. But we deserve to get there now. We've done all the hard work and it would be a shame to fall at the last hurdle.'

'It felt like a long day,' Ed wrote in his diary, 'but

we are going incredibly well. During the afternoon I couldn't stop thinking about home and Harriet and the children and felt rather homesick. It is certainly an added dimension missing them like this. In the evening I changed my underclothes for the first (and only) time. It was wonderful having clean socks and pants and thermal vest on and it felt lovely getting into my sleeping bag. We only have forty-four nautical miles (so fifty-odd imperial miles) left. We might be there in four days??? Why is the Arctic holding back and giving us an easy time? Not a huge amount of encouragement coming from Inge, but he is keeping us safe.'

'If we carry on at this pace,' said Martin, 'we should be at the North Pole in four and a half days' time. Every evening we've been checking in with Viktor Boyarsky at Barneo Ice Camp and he's impressed with the distance we're covering. He's a bit of a punchy explorer type, so for someone of that calibre and experience to think that means we're not doing a bad job. He's not the kind of man that's going to big you up for no reason. We've had a number of people telling us that what we were planning was physically impossible, so hopefully if we're successful we can demonstrate that if you get the right team, the right preparation and the right planning, you'd be surprised what you can pull off.'

Naming no names, of course!

As well as changing his clothes, Ed was tending to his sore feet with an embrocation the soldiers swore by—Elizabeth Arden's Eight Hour cream.

'This is a skin cream that girls use,' he said, 'and it's very, very good on beaten-up old feet.'

'I use it on my lips, mate,' said Steve. 'Lips and nose.'

273

'I've done that as well,' agreed Jaco.

'It's really good. You can put it on anywhere, absolutely anywhere.'

The cream had been given them by the manufacturers, but Captive Minds were nowhere in sight and these words of praise were clearly from the heart.

As well as putting soothing remedies on their feet the men were talking about their beards. Since all of them had given up shaving for the course of the trip, there was bound to be an element of competitive analysis.

'It's black,' Steve insisted of his, 'it's not ginger.'

'If that's a black beard,' said Ed, 'my name is Rumpelstiltskin.'

'I think it's black.'

'Two things are true here. One, you're Welsh and two, you have a ginger beard.'

'There's a little bit of ginger in there, but it's a good dark beard and I'm impressed and proud of it.'

'Do the Welsh even know that rugby is a competitive sport?'

'Don't even go there! All right? Stand by for the World Cup.'

On they went, into the daylit night. The end was in sight. What could possibly go wrong now?

**DAY 9. Wednesday 13 April. 89° 28' 36".
−28°C still air, −35°C wind chill. 12½ miles
+ 1½ miles N drift overnight. Clear blue sky.**

Crossing a pressure ridge at 10.30 the next morning, Guy was just ahead of Ed, negotiating his way over the usual slippery mound of ice blocks. 'I was about

274

two-thirds of the way through,' he recalls, 'and Parks was behind me by two metres. He had been pulling his pulk up, then as he was coming down the other side, instead of the pulk holding his weight it must have given a little, so he slipped forward and his back went on to a sharp point on the ice. I heard this almighty thump and crack, which was Ed's back, then two sharp screams. Inge was there very quickly. I ran over to join him. Ed had passed out, in a fairly nasty curled-up position. I thought he'd broken his back. It was just the way he went down.'

'I felt instant shooting pains across my back,' wrote Ed, 'and my first instinct was I had done something very bad and my expedition was over. It hurt like hell and I did pass out.'

'I thought it was a helivac moment,' said Martin. 'For a man who's as robust as Ed to make that kind of noise meant something was seriously wrong.'

'When I got to him,' says Inge, 'he was slipping down from the edge in great pain, screaming. He turned his body round, almost in a foetal position. I asked him how he was and where it hurt. He muttered that it was his back. Then I held his head and he fainted in my arms. But I could see from the way his body moved that there was sensation in his legs, they were pushing him and supporting him. So he hadn't broken his back.'

Inge shouted to Rune to get a tent up, so Ed could be stabilised somewhere warm. He thought they would probably be there for an hour or two, even if they didn't have to call in a helicopter.

After twenty seconds or so, however, Ed came to. 'He was a lot better then,' says Inge. 'He had calmed down. I asked him where it was painful and if he had sensation everywhere. Then I released

275

him from his harness and took his skis off and he stood up. He was in great pain, but he got his breath back and straightened up.'

Steve supplied Ed with some painkillers and Inge gave him a hot blackcurrant drink. Within twenty minutes they were on their way again, with Inge pulling Ed's pulk. 'After about ten minutes of skiing without any weight,' Ed wrote, 'I couldn't watch Inge struggle with his and my sledge so I asked to pull it again. Dags, Jaco and Inge all took some of my weight, which made it much easier. Shortly after the incident I thought of Steve's back, which actually prompted me to shut up and get on with it!'

'Parker does tend to pass out,' said Dags. 'He once slammed his finger in a door when we were training down in Cornwall and fainted. But it only goes to show. It just takes one slip and you're out. We're clambering over six, seven foot high blocks of ice with a pulk behind us and it's a difficult balancing act. Had Ed slipped a disc or broken his back, it wouldn't have been good. We're in minus thirty-five out here, we're standing still. We'd have had to work out a way to get him out. We do have helicopter back-up, but that doesn't mean a chopper can get to every single spot.

'We're not meant to be here, really, is the long and the short of it. Humans don't live here for very good reasons. We're here as guests, short-term guests who tow our lives behind us. Should we somehow become detached from that pulk, we wouldn't survive. The Arctic's been good to us so far, but it could easily turn against us. Any time.'

'It was slightly ironic,' says Guy, 'that there was always a morbid fear that something could go wrong with one of us injured, and here was a guy

276

who was completely able-bodied suddenly coming pretty close to having it over and done with.'

But by the end of the second break, Ed was fully back in the game. 'From 2 p.m.,' he wrote, 'I felt much better and actually pulled well. Must have been the lighter pulk!' Martin gave him a piece of his mother's tiffin cake, which Ed put in his pocket to enjoy in his tent later.

That evening, on the blog, there was barely a mention of the morning's incident. 'Hello my lovelies,' crooned Martin, 'and welcome to another rendition of the Officers' Mess voice blog. Today was another great day, there were some significant pressure ridges, which presented a challenge to negotiate . . .?'

Ed talked about his evening routine, with particular mention of Elizabeth Arden cream. 'So, girls, it's not just you that use those little pots in the bathroom, we boys use it too.'

Only Steve made any mention of Ed's near disaster, and that was perfunctory. 'Ed went over and hurt his back, but he seemed to be OK and walked it off. One of the lads took his pulk for a bit but he was more than adamant that he wanted to pull his own kit. The whole team is doing well and we're looking forward to what we think *might* be Saturday—the big day! Morale is really high as we sip a hot chocolate with a bit of whisky in it to help us sleep, which I especially need as Ed has been snoring the last few days. Hi to all my family and miss you loads, missing you too Emma and love you loads.'

Later, though, Dags agreed that the website blog had presented an upbeat, not to say edited version of what was really going on. 'There were two reasons for that,' he says. 'One was that we didn't want our families at home to get worried. If you're out there reading the daily blog and it says we're having a shit time, I was concerned there might be general panic. Another point to be borne in mind was that we always did the daily blog when we were in the tent, had just got warm, had our supper, everybody had had a nip of whisky and we were feeling good.'

This evening their happy mood contained an extra ingredient: a collective relief that they had avoided misadventure by a whisker, compounded with a reminder of how easily and unexpectedly disaster could still strike.

19

THE FINAL PUSH

Day 10. Thursday 14 April. 89° 40' 50". –24°C still air, –32°C wind chill. 12½ miles + 1 mile N drift overnight. Started cloudy with W wind, 2 p.m. cleared.

Having gone to bed in an upbeat mood, the team woke to face another day of hard slog across the rubble fields and pressure ridges. 'After all the euphoria of last night,' Ed wrote, 'when we were thinking about arriving at the Pole, we were struck by the reality in the morning that we still have plenty of hauling to do.'

'Everybody kind of thought,' said Dags, 'Oh well, we're nearly there—but we're not. So the energy's gone out of it. We've got to reboot ourselves and keep going. We'll still be doing this at the same time tomorrow. And the same time the day after. So we've got a way to go.'

Ed had slept badly, coughing incessantly with his flu, the bruise on his back making it impossible to find a comfortable position. Steve had been kept awake by Ed's cough and was feeling eighty years old again. 'Proper feeling it today. I started off just drained of energy.' As well as his back, the ligaments in his shoulder, which had been damaged when he was dragged from the Viking in the Shamalan canal, had started hurting again: 'It's the body's way of rebelling; it's asking me to go back home to a nice warm room.' To cap it all he had a frostbitten right ear. When the wind had veered round to the east the previous afternoon he had felt a stinging at the top of his ear, even though he had his hood up. Last night it had throbbed uncomfortably, and this morning Inge had confirmed the diagnosis. 'Inge's advice was to focus on the pain, apparently it'll make the day go faster. That's a very Norwegian thing to say, I think.'

Guy was stoic as ever. 'I'm pretty sore at the end of each day,' he admitted, 'but bearing up pretty well. We don't have far to push now and I really didn't go into this with the attitude that failure was an option. If I do hit an uncomfy point, I just think, *There's always someone who's got it worse than you have.'*

Later, back home, he elaborated on his uncompromising philosophy: 'If I'd said it was sore, it wouldn't have changed anything. It wouldn't have made it feel any better. There was nothing to be done, so no point somebody else worrying about it,

279

thinking, "Poor Guy with his sore leg." It makes no difference to me if somebody else knows it's sore. It just brings somebody else into the circle of being uncomfy. My view is, unless there's something that can be physically changed by someone else, there's no point telling them it hurts. I actually think it's slightly selfish, me giving the burden to you as well. It also shows weakness. I don't want to sound arrogant, but if you show any sign of weakness up there, it's like admitting something's wrong. When you do that it's a downward spiral. It's got to be head up and plug on.'

In their various states of pain and weariness, the team did just that. During the second session, as Guy was leading, his spirits were lifted when he spotted tracks in the snow. 'I was amazed,' he said. 'It was an Arctic fox. I pointed them out but nobody believed they were tracks. Dags thought I was joking. Somebody else thought they were ski poles from another expedition. But I showed them to Inge and he agreed they were tracks. There wouldn't be much for a fox to eat up there, except for scraps of seals left by polar bears, which must have meant there was a bear somewhere about. It was the first sign of life we had seen for seven days.'

At 2 p.m., the cloud cover cleared and with the sun on their faces, the men's moods improved—a little. The ice was flatter and they picked up pace. Around 3 p.m. they saw a helicopter in the far distance, presumably extracting one of those 'one degree' trips from the Pole. Guy was annoyed to have the fantasy of pristine empty space broken into for the first time since they had landed on the ice, but Jaco was more upbeat. 'There's about four or five other expeditions, that I know of, whilst

280

we're out here, so congratulations to those boys for reaching the Pole. We'll be there the day after tomorrow, by the grace of God.'

Around 4 p.m., Martin was up ahead, leading, when his followers saw that he had stopped and was pulling off his clothes. First his outer layer, then his fleece, then his long johns and vest, then he dropped his trousers, till he was naked bar his ankles and feet in a temperature of −30°C. They knew the Scouser was crazy, but what on earth was going on?

'When I was in 3 Para,' he explains, 'we created in the officers' mess something called the 3 Para Power Ballads. We used to do a thing called the naked dance-off. After a few beers we would all dance with the ladies, if there were ladies there, otherwise we'd just do it together. Basically you had to dominate your partner through aggressive dancing. Some would strip, some wouldn't, but if one particular song came on, we would undress and dance aggressively.'

Unfortunately for Martin—or perhaps fortunately—that particular song had come on his iPod. 'So I decided I was duty bound to stick to the bond I had created several years ago. I got naked. It was very cold indeed, but rules are rules.'

And what was the particular song? 'I'm very sorry, that's a regimental secret.'

Sadly, the others were more bemused than amused. 'During one session,' Ed wrote, 'when Dog was leading he suddenly stopped and stripped off. We were all too tired to find it funny! I looked at Jaco and Jaco didn't even bother looking at the heavens. Inge said to me, "Just go and sort Dog out." So I went over and started getting him

281

dressed. Nothing was really said. Dog's timing on this occasion was not necessarily his best. I think he probably thought it would cheer us all up. Unfortunately the mood was low. All we wanted was to get to the end of the day, get the tents up, and hot food down us.'

'It was great fun,' says Jaco, 'and a brilliant thing to do, but it just wasn't the right time of day to do it. We all got cold waiting for him to get dressed again. We all felt we'd wasted fifteen minutes when we could have done another half-kilometre.'

When they pulled in at six, they were all ready to stop. Despite everything, they had covered a good distance. They were twenty miles from their target now, so they needed to prepare for a big day tomorrow, in order to be sure of reaching the Pole the day after.

Ed went for dinner with Inge to give Steve and Jaco a bit of space. He was tired and feeling the pressure. 'My old body is holding up pretty well,' he wrote, 'but it's complaining a little. I have nerve pains in both wrists where the straps from my ski poles have been cutting in, which is uncomfortable.'

They were all tired, though from the daily blog you would never have known. 'Hello my dears,' came the chirpy voice of Martin Hewitt, sounding like some pre-war radio comedy act. 'It's us again for another rendition of the Officers' Mess voice blog. Today has been a fantastic day, though rather difficult, with pressure ridges and water leads, one or two of which we jumped. We only covered twelve miles, perhaps because we have two old men with us slowing us down . . .'

DAY 11. Friday 15 April. 89° 51' 70". 12 miles + ½ mile N drift. –25°C, –34°C wind chill. Clear blue, light N wind.

Ed must have been worn out, because in addition to his persistent coughing, he had also snored loudly, keeping Steve awake most of the night—the tables had truly been turned. Not only was he exhausted from lack of sleep, but Steve's nose was also running continually, which in this climate meant icicles of snot all over your lips: 'Not too bad in the daytime, but when you go into your tent at night, and they defrost, you've got a nice snot-flavoured Tip-top stuck to your lip.' Despite all that, he was feeling better today. They were almost there!

But as they headed off this morning, the wind was blowing from the north, straight into their faces. 'It's amazing the difference wind chill makes,' said Martin. 'When that hits you, you know about it. It stings. And the spindrift, which is when the wind picks up the top layer of snow and throws it at you, is remarkably similar to a brownout in the desert, when sand particles are blown in your face by the wind and you get covered in the damn stuff. And if you don't protect your face from it you get a good whipping.'

As if that wasn't enough, it was another day of leads, the broken ice crust liable to hold them up for even longer than pressure ridges. While they stood in front of one stretch of inky black water which was too wide for them to jump over, there was another short discussion about the use of immersion suits. In the end Inge decided that they should walk a little way and build a snow bridge across the narrowest gap they could find. He found a place where some of the free-floating chunks of ice in the black water had frozen together, creating a base on to which they piled more ice and snow to create a metre-wide bridge, albeit a rather unstable one.

'Then we slowly approached it,' said Jaco, 'making sure our balance was right. You couldn't really use your pole at this point, because if you fell that would go straight through the ice and into the water. Even the guys with two hands had to just balance. Martin and I looked at each other, because we rely a lot on our single pole—his left and my right. We approached the snow bridge really slow, keeping that balance nice and steady, pulling your pulk right up to the edge, so you've got a bit of leeway on your rope and nothing is going to pull you back. Then we slowly crossed over. Once you were over, that worked out perfectly, because you had a bit of tension in your rope again and you could just glide your pulk across. We all stood by in case anyone fell or lost their balance, but everyone crossed it fine. Ed was a bit heavier, so we threw a bit more snow on it for him.'

'As team members crossed,' Ed wrote, 'the bridge bounced up and down. We constantly had to add more snow to keep it buoyant. I was the last to go—and the heaviest member of the team. Not something I relished and as I tentatively slid across I felt the back of my skis tilting into the Arctic Ocean and myself slipping backwards. Luckily I was far enough over for Inge to grab my harness and pull me across. I felt a dip had been quite close! Not sure I am a huge fan of the open leads!'

Some time later they reached the biggest lead they had yet come across, and for a few moments it looked as if they might at last be trying the immersion suits. But Inge again decided it would be easier to look for a way round. So he led them along its edge for a mile and a quarter until suddenly the giant crack turned sharp east. 'So now we don't even have to cross it,' he said. 'We can just cut straight north after the turn here. The five or ten minutes we lost from walking west was worth it.'

As they negotiated the crossing of yet another lead a little later, they came to a point where two ice floes had just met, and where the force of the collision was creating a new pressure ridge right before their eyes. 'We actually saw one forming,' wrote Ed. 'You could feel the vibrations through the ice and hear it creaking as the rubble was slowly pushed higher. It was an extraordinary sight. The power of nature is awesome.'

'Underneath my feet I can feel vibrations,' cried Martin, as he made his way over the slowly climbing heap of ice. 'Serious vibrations. It's the force of one pack of ice hitting the other, which I have to say is very, very cool.'

'It's like tarmac that's come together in an earthquake and split up,' said Guy. 'It's absolutely incredible.'

The team crossed while the ridge was still low, then took a ten-minute snack break while they stood and watched Nature take its course. Guy was right. The ice did look like tarmac in an earthquake—albeit huge, gleaming, semi-transparent tarmac, slabs of various sizes rising up under the inexorable pressure of the moving floes, cracking, then falling back, the larger chunk of ice forcing its way over the smaller.

'The size of that one block there alone,' said

Martin, 'is six metres by six metres, probably two metres thick. You've got one pack of ice that is literally hundreds of square miles versus another that is the same, and the sheer force of their collision is creating this. It's happening very slowly, but it's extraordinary.'

'It's normal,' said Inge, 'but I am so happy we've had that experience with this group, because now they really understand the forces involved.'

*   *   *

It was Friday and Walking With The Wounded had less than twenty miles to go before reaching their destination. Unless something went seriously wrong, they would arrive the next day. 'Tomorrow is Saturday,' said Martin. 'Which means if we're lucky we'll get back to Longyearbyen in time for Saturday night. And Saturday night is smash night! I am very much looking forward to a few whiskies with the team at the end of this. And making a fool of myself on the dance floor, which I particularly like doing, swinging my paralysed arm around as I can. After that, when we get back, I'm going to take a little break. Make a few phone calls to a few friends of mine who are equally stupid and enjoy ridiculous holidays that burn the candle at both ends. We'll go away somewhere and practise a well-known activity known as lizarding. We will lizard, we will drink, we will partake in a few extreme sports, and I guarantee you we'll go somewhere hot with a beach and a swimming pool and a temperature of thirty degrees. Plus thirty, that is.'

Martin wasn't the only one to have end-of-expedition fantasies. 'I am definitely, definitely

286

going to go on holiday somewhere warm when I get back from this place,' said Steve. 'Chill out for a couple of weeks in the sunshine.' His food cravings had meanwhile changed. 'Mature blue cheese. That's what I want. And a few beers.'

'Now that it's so close,' said Jaco, 'and so nearly finished, you start thinking about the first thing you're going to eat when you get back, that first warm shower, that comfy bed, and whatever you craved out here. Steve's been driving us absolutely ballistic with his cheese cravings. Two days ago it was prawn cocktail crisps. What a nutter.'

'They were tired,' says Inge. 'They are not the kind of people who complain too much, but you see the symptoms, the way people are walking, the time they are taking with their breaks, what they are talking about: what they're going to do when they finish. How it's going to be to get back to Longyearbyen and have a few beers and a shower.'

Like the others, Jaco had been fantasising about a holiday. In his case, he wanted to go and see his family in South Africa at Christmas. That led on to very similar thoughts to those Martin had been having, about what he was going to do with his life now that he was about to leave the Army. 'I've been really wondering today, what's going to happen to me in the future. I'm going to try my very best to get something out of this. Maybe a race to the South Pole? Against other disabled teams? Or Everest? Then something in the desert. That's more my cup of tea, a warm place like that. But we'll see how it goes. I'm going to finish my education first. Run a couple more courses. Then I'm hoping to run the New York marathon for the charity in November.

'But it's quite frightening, wondering what's lying

next in line for you. Wondering how I'm going to do it. Finding a job to pay my monthly outgoings, to cover the mortgage and everything else. In the Army we were quite lucky. You knew exactly what you were getting, every month, in that bank account. How much you could spend. Now I've got to start cooking for myself too. I'll be living off takeaways, I reckon. No, I'm actually quite a good cook. I enjoy it. I've done it before. You do get spoiled when you're in the Army. Pay a minimal fee for a very nice dinner.'

*   *   *

The team had planned to push on till 7 or 8 p.m., but by 6.15 they were all worn out, so they agreed to stop. That left them just ten miles short of their goal. 'It would have been great to be a mile or two closer,' wrote Ed, 'but still, tomorrow is our last day. We will be at the Pole at 5 p.m.'

The wind had dropped and with a clear sky it was a beautiful evening, which, Ed thought, boded well for the morrow. Knowing they had enough fuel to get them to the end, with some to spare, Steve fired up both cookers in the tent for the first time. 'We were fabulously warm,' wrote Ed, 'for the first time and everything dried in no time. Before I got into the tent I emptied out a lot of excess food, which will make my sledge much lighter tomorrow. Tomorrow . . . top of the world!'

DAY 12. Saturday 16 April. 90° N. 10 miles + ¼ mile N drift. –25°C.

'So we've finally come to our last day, potentially,'

288

said Guy, as they packed up camp in the morning. His words still allowed for some final unexpected disaster: a fall on a pressure ridge, someone slipping from a snow bridge into the inky waters of a lead, a hungry polar bear appearing from nowhere. But in reality, they had all but done it now. The sky was clear blue, with no hint that anything worse was coming in. 'We've got ten miles to go to the North Pole,' he continued, 'and I have rather mixed feelings about it. I'm delighted we're going to get there. But it's also a bit of a shame that it's all coming to a close. I suppose all good things must pass.'

Even with the pain his stump was giving him, there was still a part of Guy that wanted to stay out in the freedom of the wilderness, away from the mundanity of life at home. 'So I think we'll probably get to the Pole around three or four o'clock, and then it's a case of making the odd phone call. I'll call my parents, my grandmother, catch up with them. Then it's back to life as normal, which will be a bit of a shock to the system as this expedition has been dwelling at the back of my mind for such a long time now. It's quite incredible, really, how smoothly it's all gone. But equally, with the amount of exposure we've had through the media, it got to a point where I think we realised that if it did go wrong we could all look really stupid pretty quickly.

'What's slightly ironic is that the two guys who are most looking forward to finishing—Ed and Dags—are the ones who are able-bodied. Dags is fine body-wise. No niggles at all. But Parks is pretty broken. He's got flu, which I wouldn't want to be doing this with. He's got a seriously bruised back.

He's pretty doped up on painkillers.'

Dags, interestingly, was also feeling a twinge of sadness that the trip was all but over. 'A mixture of sort of melancholy and a sense of loss because by the end of play today we will have reached our goal, achieved what Ed and myself conceived two years ago. From a personal perspective, about ten years ago, I said I'd raise over two million pounds for various charities. I've done the three events I said I'd do, and reached nearly three million, so I've achieved my own personal goals and it's the end of that chapter for me personally. When we step on that spot, that's that. End of. And it's the end of the team that's been together and been so strong and very, very close. There's never been a cross word between us, I don't think, over eighteen months. Now we go out into the world to face our new challenges, whatever they may be.

'There's also a sense of great joy. What these four soldiers have achieved is amazing. It's been incredible to watch them—their determination, their bloody determination to achieve what they've achieved in getting here in such fine form. And the sense of humour and the gusto they've got. What a privilege it's been to work with every single one of them. They will remain friends for life and my door is always open to them, as I think theirs are to me.'

Welshman Steve wasn't tempting fate. 'Hopefully it's the last day, weather dependent,' he said, looking up into the clear blue sky. 'But as you can see, absolutely beautiful. So I imagine this should be our last day. One last push up to the North Pole. Should be—fingers crossed—fairly easy going. With the boys' morale as it is we should cover that easily.

'But I think the lads have got mixed emotions

290

because it's the end of a lot of hard work getting here. For myself it's been the end of a twenty-month period in my life—at times quite a dark period. When I was first hit I was told I might never walk again. Then, after a couple of weeks, I was being told I would walk, but it might take two years, and I would need a frame or sticks for the rest of my life. So now, to have walked to the North Pole, that'll be a good way of putting all that to bed, putting it behind me. At the same time I've got really close to the lads and it'll be a shame to split us up.'

South African Jaco was not troubled with even a smidgeon of doubt. 'It finally came,' he said. 'In about eight hours we'll be standing on the Pole. So I'm very excited. We'll probably push our pace a little bit today.'

Martin echoed the others' sentiments. 'For me,' he added, 'it's really been about demonstrating that if you're willing to adapt, post injury, you can go on and do some great stuff. With the right kit and the right team and the right attitude there's no reason why you can't do things of this level and beyond. There's a number of people out there who said this was physically impossible and I'd imagine that after this they're going to be regretting saying that. Now I want to find a bigger challenge. 'Cos that's life. You do one thing and you want something harder. And on and on it goes until you're either too old or too broken to carry on.'

*   *   *

As it turned out, their progress on the final lap was relatively smooth, with only a few leads and

291

pressure ridges and some 'awesomely flat bits' too. Yet, as if to prove that on a polar expedition you could never take anything for granted, this was the day when Simon finally hit a spot of trouble. Coming over a pressure ridge with his skis off, he put his foot through some thin ice on the far side and got one of his boots wet. Then he put his hand through another patch of thin ice, ruining his gloves: 'It was the last day, so it didn't matter. If it had been another day and my gloves had remained wet it would have been a problem.'

Then, as the GPS reading came closer and closer to that moment where the numbers would confirm that they had finally made it, they reached a huge pressure ridge, the highest and hardest, they thought, since the start. 'It was the Arctic's last opportunity to throw something tough at us,' wrote Ed.

Encouraged by the fact that this surely was the final such obstacle, they took off their skis and carefully made their way over. Once they were all on the far side they formed into an impromptu line and skied the last few hundred yards together to the Pole. 'I said to the boys,' says Ed, '"You four go in front and Dags and I will hold back." One of them, I think it was Guy, said, "Absolutely not, we are all going to go together." I was looking at them all as we were skiing up. Some faces were still focussed on getting there, some were smiling, then the smiling faces would focus.'

'It wasn't planned,' says Dags. 'It just happened. It was the right thing to do and everybody did it. It was the nicest point of the whole thing. Because the joke had been: "Who's going to be first to the Pole?"'

'In a line of six abreast,' Ed wrote in his diary that evening, 'just behind Inge, who was following the GPS, we skied out into a patch of flat multi-year ice where the GPS said 89° 59' 9999999999999"— we were there! It feels unreal and hugely exciting. Our journey is over and we have succeeded. For us all it felt fantastic. Hugs and tears from everyone, but I am sure they won't be admitted to!'

'Awesome,' said Steve. 'Can't believe we're here. It's absolutely unbelievable. A few whiskies tonight, I think, in celebration.'

'Words can't express,' said Guy. 'It's pretty special, it really is.'

'An unbelievable feeling,' said Jaco. 'It's been a roller-coaster ride, it's been hard, it's been emotional, it's been fun, it's been laughter, absolutely everything in it, and I'm actually quite a bit shaky now.'

'I tell you what, mate,' said Martin. 'It feels rather good. Now I think I'm going to go somewhere hot with a beach, but not before a drop of whisky and a cigar.'

It was, of course, just another patch of polar ice, the particular segment of the particular floe that just happened to be drifting over 90° N at that moment. 'Because the ice moves all the time,' says Dags, 'our North Pole will always just be our North Pole. It will never be anybody else's because it will be a different piece of ice.'

'What was great,' says Ed, 'was that it wasn't in a lead, or on a pressure ridge, it was right in the middle of an open bit of ice.'

Inge planted a ski pole at the point where the North Pole was and the whole team ran around it, as if they were running around the world. 'We did it with our heads on the Pole,' says Ed, 'and then all got dizzy and fell over. None of us show our emotions hugely, even to each other, but it was quite an emotional moment.'

Then Dog brought out the cigars. 'Whopping, frankly unsmokeable due to the size,' says Dags, 'which Disco, Dog and I duly puffed on and then felt sick.'

There was whisky but no champagne. The huge bottle of Pol Roger they had been filmed with at Gatwick would never have made it across the ice. 'It would have frozen,' says Dags, 'and the cork would have come out. Whisky doesn't freeze, because the alcohol content is much higher.'

Cameraman Alexis Girardet and sound man Rob Leveritt were standing to one side, capturing the remarkable moment for the TV documentary. 'We wanted them to stop,' says Ed, 'because they had got to the North Pole as well. They were as much a part of the team as the rest of us were. They had been integral since the start. When the TV programme is made, you obviously won't see them, or Rune and Petter, who took their technical kit, the story will be about the four boys. But for us as individuals, the four of them were as much part of our story as we were.'

* * *

For those with wives and girlfriends back home it was time for a special call on the sat phone. 'Ed called his wife,' says Jaco. 'Simon called his wife. I think Steve called Emma, his fiancée. Disco called his dog probably.'

Tragically, Ed couldn't get through to Harriet.

She was trying on jeans in a shop in Fakenham and their fourteen-year-old son Jack, left in the car with her mobile, hadn't realised the significance of this particular Missed Call. 'Then we were driving along,' says Harriet, 'and about an hour later I got a text from my niece saying "Awesome".

'I rang her up. "What's awesome?" I asked.

'"Harriet, they got to the North Pole."

'I felt terribly upset. I rang Ed's parents. "What's happening?" I said.

'"They've got to the North Pole," his mother told me.

'I put the phone down. "I can't believe it," I said, "they said he tried to call me."

'Then Jack piped up, "Oh yeah, there was a missed call while we were in Fakenham."

'"Why didn't you answer it?"

'"I didn't recognise the number."

'I was so upset. It was awful. All I wanted to do was hear Ed. I tried to phone back the number but of course I couldn't get through.'

They had reached the Pole so fast that their supporters had been taken by surprise. Alex Rayner was with his children at a point-to-point. 'With horse racing and a really crap funfair. All I could hear was tinny disco tunes and "Roll up, roll up, hook a duck", when suddenly the phone rang and it was Ed. I had to leg it off and hide in the back of a generator to say, "Congratulations, you've done it, I can't believe it."

'Ed was saying, "Please don't tell anyone for a couple of hours because we haven't been able to get hold of our wives." I thought we would announce it nice and calmly on the Sunday morning, but alas when they did hear, the wives got terribly excited and put it all over Facebook. Which was great in a way because that was a very organic way to do it.'

Down in Tonypandy, Steve's fiancée Emma had organised a family fun day which had been planned for this Sunday to mark the half-way point of the trek. Now it turned into a celebration of the expedition's success.

*　　*　　*

Back on the Pole, despite the team's elation, the temperature was still −25°C and they were starting to get cold. It was time to put their tents up for one last evening on the ice. 'How often,' said Guy, 'do you get to spend a night on top of the North Pole?'

But while he and Jaco were happy to stay, the rest had been less keen. 'The other guys,' says Jaco, 'said, "Let's get there, do the celebrations, then get off and have a nice comfy sleep."' As it happened, the available helicopters had already made two trips out from Barneo that day, picking up other expeditions, so there was to be no Saturday night smash in Longyearbyen. They would have to wait till morning.

The Officers' Mess had sadly run out of whisky, but the members of the less gobby tent were able to oblige. Jaco unpacked his dartboard and had a game with Steve. Ed opened a letter from the Prime Minister, which had been sent over after their visit to No. 10, with instructions to be opened at the Pole (when he got back to Longyearbyen he found a text from the PM on his phone, congratulating them all).

'Cigars were lit,' wrote Ed, 'and we all had a fair few drams to celebrate. So it is over. We have

296

walked further to the Pole in 2011 than any other team. We have done it faster than anyone ever imagined. And we have done it with four wounded soldiers, two of whom are amputees, four people I consider four of the most impressive people in the world. We called in our last blog for the website. We've done it!!!'

20

WARM AGAIN

The helicopter was due early, so they were up and packing at 5 a.m. the next morning. 'I slept very badly—too excited,' wrote Ed. 'Didn't bother to have breakfast as I am completely bored of forcing down huge quantities of porridge each morning. Anyhow, I don't need it today! Our helicopter arrived at 5.45 a.m. with Jon and Viktor and they brought with them all our sponsors' flags which we were then photographed with. Steve had brought a Welsh flag with him. We think he took over a thousand photos of it!

'At 7 a.m. we loaded on to the helicopter and left. In an instant it was over. As we flew over the sea ice to Barneo it looked so innocent and beautiful. The harshness of pulling across it is so different! The warmth slowly permeated its way into everything, and for the first time the ice inside my windproof jacket defrosted! Slowly it is sinking in that we have done it.'

By 11 a.m. they had been through Barneo, transferred on to the Antonov AN-47 and were back at the airport in Longyearbyen. 'It seemed unreal,' Ed wrote, 'as if the Pole was just a brief blink of time. The world we had been living in, where we were in complete isolation, now seemed a dream. Yet during those long nine-hour days of hauling, time often went very slowly and it felt like we were never going to escape from the incessant cold. We did it far quicker than expected (three days from faster pulling and two days from ice drift) and were lucky with the weather. But you can only challenge what you are faced with, and succeed we did, and in style.'

They had completed the trip so much faster than planned that Expedition HQ had moved their flights home forward an entire week. 'If we hadn't,' said Alex Rayner, 'they would have had to spend almost two weeks in Longyearbyen, which would have killed them—or their livers.'

Marcus Chidgey had changed his plans and flown to Spitsbergen just in time to welcome the team back. 'I met them an hour after they landed, just after they'd taken their pulks back to the warehouse. They were completely dazed. They were almost on autopilot. Their bodies were in Longyearbyen, but their souls were still out on the ice.'

'They were happy to come off,' says Alex, 'and not just because they had been camping in sub-zero temperatures. I think it was also a bit like the Big Brother house. They wanted to see what had been going on in their absence. Don't forget they left with the biggest amount of media this side of the royal wedding. It was one of the biggest stories of the year, press coverage wise.'

One of the many emails they received was

from Matt Kingston, who had been following the expedition on the news: 'Please pass my congratulations around the team,' he wrote. 'I'm sitting here literally feeling physically sick. Just sent the BBC link to all involved in the Corps who stopped me going from the start with a big F@&k you in it. Very proud of you all and unbearably jealous. Hands are shaking writing this. Cheers, Pies.' It was a damn shame, those who had known Matt agreed, that he hadn't been able to reach the Pole with them.

That evening the team did go out for the beers they had fantasised about on the ice. After a dinner at Kroa, Ed and Simon retired, while the four lads partied on. At some point in the small hours, back at their hotel, Guy got stuck in a disabled lift and Martin let off a fire extinguisher, much to Inge's disapproval.

They stayed in Longyearbyen till Thursday, a slightly longer decompression period than Simon and Ed had planned. But they had access to computers and were able to catch up on everything that had been written about them, both in the press and on Facebook. There were countless messages of support, from friends, family and other wellwishers. 'I think it was very important,' says Ed, 'to all of us that we knew people were following it. But I was amazed when I got back at how many people were telling me they had been reading about us on the blog.'

Stopping over for a night in Oslo, Simon found himself surprised by what he felt as he contemplated the neat bottles of shampoo and bubble bath in his well-appointed hotel room. 'It was a strange thing, because we had all been living

299

together for so long, sharing bedrooms and tents, I got to my bedroom in Oslo and I felt really lonely. It was weird. I had a room of my own, as you would expect, but I didn't like it at all.'

Captive Minds had been in touch with the men's platoons and regiments as well as their families, so when the soldiers landed at Gatwick, there was something of a heroes' welcome. Steve's fiancée Emma was there, with a posse from Tonypandy. Harriet was there, this time with her children. Dags's wife Emma, with Felix and Oscar. Guy's mother, Jaco's sister, Martin's mum and dad from Widnes, quite apart from Army mates and colleagues, including the top brass. 'The Commander of the Welsh Guards was there for Steve,' says Alex Rayner. 'The Chief of Staff was there for his brother.'

It was a point that Ed had always been modest about: that his older brother Nick, Harry Parker's father, had all this time been the general in charge in Afghanistan. Nor, in all the ups and downs Ed had experienced with Army bigwigs, had he ever used the connection to gain an unfair advantage in his long struggle to get some wounded soldiers to the Pole: 'Ed was very conscious of not using his brother,' says Harriet. 'You don't want to be embarrassing and you don't want to get it wrong. And I don't actually think Nick having that job made any difference. But he has been incredibly supportive of Ed as a brother. And he knows that this has to be done for the wounded.'

In Wales and South Africa, Steve and Jaco had become local celebrities. 'Jaco did an interview with his local paper,' said Marcus Chidgey, 'and he was on the phone for an hour and a half. It was almost like he was a pop star. They were asking him about his hobbies, what music he liked, unrelated things. I think he became a focus for South African pride in a way, the fact that he had been part of this expedition.'

'It was massive back home,' says Steve. 'I had no idea. I walked through town the day after I got home and everybody was patting me on the back and shaking my hand and saying "Well done". It was awesome. And when I'd been on the ice, there were strangers coming up to Emma in the street and giving her money for the charity. I'm not one for standing in front of cameras and things, but it was nice to know that your friends and family are proud of you.'

Some sections of the press, always eager to hit the superlative button, were happy to hail the boys as heroes. But interestingly this was not a term they were necessarily keen to use about themselves. 'There are certain words,' says Guy, 'that make us look like complete shits. Things like "hero". You read some *Sun* article that says "Heroes do this and heroes do that" and it's just grim. At the end of the day we are in the Army, it's our job. I chose that job. We chose to go to Afghanistan. And there are hundreds of other people who have been injured and could have done this trip.

'Apart from anything else, that kind of language makes you look like a real prat in front of your regiment. I don't want to go back with the guys having read all this stuff about me being heroic. I got a bloke killed by choosing a course of action and I got my leg blown off. There is nothing heroic about that. War is not heroic. I think the media are quite naughty about selling it as a glorious thing.

301

It's not glorious, it's bloody hard work.'

'I have nothing but good thoughts about the expedition,' says Dags. 'The wounded were a very interesting bunch of people. I will probably always be closer to Martin and Guy than Jaco and Steve because we shared a tent. But all four will remain lifelong friends. People often say that, but in this case it's true. If I were at a drinks party, and I saw Guy over there, or Dog, there would be a hundred people in between and I wouldn't need to say anything. I would just look at them and they would know that I knew that they knew we had been to the Pole together. We don't need to say a word, it's just there. We did that. You can carry on talking to whoever you want, but nobody else in that room will share that.'

Harriet was both proud of and relieved by her husband's achievement. 'Before they went,' she says, 'everyone kept saying, "Are you proud?" And I said, "No, not yet. When he comes back and he's achieved it I will be the proudest person." And I am. I think it's amazing that little old Ed from Norfolk has done this. He got those four boys to the North Pole and they've raised half a million pounds for charity and it's ongoing.'

Even though the adventure was in the bag, Ed was still waking up in the night. 'It happened for about five weeks after he came back,' Harriet says. 'He woke up and he was sweating and puffing terribly. He thought he was drowning, or one of the boys was drowning, that they'd fallen into a lead and were sinking. But this was always Ed's biggest worry for the whole trip: that those boys wouldn't be safe. They had been through such hideous traumas and their families had too. My take on it

302

is that it's post-traumatic stress in reverse. Nothing happened, but the worry is still there.'

But in the broad light of day, Ed has already forgotten his fears: of Jaco losing his only good hand to frostbite or Steve ruining his back for ever, or of himself toppling into an open lead and being pulled down by his pulk four thousand feet in the inky water. 'The rose-tinted glasses do come down very quickly,' he says, looking neat and rested and fit, sitting on a bench in Green Park in the warm May sunlight in his London suit. 'I still can't feel the ends of two of my fingers, but the others have come back. You forget the cold. You forget the pain. You forget the tiredness. You forget all the bad side of it, of which there is quite a lot. Achieving the goal and the challenge is such a fabulous thing to do, so there will be more.'

AFTERWORD

Walking With The Wounded is about inspiration, courage and determination. By embarking on this extraordinary expedition and others in the future, we hope to keep the injured in the public eye so everyone can see just how remarkable these young men and women are. Their future is different to the one they would have chosen, but they still are driven to succeed. While many view the wounded from a conflict zone with pity and sorrow, our charity is adopting a rather more upbeat and positive approach to their future. While they all have to adjust to an altered life, there is an inspiring strength of mind within this group of people to push on to achieve outside the Armed Forces. But it is a huge step that they have to take, into a new career most of them weren't expecting to be embarking upon. Walking With The Wounded aims to raise money to help our injured servicemen and women with this transition, providing funding for training courses, education programmes and apprenticeships, which will ensure jobs. It is simple—a job provides security. So let's not pity them. Let's provide them with the tools for a successful future, let's help them into the civilian world and let's give them the support they deserve after what they have done for us. We need your assistance to help provide this funding so please do visit our website (www.wwtw.org.uk) where you can donate online.

Thank you.

The Trustees of Walking With The Wounded

ACKNOWLEDGEMENTS

Walking With The Wounded would never have made it to the North Pole without the support and help of many organisations and individuals, large and small. At the top of the list come our sponsors, who backed us from the start and made sure through their generous donations that every penny raised by the public goes direct to the cause. Leading the way is Artemis Investment Management LLP, closely followed by Carillion, Helly Hansen, Catlin Underwriting, Elmfield Training, Edmiston, LDC Private Equity, J. O. Hambro, Norwegian Airlines, Horlicks, Career Transition Partnership and Esri UK.

Prince Harry supported the expedition from the off: his involvement lifted its profile to a new height. We are all immensely grateful to him and his team at Clarence House: Miguel Head, Nick Loughran, Rebecca Deacon and Jamie Lowther-Pinkerton.

On the media and management side of things thanks go to Marcus Chidgey, Alex Rayner and all at Captive Minds in Spitalfields, who worked tirelessly to generate publicity, create our marketing collateral, co-ordinate our sponsors and manage our commercial partners.

Thanks to Bridget Sneyd, Alexis Girardet, Rob Leveritt and all at TwoFour, a TV production company who definitely went the extra mile; Hans Zimmer, Czarina Russell and all the staff at Remote Control Productions; Adam Strange and all his team at Little, Brown; *GQ* magazine; Duran

Duran and their people; Olly Murs; John Simmons and Katie Collins at GMG Radio; Frank Gardner and Mark Georgiou at the BBC; Chapman Bell at NBC; Bob Woodward at ABC; James Edgar and Dave Cheskin at the Press Association; and David Bailey, who gave his time and skill for free.

On the medical side: Dr Dan Roiz de Sa and all at the Cold Clinic at the Institute of Naval Medicine; the Rehab team at St Athans; the consultants and physios at Headley Court; and PACE Rehabilitation, in particular Jamie Gillespie and Scott Richardson, who did such a fine job tailoring Guy's prosthetic leg to order.

Thanks also go to the Army, whose support was wholehearted once it understood what we were trying to do; and to the Ministry of Defence for backing us, in particular Major Ben Walters for steering us along the way.

We would never have reached our goal without the expertise and dedication of Inge Solheim of Storm Adventures, along with his guides Rune Malterud, Petter Nyquist and Jon Haldorsen; as well as Stian Aker who helped on the initial training in Svalbard.

On the expedition itself, we were grateful for kit and provisions provided by Alternative Networks, Mountain Fuel, Casco Optics, Oakley Goggles, Mule Bars, Polar Tec, Blacks Outdoor, Cotswold Outdoor, Hestra, Be-well Expedition Foods, Panasonic Toughbooks, Powertraveller, Nanok, Heat Max, Therm-ic, Energizer, Gerber, Upcakes, Integral Designs, Needles Outdoor, Hilleberg Tents, Madshus Skis, Gerard Baker's Flapjacks, Equip Outdoor Tech Technologies, Garmin, Freia and Light My Fire—all secured by our enthusiastic

Head of Training and Logistics Henry Cookson. Also thanks to Mrs Hewitt for her tiffin cake, Viggo Grytbakk for his amazing reindeer stew on press day in Beitostølen and Beitostølen Ski Resort.

Harry Parker was an inspiration for the trip, and has worked tirelessly to support us in numerous unseen ways.

On the personal side, the team would like to thank their wives, girlfriends and close families for their support and belief in us; in spirit they were never far away. In particular Harriet, Jack, Kitty and Olivia Parker along with Em, Oscar and Felix Daglish, who 'always knew they would succeed'. Steve Young would like to thank his family and his fiancée Emma for all the support they gave him through the difficult times, and for their encouragement during training for the expedition. Jaco van Gass thanks his mother Aloma, father Deon and sister Lizanne van der Merwe, as well as all his friends and family in the UK and South Africa and the Parachute Regiment for their continuing support. Thanks go out from Martin to the Parachute Regiment for providing him with a new focus and drive after his injury; to lizards past and present for being good lizards, and most of all to his family: 'Mum, Dad, Phil, Pete and our Emma who I love so much and have done more for me than I could ever write in a book.' Guy writes: 'Massive thanks to my Regiment, The Light Dragoons, to my friends, my family and in particular my parents for putting up with me.'

Author Mark McCrum would like to thank his agent Mark Lucas and PA Alice Saunders; Adam Strange and all at Little, Brown; Bridget, Alexis and all who helped at TwoFour; copyeditor Steve Gove;

Ed and Simon for consistent support throughout; and all on the expedition team for being such responsive and cooperative interviewees. Finally his wife Jo for keeping him provided with cups of tea in his not very cold study.

310

EXPEDITION KIT LIST

Item and **Quantity;**
Modification/Notes

GROUP EQUIPMENT:

Tents

Polar modified Hilleberg Keron 4 GT (2)
Snow flaps, vent, fortified poles. Henry requested non-tangle guy lines, drying lines. Has more space, four side pockets, big vestibule, higher ceiling (for Ed and Steve), easier to erect etc. Three people per tent. Inge used his own Nanok Argos 'Pleasure Dome' tent

Snow pegs: 6 per tent (18)
Alternatively can use combination of skis and poles

Tent Flooring: 4mm foam cut to shape (2)
EasyFoam

Spare poles (1)
Complete set and pole jacket for repairs

Tent repair kit (see Repair section)

Tent brush (3)
To brush out snow

Large safety pins for drying line(60)
Also used mini carabiners

Shovel (3)
Lightweight. Insulated handle and shaft with gaffer tape

Camping chairs (3)
Steve, Ed and Dags took Crazy Creek camping chairs to ease strain on back and for doing cooking

Toilet tent/Windbreak and chair

Collapsible camping chair with hole cut out.
Norwegian fishing tent for shelter

Haulage, Sleeping & Storage System

Acapulka 160 (6)
No modifications for Jaco or Martin. Four grab
handles: two front, two back

Acapulka 230 (2)
Larger pulks to enable bridging the open water
leads

Harness/Backpack (8)
If using backpack, attachment points strengthened;
modification to harness with webbing-type
additions. Prince Harry and Jaco used the Deuter
35L Guide (one that Henry has used on every trip
to Antarctic, Arctic and mountains). Remainder
used standard Acapulka harnesses

Knotted trace with dampener bungie (8)
Rope that will not fray, 7mm bungie 5m, trace
5mm–7mm 32m, knotted for grip. Never utilised—
Inge's bog-standard nylon rope used instead

Carabiners (36)
Non-locking mid-sized

Nanok sleeping bags (-45) (8)
Net pocket sewn inside (above where chest would
be) to keep loose items dry and in a manageable
place (socks, gloves, hat, music, pens). 40cm ×
30cm approx

Large ridge-rest foam roll mat (8)
Large inflatable Thermarest mat (8)
Large red Nanok tent Bags (16)
For easy storage and separation of kit/food in pulks

**Stuff sacks, assorted sizes: integral design or
similar (60)**
Colour-coded for each tent so no mix-up, used to

store meals, snacks—integral design, granite gear. All drawstring-operated except the ones for Jaco and Martin which were a waterproof fold-over and clip version that are easier to open and close with one hand

Ski System
Metal-edged skis (pair) (8)
Madshus Glittertind
Spare skis (pair) (2)
Rotefella bindings (10)
3-pin bindings
Heel plate (10)
Replaced with spiked version for more grip so heel does not slip
Full skins or kicker skins (10)
Full skins used
Screws and wire for skin attachment
Metal grinder used to smooth down ends of screws
Skin glue
Swix ski poles (pair) (10)
Long, insulated handles, increased with foam and gaffer tape. Double-looped handles for different mitt sizes (not utilised)
Alpha Modre boots (8)
Specialised boots developed by Sjur Modre— soft boot with removable Katanak wool liners. Very comfortable and warm with less likelihood of blisters. Wool liner is placed in a Helly Hansen polar sock so it retains shape and does not disintegrate
Katanak wool liners with Helly Hansen polar socks (10)
Two/three spare pairs
Gaiters (optional) (8)

Outdoor Research Crocodile Gaiters
Repair and spare (see repair kit)
Inge's own

Cooking Equipment
XGK MSR stoves, pumps, repair kits (6)
Two per tent
XGK spare pumps (6)
Two per tent
MSR fuel canisters (6)
Funnels (3)
Freeze-tested, malleable plastic, same as freezer-proof Tupperware
Stove boards (3)
Custom-made to fit two stoves, lightweight and stowable in pulk with stoves attached to save time when making/breaking camp—just had to de-rig when refuelling. Plain plywood used in the end with some adaptations dependent on the tent but nothing sophisticated
Fuel containers: 5 litre and 10 litre (70 litres)
Order of 10 litres per person. 5-litre fuel cans supplied at Barneo
Koke Willy (3)
Snow-melting pot
MSR Black Mondo Pot: 4 litre (3)
For two-stove option
Pot handles (3)
Titanium spork (12)
Insulated bowls (8)
Insulated bowls made in warehouse. Option if did not have boil-in-bag breakfasts, freeze-proof
Wide-base insulated thermos mug (min. 400ml) (8)

Hydration system

1-litre wide-mouth Nalgene bottles (16)

Masking tape or rubber to help Jaco and Martin. Narrow-mouth ones were probably easier to open and close but then harder to pour into. Access was a priority

Nalgene insulated covers (15)

Nalgene pee bottles (8)

Well marked and different colour

Insulated thermos: Aladdin/Thermos (8)

Wide mouth, simple top, insulated with neoprene to prevent cold injuries on metal and help grip. Added grips for Martin and Jaco so that they were easier to open with one hand

1-litre Nalgene narrow-mouth bottles (5)

For whisky!

Navigation & Communications

Garmin GPS 60 (6)

Sponsorship item

Compass, Northern Weighed (3)

Adapted for wrist mount. Used Henry's from Antarctic trip

Compass holder (2)

Not used

Thermometers (6)

Thermometers going down to -50°C (simple, lightweight)

Wind anemometer (Kestrel or JDC Skywatch Explorer) (3)

Henry brought old sponsored ones. Not used

Solar panel (1)

Took foldable solar panel with cigarette-lighter female socket

Iridium, batteries, chargers, serial ports

For satellite blog updates
PDA
For inputting data, text and pictures for satellite blog
Panasonic Toughbook (1)
Used by Henry at base camp
Camera, Power (1)
Canon PowerShot camera with AA batteries

GENERAL INDIVIDUAL EQUIPMENT:

Carabiners: mini size for kit attachment (32)
For attaching gloves etc. to pulks/packs, harnesses, drying lines
Gerber/Leatherman Charge (8)
Suggest minimum of two Leatherman Charge for additional tool options
Toiletries (10)
Toothbrush, toothpaste, hand cream (Elizabeth Arden Eight Hour Cream), arse admin, medical lip balm, tea tree oil, foot powder. All medium-sized so they were were easier to warm up due to less volume
Small washcloth & zip-lock bag (14)
To have a tent bath. Not used!
Sunblock and lipblock
Blacks own brand
Journal, pencil, pen (7)
Moleskin journal
Reading book
Music system which works in cold, easy to power
AA battery-operated MP3 player
Marker pen
Wet wipes
Small packs of five so easy to thaw in chest pockets

Toilet paper: good quality so does not shred
Pack all in waterproof stuff sack, zip-lock for one in use. Chilli grit and glass shards to be glued to Dags's supply
Tissues small-sealed reusable pack
Easy-access emergency dumps
Small sewing kit (3)
Ear-plugs
Snoring protection. Good headphones can do this as well
Black-out masks
For sleeping in 24-hour daylight

First-Aid Kit

Expedition first-aid kit (2)
Dentistry kit
Everyone was instructed to have a check up at dentist prior to departure for loose fillings etc
Individual pain and blister kit   (7)

Emergency kit

Hypothermia (Hypo) bag
Immersion suit
Rescue/Dangerous lead cords
Flare gun and flares
Shotgun and ammo
PLB/EPIRB
Smoke and flares for aircraft signalling

CLOTHING: INDIVIDUAL

Kit bags:
Kit bags (3)

Two extra large, one medium

Top
Base layer: white crew-neck, long sleeve (2)
Personal preference is zipped for venting and pockets
Fleece medium: black (1)
Good in tent (one or other)—Helly Hansen warm loose hoody as an alternative. No full-length zip and hood great for windy days, around camp etc
Fleece thick: green (1)
Good in tent (one or other)
Odin isolator jacket **(1)** A pullover easier than no zip, also a gilet for Jaco and Martin because it keeps torso warm but allows sweat to vent out of sides
Helly Hansen expedition jacket (1)
Nanok down jacket (1)

Bottom
Underwear (2)
All access to fly needs to go in same direction as over-layers to prevent dick meander
Base layer: long johns (1)
Warmer base layer (1)
Helly Hansen expedition trousers (1)
Knee pads put in
Down trousers synthetic fill: ID (1)
Very good for tent if storm-bound, wandering round camp, filming, interviewing, bathroom calls. Easy to put on and remove, and lightweight

Feet
Inner liner socks (pairs) (2)
Coolmax
Medium socks (2)

Thicker socks (2)
One pair can be used as dry tent socks and then be replaced mid-trip
Tent boots/Down boots (1)
Nanok tent socks (1)
VBL (1)
Alternative if they fail zip-lock bags from food
Plastic supermarket bags (80) Used as a vapour barrier in order to stop the sweat from our feet freezing in the Katanak wool boots

Hands

Silk inner gloves (2)
Polartec 100 contact gloves (2)
Ext Power Dry, OR
Grip gloves (1)
Boreas, Outdoor Designs, Exrem, action stick wind
Thick gloves: Hestra Army Leather Heli Ski (1)
One or other—both have removable liners so can dry
Mittens: Hestra Army Leather Heli Ski (1)
One or other—both have removable liners so can dry. Can use finger liners in mitt in order to have better dexterity
Mittens wind shell (1)
Wristlets (2)
You may look like Prince but these are extremely effective as they warm the blood in your wrists going into your fingers

Face/Head

Goggles and nose guard (10)
Nose guards (7)
Neck warmers (7)
Neoprene face(7)

Hat with ear protection (10)
Balaclava (7)
Windpro Balaclava: Outdoor Designs
Sunglasses: leash (9)
Head torches (winter training) (7)

Repair, General and Suggestions

Tent fabric
Spare laces
Glue for boots
Skin glue
Screws
Hand drill
Snap locks
Cooking gloves
1-litre pouring jug (1)
Medium Phillips screwdriver
Medium screwdriver
Lightweight pliers
Duct tape: assorted rolls
2-metre bungee cord
Superglue
Lighters (14)
Pole repair jacket (1)
Spare velcro
Box of matches
Rolls of thin cotton
Miscellaneous needles
Zip-locks (300)
Parachute cord
Rope
Spare fleece material
Thermarest repair kit
Energizer lithium batteries (AAA and AA) (180)

Therm-ic electric heating elements
Heat Max chemical heat packs

FOOD

A typical day's diet

	g	cal
Breakfast		
Granola, Quaker	200	960
Powdered milk	0	
Hot chocolate × 2	80	336
	280	1296
Snacks & lunch		
Crackers	50	215
Dry salami	70	325
Cheese	70	325
Flapjacks	50	250
Granola bar	0	
Chocolate pieces	50	250
Dried fruit	50	200
Mixed nuts	100	600
Juice Crystal × 1 litre	50	200
	490	2365
Dinner		
Soup	30	125
Noodles	30	165
Couscous	136	536
Ground beef	17	137
Butter	30	216
Shortbread	50	255

Hot chocolate × 1	40	168
Herbal or regular tea	2	0
	293	1434
Total	**1063**	**5095**